Mathematical Literacy

Helping Students Make Meaning in the Middle Grades

Denisse R. Thompson

Gladis Kersaint

Janet C. Richards

Patricia D. Hunsader

Rheta N. Rubenstein

HEINEMANN • PORTSMOUTH, NH

Heinemann
361 Hanover Street
Portsmouth, NH 03801–3912
www.heinemann.com

Offices and agents throughout the world

The authors and publisher wish to thank those who have generously given permission to reprint borrowed material:

"Day Care Center Problem" from *A Collection of Performance Tasks and Rubrics: Middle School Mathematics* by Charlotte Danielson. Copyright © 1997. Reprinted with permission from Eye on Education.

"Lesson 1-2" from *UCSMP Transition Mathematics, Third Edition* by the University of Chicago. Copyright © 2005. Published by the Wright Group-McGraw Hill. Reproduced with permission of The McGraw-Hill Companies.

Cataloging-in-Publication data is on file at the Library of Congress.
ISBN-13: 978-0-325-01123-3
ISBN-10: 0-325-01123-0

Editor: Victoria Merecki
Production: Vicki Kasabian
Cover design: Jenny Jensen Greenleaf
Cover photography: Brian Beecher of See Photography, Sarasota, Florida
Typesetter: Publishers' Design and Production Services, Inc.
Manufacturing: Steve Bernier

Printed in the United States of America on acid-free paper
12 11 10 09 08   VP   1 2 3 4 5

Contents

Acknowledgments vii

Introduction ix

SECTION 1 *Theoretical Perspectives on Meaning Making* 1

   1. Meaning Making in Mathematics 3

   2. Communication and Mathematical Literacy 10

   3. Reading and Language Issues 20

Section 1 Summary: *Learning from Theoretical Perspectives* 38

SECTION 2 *Classroom Environments to Facilitate Meaning Making* 40

   4. Toward a Discourse Community 44

   5. Zoom In–Zoom Out: Using Reading Comprehension to Enhance
      Problem-Solving Skills 53

   6. Multiple Representations Charts to Enhance Conceptual Understanding 65

   7. You Be the Judge: Engaging Students in the Assessment Process 76

Section 2 Summary: *Developing Classroom Environments to Facilitate Meaning Making* 87

SECTION 3 *Teaching Practices That Encourage Meaning Making* 90

   8. Building Meanings Through Concept Development and Communication 91

     Models for Mathematical Concepts 92

     Graphic Organizers 96

         Comparing and Contrasting Concepts: Venn Diagrams and These Are/These Are Not 96

         Illustrating Relationships Among Concepts: Concept Maps and Semantic Feature
         Analysis Grids 99

     Concept Development Through Body Motion 103

   9. Building Meanings Through Language Development 107

Daily Practices 108

Word Origins, Prefixes, and Suffixes 111

Venn Diagrams 113

Distinguished Pairs 116

Invented Language 116

Literature Connections 119

10. Building Meanings Through Speaking and Listening 124

Cooperative Learning Practices 124

Think-Pair-Share 125

Roundtable 126

Co-op 127

Jigsaw 128

Other Practices to Encourage Language Use 128

Silent Teacher 129

Symbol-Language Glossary 129

Give and Take 130

Make My Day 132

11. Building Meanings Through Reading 135

Prereading Practices 138

Using Textbook Signals to Generate Questions for Reading 138

Brainstorming 139

PreP 140

K-W-L (Know, Want to Learn, Learned) Prompts 140

Anticipation Guides 142

Prereading Graphs and Displays 142

During Reading Practices 143

Read Aloud and with a Purpose 143

Teacher Think-Alouds 143

Pairs Read 144

QAR (Question-Answer-Relationship) 144

Sketch the Text 145

Postreading Practices 146

Strategies That Engage in All Three Phases of Reading 146

SQ3R (Survey, Question, Read, Recite, Review) 147

DRTA (Directed Reading-Thinking Activity) 147

Reading Word Problems 147

12. Building Meanings Through Writing 150

Mathematics Autobiography 152

Writing Opportunities for Concept and Language Development 153

    Personal Glossaries 153

    Multiple Representations Chart 153

    Analogies 153

    Compare and Contrast 156

Writing About Problems or Processes 159

    Symbols-Meanings Writing 159

    Write Your Own Problem 161

Notes and Portfolios 161

    Guided Notes 161

    Build Your Test Notes 164

    Test Corrections 165

    Portfolios 165

Journals 165

Creative Writing That Enhances Understanding 166

    Mathematics Bumper Stickers 168

    Mathematics Graffiti 168

    Short Stories, Poems, Songs 169

Section 3 Summary: *Encouraging Meaning Making in Your Classroom* 174

Appendix: Sample Middle Grades Mathematics Textbook Lesson 177

References 184

Index 191

About the Authors 195

Acknowledgments

The development of this book grew from insights obtained through interactions with preservice and inservice teachers in schools and in our university classes about integrating communication into the mathematics curriculum. Many practicing teachers have graciously welcomed us into their middle grades classrooms and given us opportunities to work with their students. These classroom experiences allowed us to think more carefully about issues and challenges related to mathematics communication and enabled us to enact practices and strategies for addressing them.

Although we cannot mention all of these colleagues by name, we want to give special acknowledgment to Denise Robinson of Hazel Park Schools in Hazel Park, Michigan; Joshuah Thurbee of the University of Chicago Charter Schools, Woodlawn Campus; and the seventh- and eighth-grade mathematics teachers at DeSoto Middle School in Arcadia, Florida. The vignettes stemming from these visits are not transcripts, but represent classroom discussions that occurred while an author taught or observed similar lessons in a teacher's classroom.

We also want to thank our editor at Heinemann, Victoria Merecki, whose suggestions enhanced the content of the book. We appreciate her patience with our progress toward completion of the chapters. We also thank our production editor, Vicki Kasabian, for her efforts with the design and final publication of the book. Their support, and the support of Heinemann, helped turn a glimmer of a dream into a reality.

Introduction

Learning mathematics in the middle grades is a critical component in the education of our nation's youth. The mathematics
foundation laid during these years provides students with the
skills and knowledge to study higher level mathematics . . . ,
provides the necessary mathematical base for success in other
disciplines . . . , and lays the groundwork for mathematically
literate citizens.
—National Research Council, *Educating Teachers of Science,
Mathematics, and Technology*

This book focuses on the importance of meaning making in middle grades
mathematics classrooms. We chose this focus because the middle grades
(generally, grades 6–8) are an important period in the mathematical education of students. During this time, students solidify their understanding of many
concepts they initially studied in elementary school, such as rational numbers and
their operations, and begin more formal study of geometric and algebraic concepts.
These critical mathematical turning points open doorways to later studies and ca-
reers that require mathematics prerequisites. In addition, adolescents are in a stage
of development in which they particularly value peer opinions and interactions.
Therefore, they need and seek opportunities to communicate with one other. We
can capitalize on their need for socialization to build learning communities in which
students work with their peers and the teacher to make sense of mathematics.

In this book, we share teaching practices related to communication (reading, writing, speaking, listening) that teachers can use to "establish a communication-rich
classroom in which students are encouraged to share their ideas and to seek clarification until they understand" (National Research Council 2000, 270). In such classrooms, students are expected to explain their thinking, question and debate responses
from their peers, and assume responsibility for their learning. Communication-rich
mathematics classrooms are environments in which atmospheres of respect and trust
have been developed and teachers encourage students to explain their struggles, partial understandings, and conjectures and insights about mathematics.

This book is a collaborative effort of mathematics educators and content literacy
experts who have brought together their diverse classroom experiences and discipline
perspectives to help clarify issues related to communication and mathematics. Many

states now require teachers to have preparation in reading in the content areas, either as a requirement for initial certification or as continuing education to maintain a teaching certificate. Too often, such preparation is generic and mathematics teachers are left to determine for themselves how ideas and strategies from general content-reading courses apply to mathematics. From our experiences in teaching content-specific courses related to reading the language of mathematics, we are convinced that language-rich mathematics practices can lead to deep understanding of concepts as students work to explain their thinking to themselves and others. In the process, teachers gain valuable insights about students' emerging understandings that can inform instruction.

We have structured this book into three main sections, each with a slightly different focus. We begin each section with a brief overview that describes the format of the chapters in the section. We end each section with a brief synthesis that connects the chapters in the section.

- Chapters 1–3 in Section 1 provide a theoretical perspective on an issue related to developing mathematical literacy and meaning making. The chapters progress from general issues related to meaning making across all disciplines to broad issues about communication in mathematics to specific issues related to reading and the language of mathematics. The section introduction provides a rationale for integrating communication into the mathematics classroom from the perspective of national recommendations and describes the nature of each chapter. Chapter 1 introduces you to semiotics, a discipline that describes how individuals give and receive meaning from culturally agreed-upon sign systems, and illustrates how mathematics is such a system. Chapter 2 extends this discussion of meaning making to the role that multiple literacies (speaking, reading, writing, and listening) play in helping students make sense of mathematics. Chapter 3 follows with issues related to reading mathematical text, including issues with vocabulary and symbols, which can influence students' success with mathematics. Finally, the section concludes with a brief synthesis designed to help you connect the ideas to the mathematics classroom.

- Chapters 4–7 in Section 2 focus on literacy strategies as they might play out in a middle grades mathematics classroom. The introduction provides a rationale for the use of worthwhile mathematics tasks to engage students in communication activities to facilitate the development of mathematical literacy. The subsequent chapters provide vignettes to illustrate how communication and literacy ideas might look and sound in a classroom and how mathematical literacy can be a routine part of classroom instructional practice. Through the vignettes, we encourage you to visualize how such strategies can help with reading comprehension, vocabulary development and writing in mathematics, assessment, and the creation of a discourse community. Analysis of students' work generated with each strategy helps you understand how communication can inform instruction. The section ends with a synthesis of issues that teachers need to consider as they develop classrooms that support mathematical literacy and meaning making.

- Chapters 8–12 in Section 3 provide classroom practices that address each of the literacies (reading, writing, speaking, and listening) that we have discussed throughout this book. In addition, the first two chapters of the section describe practices that integrate multiple literacies as students build conceptual understanding and the mathematical vocabulary necessary to discuss mathematics effectively. The summary provides opportunities to connect the practices to your own classroom.

Integrated throughout each chapter, you will find brief prompts in a callout box labeled Reflect. These prompts are designed to help you reflect on ideas presented in the chapters; we encourage you to stop and try to respond to the prompts as you read. If this book is being used as part of professional study, either as a text in a university course or as a book read by a professional learning community, the reflection prompts in each chapter provide points of discussion. At the end of each chapter, you will find two additional types of questions or prompts: Expand Your Understanding prompts are designed to help you think deeper about the issues raised in the chapter; Connect to Practice prompts provide an opportunity for you to bring the concepts you're learning into your own classroom instruction.

Whether you are a preservice, beginning, or veteran teacher, we believe this book will stimulate your thinking about enhancing communication practices in your classroom. We welcome your comments and thoughts.

Theoretical Perspectives on Meaning Making

People are not recorders of information but builders of knowledge structures. To know something is not just to have received information but also to have interpreted it and related it to other knowledge.
—Lauren B. Resnick and Leopold E. Klopfer, "Toward the Thinking Curriculum"

The three chapters in this section provide theoretical underpinnings for the mathematical literacy practices that are the focus of this book. Specifically, we use a perspective called *semiotics* as a foundation for the development of language-rich classrooms in which students make sense of mathematics; semiotics encapsulates many of the recommendations for communication espoused by the National Council of Teachers of Mathematics (NCTM). Chapter 1 introduces you to semiotics, a discipline that studies and explains how individuals give and receive meaning from sign systems. Mathematics is a sign system. The chapter also illustrates how mathematically powerful students are able to transmediate from one sign system, such as words, to another sign system, such as symbols or diagrams.

Semiotics provides a theoretical perspective for the communication and language perspectives of Chapters 2 and 3, respectively, because semiotics focuses on meaning making. Communication between teacher and student, student and student, student and the text, or student with himself or herself is essential to making sense of mathematics. As indicated in the *Curriculum and Evaluation Standards for School Mathematics*, "The communication process requires students to reach agreement about the meanings of words. . . . Opportunities to explain, conjecture, and defend one's ideas orally and in writing can stimulate deeper understandings of concepts and principles" and help students "assume more responsibility for validating their own thinking" (NCTM 1989, 78–79). Recognition of the importance of communication continues in the *Principles and Standards for School Mathematics* (NCTM 2000) as communication remains one of ten standards for all grades preK–12. This reflects continued emphasis on the importance of reading, writing, speaking, and listening to the development of mathematical literacy.

To develop mathematically literate students, we need to recognize that "All students can learn to think mathematically" and that "What students learn is fundamentally connected with how they learn it" (NCTM 1991, 21). If students are to develop more than just procedural knowledge, they must have experiences that support the development of conceptual understanding. They need opportunities to explore concepts, make conjectures, and explain their thinking. That is, students need experiences in which they behave as mathematicians.

Teachers are responsible for providing those experiences. In its *Professional Standards for Teaching Mathematics*, NCTM (1991) suggests that teachers are responsible for (1) posing tasks to students that encourage communication, (2) listening to students' ideas and expecting them to clarify and defend those ideas as necessary, and (3) monitoring small-group and whole-class discussions as students work toward developing meaning in mathematics. That is, mathematics teachers need to encourage discourse in a manner that facilitates mathematical understanding. Many students are successful at listening to the teacher and emulating what the teacher does, sometimes without understanding. Asking students to move out of their comfort zone to talk and write about mathematics can lead to resistance because students do not see these activities as something associated with mathematics class. Nonetheless, if the goal is to develop students who are able to attach meaning to mathematics and to make sense of what they learn, then we need to persevere until students are comfortable at communicating mathematically.

This communication requires that students become proficient with using the language of mathematics, including its words and symbols. Just as students learn spoken language as toddlers through immersion in language-rich environments, middle grades students need immersion in the words and symbols of mathematics in order to develop fluency with mathematical language. Dealing with issues related to that immersion in mathematics language is the focus of Chapters 2 and 3.

In particular, Chapter 2 highlights research related to communication in the mathematics classroom in its various forms (e.g., reading, writing, speaking, and listening). By viewing all students as *mathematics language learners*, teachers can think about the types of language practices needed to help students become fluent in the language, in much the same way that language teachers help English language learners develop fluency in English. Chapter 3 then focuses on specific challenges related to reading mathematical text, including similarities and differences between English usage of words and mathematics usage as well as different ways in which symbols are used.

Taken together, the three chapters in this section provide you with research and theoretical perspectives to support the hard work needed to develop a communication-rich classroom in which students share their ideas, debate with their peers, and make sense of mathematics, individually and with others. These chapters provide a rationale for why we need to engage our students in the mathematical literacy practices detailed in Section 3.

CHAPTER 1

Meaning Making in Mathematics

The learning of mathematics entails both the interpretation of mathematical signs and the construction of mathematical meaning through communication with others.
—Adalira Saenz-Ludlow, "Classroom Interpreting Games with an Illustration"

We have no capability or power to think without signs.
—Charles Peirce, *Collected Writings*

As the quotes suggest, the interpretation of mathematical signs is essential to learning. But, what are mathematical signs and how do they relate to the meaning-making perspective that is the basis for this book? Before introducing definitions or theory, we illustrate this perspective through a vignette. Ms. Greenwood, a seventh-grade mathematics teacher, offers her students opportunities to make individual and group meaning about a set of data and how the data are displayed.

Ms. Greenwood was preparing a lesson on stem-and-leaf plots and knew that her seventh-grade students had little prior experience with such plots. She wanted to design a lesson to help students construct meaning for this type of display. She decided to hand out the following data to her students and told them the display represents the ages of U.S. presidents at the time of their inauguration. The students' job was to collaborate to determine the ages of the presidents.

```
4 | 2  3  6  6  7  8  9  9
5 | 0  1  1  1  1  2  2  4  4  4  4  4  5  5  5  5  5  6  6  6  7  7  7  7  8
6 | 0  1  1  1  2  4  4  5  8  9
```

As her students worked in small groups, she circulated around the room and listened to their conversations. She heard comments such as the following:

- Presidents are usually old.
- We learned in social studies that you can't be president unless you are 35 years old or older.
- We learned that President Kennedy was only in his 40s when he was killed.

The students began to wonder if the numbers in the first row were ages of presidents. They concluded that the first row might represent U. S. presidents' ages of 42, 43, 46, 46, 47, 48, 49, and 49.

When Ms. Greenwood brought the groups together for a whole-class discussion, she used her students' comments to help them develop meaning about how stem-and-leaf plots are constructed.

REFLECT

- In a traditional approach, the teacher typically tells students that data can be organized using a stem-and-leaf plot and then instructs students about the components needed to generate such a plot. How is the approach used by Ms. Greenwood different from traditional approaches? Compare the locus of responsibility for making sense of the mathematics in Ms. Greenwood's lesson with that in a traditional lesson.

- What did Ms. Greenwood learn about her students when she provided opportunities for them to generate their own ideas?

- What did Ms. Greenwood's students likely learn from this experience?

In this scenario, Ms. Greenwood gave her students a new symbolic representation (i.e., a stem-and-leaf plot) and asked them to investigate it in order to attach meaning to it. We all engage in such investigations whenever we encounter unknown or new signs and symbols.

Meaning Making: A Semiotic Perspective

We approach this book from a meaning-making or *semiotic* perspective. Briefly defined, semiotics is the study of how human beings *get and give meaning* through multiple, culturally agreed-upon systems of communication that include such disciplines as visual art, music, oral and written language, and mathematics.

Mathematicians, like all meaning makers, use many interrelated *sign systems* to make meaning and communicate with others. Sign systems (i.e., multiple modes of communication) include all of the diverse ways human beings come to understand and make meaning in their world, including social context, cultural and family experiences, shared understanding with others, personal and collective beliefs, and assumptions about reality (Short, Kauffman, and Kahn 2000). Each sign system has its own *elements*. For example, visual artists work with lines, shape, color, and form. Readers of print text work with words, punctuation, and paragraphs. Mathematicians work with meaning-making elements that include the English language, mathematics specific terminology (e.g., hypotenuse), implicit assumptions (e.g., the meaning of point), numerals, symbols, tables, diagrams, graphs, understandings about what is logical, and proofs (Rotman 2000).

According to Semali and Fueyo (2005), "At its most basic, semiotics is the study of sign systems: what signs mean, how they relate to one another, and how they are manipulated" (1). Mathematics teachers who understand the principles of semiotics recognize that mathematics is a culturally agreed-upon abstract system with characteristic ways of doing things—counting, computing, and analyzing (Lemke 2005). But, mathematics is much more than manipulating a culturally agreed-upon set of abstract symbols. *The goal of mathematics, like every other sign system, is to make and give meaning.*

Meaning making is reciprocal in mathematics learning: we give meaning to sign systems and the elements within sign systems, and in turn, sign systems give meaning to us. Regardless of pedagogical stance, we need to communicate mathematical ideas to others. Mathematics is a language that uses various signs (e.g., words, symbols, notations, icons, diagrams, graphs, representations) to convey information. Through the interpretation of these signs, individuals make meaning and gain understanding about mathematics concepts.

Consider the following description of the use of signs in algebra described by Goldin and Kaput (1996):

> The numerals, letters, and arithmetical symbols of an algebraic system of notation are *signs*. Certain configurations of those signs are permitted (e.g., the equation "$y = 3x - 6 = 0$"); other configurations are not allowed [and as a result are considered] nonsensical (e.g., "$y3x + = 6\ 0\ -$"); and still others are . . . ambiguous (e.g., depending on the context of the expression "$y = x3 - 6$" might be understood to be a rather sloppy way of writing "y equals x cubed minus 6"; or alternatively, x could be construed in the original expression as a missing digit in [a] two-digit number; or the expression might simply be rejected as erroneous). (404)

This description highlights three important ideas related to teaching and learning mathematics:

- Signs play a significant role in understanding and making meaning in mathematics.
- Understanding is based on an individual's interpretation of the presented signs.
- Functioning within a mathematics environment requires one to make and give meaning to signs that are encountered.

Because of these principles, mathematics instruction needs to focus not only on the meaning of concepts (e.g., slope), but also on "whose meaning and whose interpretations" (Saenz-Ludlow 2006, 194). Therefore, as part of mathematics instruction we need to consider students' personal interpretations and the origins of those interpretations, and evaluate the processes that students use to make sense of mathematics. That is, the process of meaning making needs to be visible with all of its possible messiness and struggles. Success in making sense of mathematics is often a result of steps forward followed by steps back or to the side before moving forward again.

Making meaning through the use of multiple sign systems is termed *transmediation* (Siegel 1995), which is a process of translating meaning from one or more sign systems (e.g., graphical display) to other sign systems (e.g., language). This was the situation with the stem-and-leaf plot in the vignette at the beginning of this chapter. Consider the following five tasks that middle grades students might encounter.

1. A gallon is 4 quarts. If a container holds g gallons, which expression shows the number of quarts the container holds?

   $g + 4$ $4g$ $g \div 4$

2. Write two fractions that name the shaded part.

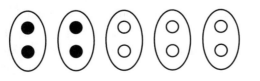

3. Write a story that describes the bicycle trip displayed by the following graph.

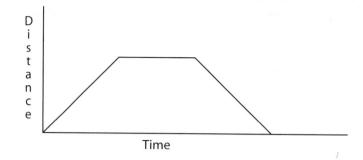

4. Two number cubes are tossed. Find each probability expressed as a fraction.

a. *P*(even sum)

b. *P*(sum of 5)

5. Two figures have a perimeter of 12 units. Can they have different areas? If so, draw the figures and label the dimensions. If not, explain why not.

In each task, students must move flexibly within or between semiotic systems (ordinary language, mathematics language, mathematics notations, diagrams, and graphs) and determine the connection between the systems in order to be successful. Many students struggle in mathematics because they have not developed the ability to translate from words to symbols (e.g., task 1) or from symbols to words (e.g., task 3).

Students in meaning-making mathematics classrooms engage in a range of activities and methods involving transmediation. Teachers may pose challenging worthwhile tasks, have students solve problems using multiple approaches, ask students to collaborate with peers and try to understand one another's modes of thinking and representing, encourage students to make conjectures and generalizations, and provide opportunities for students to debate and justify their reasoning. Teachers also prompt students to make sense of mathematics within the context of their own lives and cultural settings by keeping logs and journals in which they record personal reflections about their mathematics understandings and confusions (Smith 2005). Students listen to their teacher's and other students' explanations and they use *strategies* (i.e., plans of action to achieve a specific goal) that promote inquiry and problem solving. Students question teachers and fellow students, engage in calculations, read from their mathematics textbook, listen to their classmates' responses to teachers' questions, and look for and examine relationships and differences between previously acquired and newly formed ideas. In addition, they may copy information (e.g., definitions and diagrams) presented by others, view a mathematics video, work collaboratively with classmates, and employ various forms of technology (Lemke 2005).

Students in meaning-making classrooms have opportunities to construct knowledge about mathematics connections to the real world and to the mathematical demands of specific contexts (Smith 2005). These real-world activities or larger complex networks extend far beyond the classroom. As Lemke (2005) explains:

People make mathematical meanings as an integral part of activities, such as building and operating a power plant, sending an expedition to Mars, creating global climate models, or trying to find more efficient compression algorithms for digital video. (8)

As teachers, we need to remember that students cannot skillfully *make or give meaning* in mathematics unless they have experiences with the elements within the sign system of mathematics (e.g., mathematics language, ways of problem solving, definitions, symbols) (Albers 2003). Usually, it is only through their experiences in the mathematics classroom that they will understand how elements within that sign system operate, relate to one another, and connect to other sign systems.

R E F L E C T

- What type of mathematics instruction did teachers provide you in the middle grades?

- How were you encouraged and helped to engage in transmediation and meaning-making activities?

Implications for Teaching and Learning

Throughout this chapter, we have argued that effective mathematics teachers follow a semiotic perspective by emphasizing meaning. Teachers who promote meaning making provide opportunities for students to have numerous experiences with mathematics and to consider mathematics applications within multiple contexts, including the real world. In addition, such teachers help students understand the elements within the sign system of mathematics and extend students' abilities to coordinate (i.e., transmediate) meaning from mathematics into other sign systems (Hitt 1998). These teachers encourage students to consider mathematics tasks from multiple perspectives, and to recognize that knowledge is social and negotiated (Smith 1997). Most important, exemplary mathematics teachers understand that mathematics is best learned and taught as part of larger sense-making systems.

Here we summarize actions of mathematics teachers that help build a classroom environment in which meaning making is the norm. Teachers in meaning-making classrooms

- remember that learning mathematics concepts should not be confined to abstract, linear tasks because the discipline of mathematics extends beyond the classroom to real-life meaning-making activities (Smith 1997);

- know in what ways students make sense of what they are learning and emphasize understanding rather than memorization;

- provide opportunities for students to work collaboratively within a community of mathematics meaning makers to share ideas and understanding;

- provide opportunities for students to make and test conjectures, investigate ideas, debate solution strategies, and justify reasoning;

- respect individual students' perceptions and ideas and recognize that students' constructions vary according to prior experiences and cultural framework;

- expand students' understanding by encouraging them to transmediate mathematical concepts into a range of sign systems;

- teach strategies that encourage students to make meaning from mathematics symbols and terms and then use the terms and symbols;

- acknowledge "the multidirectional nature of learning and meaning making that must be achieved by all learners, including the teacher" (Smith 1997, 14);

- recognize that mathematics "teaching that is educative rests upon three essential dimensions: knowledge of the developing learner, of subject matter, and of the semiotic means by which the subject matter is rendered comprehensible for the learner" (Gavelek 2005, 2).

Summary

Effective mathematics teachers recognize that students make meaning in mathematics in different ways and that "meaning makers situate their meaning within their own experiences" (Albers 2003, 151). Students are influenced by their background knowledge, culture, ethnicity, first language, competence with oral and written language, and their understanding of and facility with the elements associated with the sign system of mathematics.

The study of semiotics provides a framework for our understanding of personal and group meaning making in mathematics. In the following chapters, we discuss how communication is central to meaning making in mathematics and we consider issues related to mathematics language, vocabulary, and symbolism that are critical elements of such communication.

Expand Your Understanding

1. Think of some signs that transcend cultures (e.g., a red regular octagon for a stop sign, a circle with an image and line drawn through it). What aspects of the sign system help the sign transcend cultures?

2. What are some universal gestures that can be used to communicate among people who speak different languages? In what ways would such gestures be considered a sign system?

3. Conduct a semiotic experiment. Survey ten middle grades students or your teaching peers and ask them the meaning of the following mathematical terms: *divisor, dividend, geometry,* and *algebra.* Audiotape or transcribe the responses so you can analyze them carefully. Did all ten respondents define the terms similarly? What divergence of responses did you note? How might a semiotic perspective explain the disparity or similarities in the respondents' understanding of the terms? Remember, from a semiotic perspective we recognize that individuals see and understand mathematics differently from one another depending on prior experiences (Smith 1997).

4. Devise a code without words. Use it to write a set of directions to guide someone from location A to location B. When you have used your code to write your directions, ask some peers to read it and try to get from location A

to location B. What did you find out about your code? Was your code a combination of two types of signs? Was your code an example of a socially agreed-upon sign system? How might you help students or peers understand your code? How is your code similar to mathematics symbols?

Connect to Practice

5. Consider some middle grades mathematics concepts that you teach (e.g., "The sum of the angle measures of any triangle is 180 degrees"; or "Rate times time equals distance"). How might you extend your students' understanding of these concepts through transmediated meaning-making activities? Record your ideas and compare/contrast them with ideas suggested by your colleagues.

6. Some middle grades teachers use songs or mnemonic devices to help students remember mathematics concepts. Consider such practices from a semiotic perspective.

   a. To what extent would you consider such practices to involve meaning making?

   b. What characteristics would need to be present for songs or mnemonic devices to lead to understanding rather than to memorization without understanding?

CHAPTER 2

Communication and Mathematical Literacy

> The development of students' power to use mathematics involves learning the *signs, symbols, and terms* of mathematics. This is best accomplished in problem situations in which students have an opportunity to read, write, and discuss ideas in which the use of the *language of mathematics* becomes natural. As students communicate these ideas, they learn to clarify, refine, and consolidate their thinking.
> —NCTM, *Curriculum and Evaluation Standards for School Mathematics; emphasis added*

Imagine you are a middle grades mathematics learner and a teacher asks you to read and solve the following problem:

> Die Skala einer Landkarte ist 1 Inch für je 5 Meilen. Wie Weit würde der Abstand auf der Karte sein für eine gerade Straße, die 20 Meilen lang ist? Bitte erklären Sie.[1]

Could you complete the task? Your success would depend first on your ability to interpret the *language* used in the problem (in this case German), and second on your ability to solve the problem.

Many middle grades mathematics students are challenged by the language of mathematics. To them, mathematics is a foreign language that contains unfamiliar symbols, signs, words, phrases, and longer *discourse* (i.e., oral or written communication). The *Professional Standards for Teaching Mathematics* (NCTM 1991) states, "the nature of . . . classroom discourse is a major influence on what students learn about mathematics" (56), and research shows that classroom discourse plays an essential role in mathematics learning (Lampert and Blunk 1998; Sfard 2001; Steinbring, Bartolini Bussi, and Sierpinska 1998). Communication in the mathematics classroom provides opportunities for students to discuss and justify their ideas, reflect on ideas presented by others, amend their ideas, and make meaning as they integrate shared knowledge. Simply stated, engaging in classroom discourse communities offers students opportunities to reason, learn from each other, and clarify their thinking. Accordingly, the continual construction of mathematical meaning through sign interpretation during the act of communication should be the essence of teaching and learning mathematics.

All Students Are Mathematics Language Learners

Because communication is central to learning mathematics, as teachers we should consider *every* student a *mathematics language learner* regardless of his or her level of English language proficiency: that is, whether he or she is an English language learner (ELL) or a proficient speaker of English. Although we readily acknowledge the need to develop language skills in students with limited English proficiency, we may not always recognize the overt need to develop language skills in students whose first language is English. Within the mathematics classroom, the range of language proficiency in mathematics, even among students whose first language is English, makes a focus on communication an essential feature of the mathematics activity of students and teachers.

Students' abilities to participate in the discourse community established as part of their mathematics classroom are directly linked to the language experiences teachers provide for the class. These experiences, in turn, help develop students' mathematical literacy. Teachers who teach from a semiotic, or meaning-making, perspective recognize being literate in any sign system (in this case mathematics) involves more than the ability to give and get meaning. Being literate in a specific sign system means that students not only understand the elements that operate within that system but also that they can "use, interpret, and invent within and across sign systems to become more literate" (i.e., use *multiple literacies*) (Albers 2003). In this chapter, we demonstrate how the use of multiple literacies can enhance students' understandings of mathematics as they learn to move easily among sign systems and become skillful in representing meaning in semiotic ways. In particular, we focus on classroom communication or discourse as a means to *negotiate meaning* in the mathematics classroom.

> ### REFLECT
>
> - Reflect on your mathematics classes during your middle grades years. Who did most of the talking? How often did your teachers lecture as you listened and took notes? To what extent did your teachers encourage you to collaborate with peers to discuss and solve mathematics problems?

Developing Mathematical Literacy Through Classroom Discourse

The primary focus in a semiotic perspective is on communicative activity in mathematics utilizing signs. This involves both sign reception and comprehension via listening and reading, and sign production via speaking and writing or sketching. (Ernest 2006, 69)

Discourse in the mathematics classroom encompasses many areas that have not been traditionally associated with mathematics instruction. Discourse involves the complete *literacy spectrum: listening, speaking, viewing, reading, writing, and interpreting representations* (i.e., *learning through and employing multiple literacies*). Specifically, discourse involves the ability to attend to and interpret what is being communicated verbally, or in writing. Genuine discourse occurs when the *sign receiver* (*listener* or *reader*) understands the information that the *sign producer* (*speaker* or *writer*) intends to convey.

Pirie (1998) identifies six means of communicating in a mathematics classroom:

- ordinary language (common everyday language),

- mathematics verbal language (using words),

- symbolic language (using mathematics symbols),

- visual representations (using visuals to communicate mathematics ideas),

- unspoken shared assumptions (means for generating understanding), and

- quasi-mathematical language (typically, student utterances that may not necessarily be coherent).

Each of these means of communicating influences students' mathematical growth. "Mathematics knowledge cannot be revealed by mere reading of mathematical signs, symbols, and principles. These signs have to be interpreted, and this interpretation requires experiences and implicit knowledge" (Steinbring 2006, 136). In mathematics, the various means of communication provide opportunities for students to make sense of mathematics and facilitate the exchanging and recording of mathematical ideas. In addition, each mode of communication (listening, speaking, reading, and writing) provides a lens for accessing and assessing what students understand and how they understand the mathematics they are expected to learn. That is, communication helps make evident what mathematics content or processes (e.g., meaning or operations with rational numbers) our students know as well as how they know it (e.g., procedurally, conceptually, through memorization, or by making connections to real-world problems). Each facet of communication needs to receive specific attention to ensure its effective use in the mathematics classroom.

The Communication Standard in the *Principles and Standards for School Mathematics* (NCTM 2000) outlines goals related to mathematical discourse. Specifically,

> Instructional programs from prekindergarten through grade 12 should enable all students to
>
> - organize and consolidate their mathematical thinking through communication;
>
> - communicate their mathematical thinking coherently and clearly to peers, teachers, and others;
>
> - analyze and evaluate the mathematical thinking and strategies of others;
>
> - use the language of mathematics to express mathematics ideas precisely. (60)

These goals for mathematics education reinforce the belief that mathematics and language are interconnected. In fact, many scholars agree that mathematics is a language (see, for example, Pimm 1987; Usiskin 1996), and that there are technical aspects to that language that teachers and their students need to consider and address in order to comprehend the subject matter (see, for example, Rubenstein and Thompson 2001; Thompson and Rubenstein 2000). Unlike English used in everyday situations, the language of mathematics is learned primarily in the mathematics classroom. Consequently, regarding *all* students as *mathematics language learners* may be essential to ensure they have opportunities to learn and use the language of mathematics.

The recommended inclusion of various modes of communication in the mathematics classroom has resulted in a need to enhance the methods used to access and evaluate students' mathematical understandings. In today's world, teachers need to differentiate between students' rote learning of procedures and their conceptual understanding of mathematics concepts. As a result, mathematics teachers are using a variety of assessment strategies to collect evidence about students' mathematics learning, including classroom discussions, oral problem solving, and written assessments that include open-ended tasks, journal entries, or writing prompts. These assessment strategies require students to represent and record what they know by expressing their solutions and thought processes both orally and in writing.

Speaking and Listening

Speaking and listening in the mathematics classroom can occur in two types of settings: monologue or dialogue (Coulter 1999). In a typical mathematics classroom, students may be asked to attend to a teacher's monologue, where the teacher is solely in control of the communication and the students are limited to listening. Consider the following monologue in Ms. Jones' class:

MS. JONES: Today we are going to study how to find the volume of a cylinder. Remember that a cylinder is a shape that looks like a can. You can imagine the cylinder as a set of circles stacked on top of each other. The volume is the amount that the cylinder holds. How can we find the volume? Well, think again about a cylinder as circles stacked on top of each other. Remember that we find the area of a circle by using the formula $A = \pi r^2$. Then, if the circles are stacked h high, the volume would just be the area of the circle multiplied by h, or $V = \pi r^2 h$.

Let's try an example. Suppose we want to find the volume of a soda can whose diameter is 3 inches and whose height is 6 inches. In our formula $V = \pi r^2 h$, we need the radius. Remember that the radius is half of the diameter. So, the radius is 1.5 inches. If we substitute 1.5 for the radius and 6 for the height in the formula, we get $V = \pi \cdot (1.5)^2 \cdot 6 = \pi \cdot (2.25) \cdot 6 = 13.5\pi$. Volume is measured in cubic inches, so the volume of the soda can is 13.5π cubic inches. If you approximate π by 3.14, you find that the soda can is 42.39 cubic inches.

Throughout this monologue, Ms. Jones directs all the conversation in the classroom. Students are relegated to observing the teacher provide a justification for the formula and then watching as the teacher uses the formula in an example to find a specific volume.

In contrast, during an interactive dialogue there is genuine involvement by participants, requiring that each individual engage in the act of speaking and listening. The listener in each setting is required to make sense of and interpret the utterances of the speaker and then offer a response. Consider the following dialogue in Ms. Wade's class that focuses on the same concept as in Ms. Jones' class.

MS. WADE: Today we are going to study how to find the volume of a cylinder. Who can remind us what volume is?

RACHEL: How much something can hold.

MS. WADE: Absolutely! Any other ideas?

CARLOS: The amount of space inside.

MS. WADE: That's another great idea. When do we need to find volume? [*Several students raise their hand to share.*]

SAMANTHA: When you want to know how much something holds.

JONATHAN: When you need to find the amount of liquid in a container.

YAN-YAN: When you want to find out how much it takes to fill something up.

MS. WADE: These are all good examples of finding volume. What are some examples of cylinders that you see every day?

JOHN: Soup can, soda can, or any type of can.

MS. WADE: Yes. Let's see if we can find the volume of a soda can. I just happen to have an empty soda can here. If I asked you to estimate its dimensions, what would you say? Talk with a neighbor and come up with some reasonable values for the distance across the can and the height.

[*Ms. Wade gives students a couple of minutes to talk with their neighbor before bringing the class back together.*]

DAVID: Lynne and I think the can is about 4 inches across and about 7 inches tall.

NEAL: Soho and I think the can is about 5 inches across and about 6 inches tall.

MS. WADE: How many of you have estimates that are close to those of David and Lynne or Neal and Soho? Raise your hands if your estimates are in the same ballpark. [*The majority of students raise their hand.*] Last week we learned how to find the volume of a box. Who can remind me of the formula and how we thought about it?

NATHANIEL: Volume = length × width × height.
Length × width is the area of the bottom of the box.
Then you multiply that number by the height.

MS. WADE: Excellent. How could we use that idea to find a formula for the volume of a can? I will give you 3 minutes to work with a partner to try to find a formula for the volume of our soda can.

[*Ms. Wade walks around the room while students work and is pleased with the way students discuss their thinking. Some pairs make good progress and others have difficulties. Still, she thinks students will be able to offer some good ideas when they come back together as a class.*]

MS. WADE: Okay. Let's see what you came up with. Anybody want to share?

BETH: We decided the bottom of the can is a circle. So, we used Nathaniel's idea. We found the area of the circle and then multiplied by the height of the can. But we forgot how to find the area of a circle.

MS. WADE: Beth, you and your partner have some good thinking there. Can anybody help them with the area of a circle? Remember we studied this formula several weeks ago.

JOSHUA: $A = \pi r^2$.

MS. WADE: Okay, then if we use Joshua's formula and Beth's idea, what do we get for a formula for the volume of our cylinder?

BETH: πr^2 times height.

Notice that in this dialogue, Ms. Wade actively engages her students in concepts related to the topic at hand. She activates students' previous knowledge about volume and she tries to have students develop a formula on their own. The discussions provide participants opportunities to negotiate meaning by introducing new ideas, clarifying ideas, and questioning current understandings.

Through listening, teachers and students acknowledge that information may be shared using multiple semiotic systems, including natural language, gestures, drawings, or a combination of such activities. Active listening in a mathematics classroom is different from simply hearing. Listening, by both teacher and students, is an intentional process in which participants are fully engaged.

> Because listening is interpretative, what one is able to hear (understand) is also largely dependent upon the context in which the listening occurs. The context provides us with clues to interpret the words and actions of the speaker. It is thus that the same statement made in a different setting can take on new meaning or perhaps lose its meaning. (Davis 1994, 277–78)

This focus on listening and speaking in mathematics classrooms is particularly important given the proliferation of multicultural and multilingual students in middle grades classrooms. Teachers not only need to be fully engaged in classroom discourse (both listening and speaking); they also need to be skilled at making sense of students' attempts at meaning making that may be fragile, partial, or poorly stated (i.e., quasi-mathematical language).

> Listening across the chasms of age, culture, and class, teachers face a problem common to most forms of cross-cultural communication. The problem is one of trying to understand what students mean with their words, pictures, gestures, and tone. Students do not represent their thinking in ways that match adult forms. (Ball 1997, 735)

As a result, teachers need methods to navigate students' mathematical knowledge, their use of common language, and the inarticulate ways in which they may express themselves.

Davis (1996) proposes three modes of listening in the teaching act: *evaluative, interpretative,* and *hermeneutic.* Evaluative listening occurs when teachers listen to students' utterances for particular feedback. For example, a teacher might listen to students' contributions to determine whether they are correct or incorrect. Typically, listening is primarily the responsibility of the learner in settings in which the teacher focuses on evaluative listening.

During interpretative listening, a teacher's goal is "to *access* . . . rather than to merely *assess* what [has] been learned" (52–53; italics in original). In the initial parts of the sample dialogue, Ms. Wade used interpretative listening as she accessed what her students already knew about volume in terms of its meaning and its use. With both evaluative and interpretative listening, Davis argues that there is a dichotomy between the roles of teacher and student.

However, in hermeneutic listening this dichotomy does not exist.

> "Hermeneutic listening" is an imaginative participation in the formation and transformation of experiences through ongoing interrogation of the taken-for-granted and the prejudices that frame perceptions and actions. The focus is on the dynamic interdependence of agent and setting, thought and action, knowledge

and knower, self and other, individual and collective—rather than on autonomous constitution or construction. (53)

That is, hermeneutic listening requires the listener and the speaker to negotiate meanings in order to understand each other. The listener, in this case, does not make assumptions about messages conveyed by the speaker but attempts to understand based on the speaker's terms. Educators have argued that hermeneutic listening is the type that is encouraged in classrooms that support the NCTM process standards, such as communication (D'Ambrosio 2004). We suggest that Ms. Wade understood ideas from hermeneutic listening when she negotiated with students to develop the formula for the volume of the can by using Nathaniel's and Beth's comments about volume, even though Beth and her partner's understanding was incomplete. Simply put, hermeneutic listening explains how each learner interprets and comprehends discourse according to individual experiences and perceptions. Beth used Nathaniel's ideas to outline an approach to find the volume, even though her lack of knowledge about the area of a circle made her less than successful.

The ability to speak mathematically (describing, explaining, justifying) is developed as teachers provide students with opportunities to verbalize what they understand about the subject matter. During this verbalization process, students have to pull together ordinary and mathematical language to convey their intended message. Giving students opportunities to verbalize their thinking gives teachers access to students' understandings, misconceptions, and mathematics language development. Further, during these interactions teachers can develop students' mathematics language skills by helping them pronounce mathematics terms (e.g., *Pythagorean, commutative, Euler*—pronounced "Oiler") or build vocabulary (i.e., introducing or encouraging the use of appropriate mathematics vocabulary). Teachers also can extend, paraphrase, or ask students to paraphrase attempts at communicating their ideas (e.g., "I think you were trying to say. . . ." or "How could you rephrase that so that you could include some of the math words we have studied?"). Asking students to express themselves verbally could be considered an initial step in helping them to write mathematically (e.g., see Huinker and Laughlin 1996).

R E F L E C T

- Think about your history as a mathematics learner. Describe any time when you thought you were not understood. Have you ever asked your mathematics teacher a question, but he or she provided an answer unrelated to what you asked? In what ways was the teacher listening to you?

- As a teacher, how often have you assumed you knew or anticipated what students would say? To what extent have you listened to your students in the hermeneutic way described above?

While speaking, the speaker can respond to the feedback the listener provides in terms of facial expressions, body language, or questions. This feedback provides opportunities for speakers to elaborate or clarify what they intend to say. As teachers, we need to recognize when students speak they take a risk by opening themselves to public scrutiny.

Reading and Writing

Reading and writing enhance each other and are complementary processes that can aid students in their mathematical development. However, students may have difficulty with reading mathematics text and writing mathematics solutions because of the specialized nature of mathematics vocabulary, symbols, and structure.

> To read mathematics texts means to take the global meaning from the page, not just to be able to read a few sentences. It means to appreciate the structure of a question and the various graphs, diagrams, and pictures related to it. Reading mathematics text requires different skills and knowledge on the part of the reader to achieve acceptable levels of reading comprehension. . . . The reading of a mathematics text is far more complex than simply being able to read the words on the page. It is about comprehending the mathematics ideas being put forward. (Noonan 1990, 79)

Reading the language of mathematics in the classroom involves:
- making sense of mathematics terms, symbols, notations, and syntax;
- interpreting pictures, diagrams, charts, and graphs;
- discerning differences between the meaning of a word in a mathematics context and when used as part of everyday language (e.g., the word *mean*);
- understanding the significance of the sentence structure in mathematics problems; and
- integrating different modes of communication (e.g., the written text to the spoken text).

When students read mathematics, they not only take meaning from the text, they also generate meaning based on their prior experiences and knowledge (Siegel et al. 1996). Prior experiences and level of proficiency in reading and interpreting mathematics influence students' ability to *make meaning* in the mathematics classroom. The complexities related to reading suggest that teachers need to help students learn specialized reading and interpretation skills as part of mathematics instruction so they can make sense of the words, symbols, graphs, and diagrams they encounter during mathematics lessons as detailed more in Chapter 3.

Writing in mathematics provides opportunities to access and assess students' mathematical understandings as they organize their thinking, reflect on what they understand and what is still unclear, and create a record of their knowledge. When students are required to describe, explain, or justify their thinking, they are able to make visible what they know and understand. This written record can be used to chart mathematical concept and language development over time.

> Many types of information can be gained from students' writing. It may illustrate diagnostic details concerning computational error patterns and allow insights regarding where to begin instruction. Writing may suggest reasons why a student has failed to make connections between strands of the mathematics curriculum. . . . It may help clarify students' understanding of mathematics concepts and procedures, or provide insights regarding students' beliefs and attitudes about mathematics. (Drake and Amspaugh 1994, 43)

Overall, writing provides a *window* into what students understand and how they understand the mathematics topics they are learning. Many current classroom and high-stakes assessments require students to write solution strategies or explain their

- When have you been unable to understand an explanation provided by someone else?

- On an assessment, one item has the following directions: *show all your work.* A second item has these directions: *explain your thinking while completing the problem.* Compare and contrast what you would expect to learn from responses to items with these different directions.

reasoning. These assessment practices necessitate helping students learn how to write for a mathematical audience.

Summary

In this chapter, we have recommended that all students be considered *mathematics language learners.* To support students as active, authentic learners, we encourage mathematics instruction that focuses on classroom discourse and language development that engages the entire literacy spectrum. Communication should focus not only on the development of mathematical concepts but also on the meanings and interpretations that students take from those discussions. Students develop mathematics language skills within a social context that provides direct experiences with *multiple sign systems* so that they can get, make, and negotiate meaning in order to demonstrate what they know and understand. As such, mathematics instruction that emphasizes the development of students' *mathematical literacy* provides them ample opportunities to listen, speak, read, and write about mathematics.

However, it is not sufficient for teachers to expect that students will communicate just because they are encouraged to do so. Students and teachers must have ownership of strategies to ensure the type and quality of classroom interaction (talking, representing, and recording) are useful for developing mathematical understandings. The quality of classroom discourse determines the effects discourse has on what students are able to learn in mathematics classrooms (e.g., Cobb, Yackel, and McClain 2000; Elliot and Kenney 1996; Lampert and Blunk 1998). Establishing this type of discourse community can be a challenging task (see, for example, Rittenhouse 1998; Silver and Smith 1996). In Sections 2 and 3 of this text, we share instructional strategies and approaches that can facilitate the type of classroom discourse described in this chapter in order to enhance students' mathematical literacy.

Expand Your Understanding

1. Collaborate with your peers and discuss how teachers might help students improve their listening or speaking skills in a mathematics class. Discuss how appropriate instructional approaches can be established to support the type of discourse that leads to mathematical growth.

2. Observe a mathematics class and make note of the number of times the teacher provides students with opportunities to share or present solution strategies to their peers, has students assist in the formation of concepts, expects students to clarify their language, or has students write about their mathematics thinking. What do your findings indicate about students' opportunities to develop language skills in that class?

Connect to Practice

3. Select a passage from your middle grades mathematics textbook. In what ways might *language* influence students' abilities to understand the information provided in the passage? What common or mathematics words might you need to clarify for students? Are there additional words you would need to clarify for English language learners? How might clarifying the meaning of these words help with students' mathematical understandings?

4. Select a section, chapter, or unit of your mathematics book that contains a large amount of written text.

   a. Make a list of English words (i.e., *general vocabulary*) and mathematics terms (i.e., *technical vocabulary*) contained within the chapter that you might need to clarify for students.

   b. Why might these general and technical vocabulary words be unfamiliar? Is there some vocabulary that might be more familiar to students from certain regions of the country (e.g., snowboarding, waterskiing) or diverse experiences (e.g., tobogganing, curling, riding a subway)?

   c. How might the words you identify interfere with your students' abilities to show what they know mathematically?

   d. What words or contexts are used in the word problems that might cause difficulties for students who have not had certain life experiences?

Note

1. The English translation is "The scale for a map is 1 inch : 5 miles. How long would the distance on the map be for a straight road that is 20 miles long? Please explain." (Translation provided by Tony Erben, University of South Florida.)

CHAPTER 3

Reading and Language Issues

The text is simply ink on paper until a reader comes along.
—Robert E. Probst, "Adolescent Literature and the English Curriculum"

It might be that problems of vocabulary are considered to be fairly superficial within the whole issue of language and mathematics learning, but it is nevertheless critical that such problems are not ignored in the hope they will go away.
—Anthony Orton, *Learning Mathematics*

The National Council of Teachers of Mathematics (NCTM) describes a mathematically literate individual as one who is able "to explore, conjecture, and to reason logically, as well as use a variety of mathematics methods effectively to solve problems" (1989, 6). Students who are mathematically literate must be able to communicate effectively using the language of mathematics as they speak, read, and write mathematics as well as listen to mathematics. As indicated in Chapter 2, middle grades students are often challenged by mathematical language. For many, mathematics is a foreign language; our students are *mathematics language learners* with many of the same issues and difficulties faced by English language learners. The fluency with which students are able to use mathematics language to express their understanding of mathematics concepts provides insights into the robustness of their thinking.

Many middle grades students bring reading skills with them to the mathematics classroom. They may have learned to read for the main idea of a passage. They may have learned to predict what will come next based on what they have read and their background knowledge. They may have learned to make inferences by connecting information in text to information gleaned from their world experiences. And, they may have learned to compare and contrast text passages to look for similarities and differences (Geskus, Borden, and Burnett 1999). Whatever general reading strategies students have, they face further challenges when applying these strategies to reading mathematics.

As teachers, we want our students to make sense of mathematics and to develop abilities to learn on their own and not rely solely on us for knowledge. We want our students to view the textbook as a source of information and not as just a source of homework exercises. To help our students become independent learners in our classes and to prepare our students for advanced study in the future, we need to help them learn the language of mathematics, including the way that it is presented in technical text. That is, they need to learn how to apply their existing reading and interpretation skills to mathematics language (written and oral), including attention to the unique characteristics of mathematics vocabulary and symbols that influence their ability to read mathematical text with understanding.

Reading Mathematical Text

Reading is a complex, multidimensional process. We know that reading "is much more than being able to decode print" (Gipe 2005, 4). We also know that readers need to relate personally with text, or comprehension does not occur. Our students need to interact with mathematics text in at least three distinct ways: *within the text, beyond the text,* and *about the text* (Scharer et al. 2005). They need to think *within the text* to comprehend the topic they are reading, to learn relationships among the concepts, and to keep in mind where important information can be found. They also need to read *beyond the text* as they bring their own experiences to bear to make conjectures about the meaning of a passage or to understand inferential language in a word problem. For instance, consider the following word problem:

> Carla had $50 but wanted to buy a prom dress for $80. She decided to borrow money from her parents. How much will she be in the red if she buys the dress?

Students who do not understand the meaning of the metaphor "be in the red" may comprehend "in the red" literally, and have difficulty realizing that the operation needed to solve the problem is subtraction. Students need to bring considerable life experience to bear to read the problem with understanding. Finally, students need to read *about the text* to notice organization and how that organization can help to convey meaning (e.g., Are headings used? How are definitions identified?). In this chapter, we highlight some special characteristics of mathematics text that provide the foundation for the instructional practices described in Chapter 11.

Students need to learn to read mathematics text at a slower pace than they read many other types of text. Students need to read with paper and pencil at hand in order to work problems and follow along with the authors. Students who skim through a mathematics text may not grasp essential meanings. Rather, students need to attend to every single word in mathematics. For example, in a novel, students can gloss over some words without losing the essence of the story. Consider the sentence, "The handsome man left the movie theater with the girl on his arm." If students miss the word *theater*, they have not lost the main meaning of the sentence; if they miss the word *movie*, however, they have lost meaning because the word *theater* applies to a dramatic enactment of many types. So, students often become accustomed to glossing over a word now and then because they are still able to understand the meaning of a story. In contrast, every word in mathematics conveys essential information. For instance, consider the sentence, "A regular octagon has interior angles that each measure 135°." The word *octagon* informs the reader that the figure is a polygon with eight sides. But the word *regular* identifies the octagon as one with all sides the same length and all angles the same measure. The adjective *regular* in the mathematics sentence becomes part of the phrase *regular octagon* and is more than just a modifier. A great deal of information is conveyed in the phrase *regular octagon*.

Furthermore, mathematics text often lacks the predictability of ordinary stories. For instance, students learn patterns in particular genres of literature that help them know how to decipher what they read. For instance, when students read a fairy tale, they know there will be an underdog, there will be someone wicked, there will be elements of magic, and there will be a happy ending. When students read fiction, they know there will be characters, settings, problems, and solutions. There is much that students understand about the story without attending to every detail and every word. But mathematics text lacks this predictability. Every new concept is a new tale. Although each lesson of a mathematics text generally has some narrative and some examples, reading one lesson does not allow one to skip over parts of a second lesson.

Mathematics textbooks are not just different from fiction in the pace at which they are read or their predictability. A typical mathematics lesson contains text of different types and students interact with these types for different purposes. Specifically, Shuard and Rothery (1984, 9) identify five types of mathematics text:

- *Exposition* is the narrative body of text that contains explanations of concepts, introduction of vocabulary and notation, summaries, important rules and properties, and completed examples students use to guide them in solving problems on their own.

- *Instructions* tell the reader to do something, such as draw, solve, simplify, compute. Instructions tell the reader to complete a task away from the text.

- *Exercises* are the problems that students are expected to complete.

- *Peripheral writing* contains introductory remarks or clues for the reader. Peripheral writing does not contain important information, so readers can read without the level of attention required to make sense of exposition. A beginning sentence to a lesson, such as "In the last lesson you studied . . . ," is an example of peripheral writing.

- *Signals* are the headings, boxes, letters, or numbers for the problems. Signals should be read carefully because they alert readers about what content comes next.

Within the narrative, most mathematics texts, as well as other discipline-based texts, often highlight vocabulary in some way. One might consider the use of bold, or italics, or boxes around definitions to be signals to clue the reader these are important ingredients of the lesson.

REFLECT

- Think about a time when you read a story and found an unfamiliar word. To what extent did you need to find a dictionary? Were you able to skip over the word and still understand the story?

REFLECT

- Review the sample lesson taken from a middle grades mathematics text (see the appendix). Identify examples of different types of text.

If students use their mathematics textbook as a source of information and not just a problem book, then they need to become familiar with features of the text that the authors have incorporated to assist in learning. As you read the following vignette, reflect on the benefits for students in learning how to use their textbook efficiently.

Mr. Howard knew that his classes the first few days of school would be shorter than normal. But he also wanted to ensure that his students engaged in meaningful activities. Therefore, he decided to have them work in small groups on a Mathematics Textbook Survey. He planned to focus this year on helping students begin to read technical text and he thought the survey would be a good start.

Mr. Howard gave students the questions in Figure 3.1 based on the middle grades text from which the lesson in the appendix is taken. His students worked together to find the answers. Toward the end of class, he had students share their answers as a class. During this sharing, he had a chance to engage students in dialogue about how to use some of these features.

Use your book to answer the following questions.

1. Find the Table of Contents. What is the mathematics topic of study in Chapter 9?

2. How does your book identify definitions?

3. Use the glossary to find the definition of *variable*.

4. According to the index, on what page is the topic of regular polygons addressed?

5. What materials are found at the end of each chapter in the text?

For questions 6 through 11, use Lesson 1-2 in your book.

6. What two features are found at the beginning of each lesson?

7. What should yo do when you find a Quiz Yourself in the lesson? On what page will you find the answers to the Quiz Yourself in Lesson 1-2?

8. How does the book identify important vocabulary?

9. Look on page 12. What headings do you find?

10. Look at the question set at the end of the lesson. What types of problems do you find? On what page do you find the answers to the questions?

11. At the end of question 18 on page 16, the problem has (Lesson 1-1) written after it. What does this mean?

FIG. 3.1
Sample questions for a Mathematics Textbook Survey

MR. HOWARD: Why do you think the authors put the Quiz Yourself questions in the lesson?

JIMMY: To see if you understand.

ALYESSA: To make you read.

MR. HOWARD: Those are both good reasons. When we get ready to have a quiz or a test, you might go back over the Quiz Yourself questions in the chapter. They don't cover everything you need to know, but they are a way to see if you know the basics in the lesson.

CARLA: What did they mean by the Activity heading?

MR. HOWARD: Well, take a minute and read it. [*Mr. Howard waits a few minutes.*] Anybody have an idea what this heading signifies?

CARLA: It's questions we have to answer.

MR. HOWARD: Activities are questions to answer. The questions in the activity will usually require that we do something to get an answer. I want you to put your Textbook Survey in the front of your notebook. Remember that your textbook has lots of features to help you be successful; you should refer back to the survey if you forget where to look to find certain things in your book.

Teachers can customize a survey to focus students' attention on specific features of their text. We believe that using such a survey is an important first step in helping students understand the structure and layout of their text so that they can use its important features.

Reading Principles

There are several principles that we need to consider as we encourage students in the reading process (Daniels and Zemelman 2004).

- *Reading is more than decoding.* It is not enough for students to translate a mathematics sentence into spoken language; they must also comprehend that translation.

- *Reading is an active, constructive process.* As students read, they need to engage with the text. They need to ask themselves questions about what they read, what they understand, and what does not make sense.

- *Reading requires a repertoire of thinking strategies.* As teachers, we need to help our students monitor their thinking and develop strategies to help them make sense of the text. Can students create a mental image of what they read? Does the reading connect to previous lessons or other life experiences? What question is the text trying to answer? Can students summarize what they read?

- *Prior knowledge is the main determinant of comprehension.* Students' prior experiences with mathematics content influence their ability to make connections with new content. In addition, students' life experiences with contexts used in problems can influence their ability to comprehend a problem. As we discussed in the beginning of the chapter, phrases such as "in the red" can cause difficulties for students if their experiences do not provide the background to recognize how the meaning of the phrase clues the reader to a solution. As teachers, we need to be alert to potential contexts or phrases that may be unfamiliar to our students, particularly English language learners, and ask questions to ensure that they have the contextual background needed to make sense of the text.

- *Reading is a recursive process.* Reading is not a linear, all-or-nothing process. We read a piece of text, try to make sense of it, and reread as needed. We move back and forth as we work to comprehend text. We need to help students recognize that it is natural to read mathematics text more than once to understand it.

Just as we communicate in English with words arranged in sentences that give meaning, we communicate in mathematics using meaningful sentences as well. However, because mathematical language consists of both words and symbols, sentences in mathematics often look quite different from sentences in English. The combinations of words and symbols lead to three types of mathematics sentences (Kane, Byrne, and Hater 1974):

- Sentences comprised of only words. (e.g., *The area of a rectangle is the product of its length and width.*)

- Sentences containing both words and symbols. (e.g., *The median of the set of numbers 14, 10, 18, 24, 6 is 14.*)

- Sentences limited to symbols. (e.g., $2n + 15 = 21$)

R E F L E C T

- What different issues might students face when they deal with each type of sentence?

- What sentence types likely create the most difficulty for English language learners in the mathematics classroom?

- What sentence type appears most often in the materials you prepare for your students?

Comprehending the Language of Mathematics

Middle grades students are continuing to refine their reading strategies. Applying and extending those strategies to reading mathematics is even more challenging. In the next few sections of this chapter, we detail challenges related to mathematical language, symbolism, and graphs.

Issues Related to Mathematics Vocabulary

As mathematics teachers, we are fluent in the language of mathematics and have dealt with many of its aspects that might be problematic for our students. Mathematics language is second nature to us. For many of our students, however, the language of mathematics is similar to a foreign language; thus, our job is to provide opportunities for students to learn the components of that foreign language so they, too, can become fluent in it. Our goal should be to help our students use mathematics as second-naturedly as we do.

The vocabulary of mathematics poses special challenges for students and teachers. Teachers typically introduce and use mathematics vocabulary in the classroom. But for students to develop mathematical literacy, they must also use that vocabulary enough so that they internalize the vocabulary and make it their own. Some practices that we employ in our classrooms can facilitate that language development. We start our discussion with a brief vignette.

During the summer, Mr. Baker attended a professional development workshop on mathematics language. As a result, he set a goal to help his students become proficient in communicating mathematically. One instructional practice discussed in the workshop was the use of a word or sentence wall, in which the class would construct a visual dictionary to help students grasp the vocabulary and symbols that were part of the curriculum. He thought this practice had potential to make the words and symbols public and to make them readily available to his students. He hoped the constant reminders would make it easier for students to use correct terminology when they discussed mathematics in the classroom.

At the beginning of the school year, Mr. Baker decided to set aside one section of a classroom wall for this purpose. Each time students encountered a new word or symbol, he planned to have students work together to write the entries (a word, a phrase or an authentic sentence to give a definition, and a picture) on large pieces of construction paper. He planned to encourage students to look at the wall whenever needed, including when they took tests. Figure 3.2 contains two sample entries his students made during the year.

As the school year ended, Mr. Baker reflected on how well this practice had helped him meet his goal. Students referred to the word wall throughout the year and enjoyed making entries for the wall. He decided he would continue to use this practice in subsequent years. But he wondered what else he could do to make sure his students internalized all the entries on the wall.

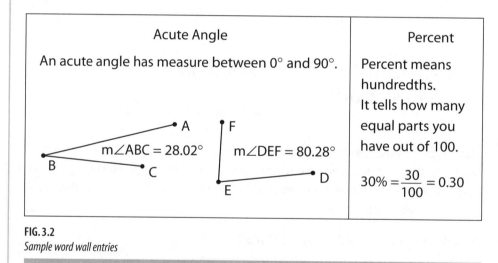

FIG. 3.2
Sample word wall entries

Mr. Baker's use of a word wall is an example of an attempt to establish a classroom environment in which students are expected to develop understanding of mathematical language and become fluent mathematics language learners. A *word* or *sentence wall* is one way to assist mathematics language learners by helping them connect a word and its verbal and/or pictorial meaning on a regular basis; that is, Mr. Baker immersed his students in the language of mathematics. Just as English language learners must see new words regularly while learning them, *mathematics language learners* must see the words in their language as well.

Usiskin (1996) argues that mathematics is a language in the same way that English, French, or Chinese is a language, with symbols that permit us to write in the language of mathematics. The components of mathematics language, namely its vocabulary and symbols, are the building blocks for communication, and they, along with syntax, are the elements for the sign system of mathematics that students must learn to negotiate to make meaning of mathematics. Just as students must use new language words regularly to integrate them into their existing vocabulary, they must also use mathematics terms regularly in order to make them their own. In fact, Murray (2004) suggests that students need to use a word at least 30 times in order to own that word; we would add symbols to this usage as well. Given that the mathematics classroom is the primary place where students have an opportunity to use mathematics language, it is our responsibility as teachers to provide a range of opportunities for students to use the vocabulary and symbols of mathematics if they are going to internalize and personalize those components of language.

Miller (1993) studied students' comprehension of vocabulary. Teachers in Australia gave their eighth-grade students the following twenty common mathematics terms and asked them to provide a meaning for each term, using words, examples, or diagrams.

- sum
- quotient
- angle
- fraction
- factor
- perimeter
- measure
- product
- difference
- remainder
- digit
- equal
- diameter
- meter
- denominator
- average
- circle
- whole
- divide
- subtract

Students' responses were scored as an acceptable meaning in words; an acceptable diagram, example, or symbol; or an acceptable combination of words, symbols, examples, or diagrams.

Miller reported that the average number of terms described in words was four; when symbols, diagrams, or examples were accepted as well, the average number of terms described increased to eleven. Nevertheless, the teachers thought that their students should have been able to describe all twenty terms.

What lessons should we take from Miller's research? The fact that students were not able to describe mathematics terms related to concepts they had been studying for several years suggests that teachers *need* to spend time helping students make sense of vocabulary. Mathematics vocabulary forms the foundation for the language students use to build understanding of important concepts. When students lack knowledge of

REFLECT

- Think about a situation in which you thought you understood a mathematics concept but had difficulty explaining the idea to a peer. What did such difficulties suggest about your understanding of the concept? To what extent did language issues contribute to your difficulties?
- Consider the following expression: $\frac{3}{4} + \frac{2}{3}$. What language issues arise for a student who needs to justify the algorithm rather than just complete the computation? What vocabulary and symbol issues might create difficulties for mathematics language learners in this situation?

REFLECT

- Before reading further, decide how you would describe a few of these terms. Then, predict the average number of terms for which your eighth-grade students would be able to provide a meaning.
- Understanding and using a word is different from writing a definition of the word. Compare and contrast the skills needed to define a word with the skills needed to understand and use the word.

essential vocabulary, they often have difficulty speaking mathematically or reading mathematics with understanding. As teachers listen to students' oral communication, they gain insight into students' use of language, either appropriately or inappropriately, and can modify instruction as needed. For instance, if students read 32 ÷ 8 as "thirty-two divided into eight" they may experience difficulty with fractions or with using technology appropriately to handle complicated division problems.

Miller also reports a case in which a teacher assigned students to write about fractions. The teacher was dismayed when students failed to use terms such as *denominator* or *numerator*. However, when observers spent some time in the teacher's classroom, they noticed the teacher never used the formal terms. Instead, he only used informal language, such as *bottom number* or *top number*. The teacher thought he used mathematics language, but he did not. If teachers fail to use appropriate mathematics vocabulary, how can students be expected to use it?

When students first learn concepts, it may be appropriate to use informal language until they are ready to attach the accepted mathematics terminology to the concept. However, Miller's work suggests that as teachers we must make a conscious effort to help students move from informal to formal language if students are to have opportunities to learn the language that permits them to communicate with others. Combining the formal language, *numerator*, with the informal language, *top number*, and using the two in conjunction with each other is one instructional practice to help students make bridges from the informal to the formal. Moreover, the roots of numerator and denominator can help students grasp their meanings. (Word roots to help students understand vocabulary will be explored in Chapter 9.)

Thompson and Rubenstein (2000) identify several issues related to potential sources of difficulty for students' understanding of mathematics vocabulary.

1. Some words have different meanings in mathematics and everyday English (e.g., *volume, factor, plane*) (i.e., special vocabulary).

2. Some words have only a mathematics meaning (e.g., *hypotenuse, integer, octagon*) (i.e., technical vocabulary).

3. Some words have meanings that are comparable in mathematics and everyday English, but the meaning in mathematics is more precise (e.g., *similar, divide*).

4. Some words have multiple mathematics meanings (e.g., *median, base, round*).

5. Some words have different meanings in different disciplines (e.g., *radical* in mathematics versus science versus social studies, *solution* in mathematics versus science).

6. Some words are homonyms with common English words (e.g., *plane* versus *plain, sum* versus *some, arc* versus *ark*).

7. Some mathematics phrases must be learned in their entirety (e.g., *if-then, at most, box-and-whiskers*).

8. Some related words have different meanings that are often confused (*factor* and *multiple, hundreds* and *hundredths*).

For English language learners, the nontechnical, or nonmathematical, meaning of a word is often the first meaning that is learned. Therefore, it is especially important for these students that teachers draw comparisons and contrasts between the everyday meaning they know and the unfamiliar mathematical meaning. For instance, students know that the *median* of a highway is a strip down the middle of the road; so the *median* of a data set should have something to do with the middle of the data. Likewise, a *tree* has branches from the trunk; a *tree* in mathematics has branches to indicate decision points from a main question or different possibilities or outcomes.

For all learners, and particularly for English language learners, personal dictionaries can be a useful strategy to support students in their learning. Personal dictionaries might contain an authentic sentence (i.e., a sentence in everyday language) with the target word or group of words highlighted. In addition, personal dictionaries often contain one or more examples, including illustrations when appropriate, and one or more non-examples. Both examples and non-examples should include reasons to justify their status as an example or non-example. For instance, Figures 3.3 and 3.4 contain dictionary entries for *prime number* and *equation*, respectively.

When English language learners use personal dictionaries, they can be encouraged to include the corresponding term in their native language if known, perhaps having parents help. For parents whose mother tongue is not English, their ability to supply vocabulary in the native language can provide a useful home-school connection.

REFLECT

- What are some mathematics terms with which you had difficulty in the past? Into which of the eight categories identified by Thompson and Rubenstein do these terms fall?

- Think of at least one additional term from your middle grades mathematics curriculum that would fit into each of the previous eight categories.

REFLECT

- What might be some advantages for students to create their own personal dictionaries of mathematics terms and symbols rather than just use the glossary in the back of their textbook?

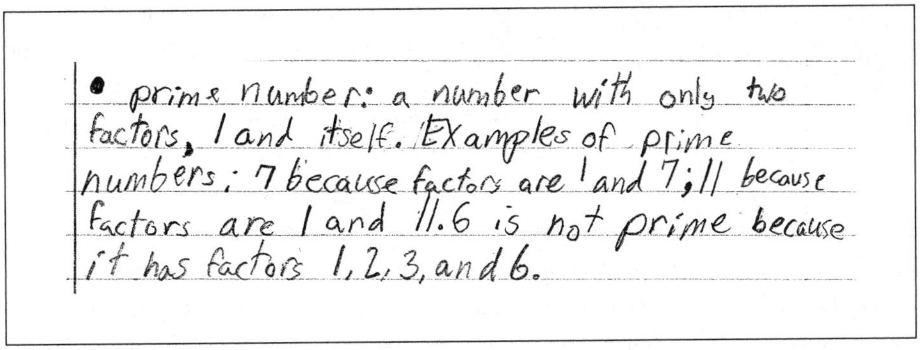

> • prime number: a number with only two factors, 1 and itself. Examples of prime numbers: 7 because factors are 1 and 7; 11 because factors are 1 and 11. 6 is not prime because it has factors 1, 2, 3, and 6.

FIG. 3.3
Sample personal dictionary entry for prime number

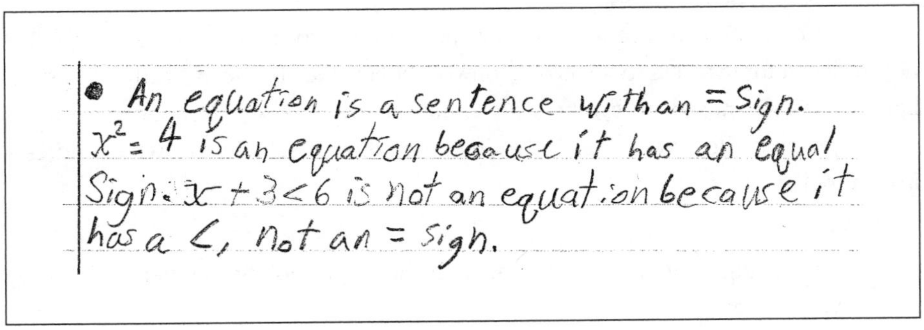

> • An equation is a sentence with an = sign. $x^2 = 4$ is an equation because it has an equal sign. $x + 3 < 6$ is not an equation because it has a <, not an = sign.

FIG. 3.4
Sample personal dictionary entry for equation

The categories identified by Thompson and Rubenstein (2000) suggest that teachers must be sensitive to vocabulary issues and ensure that vocabulary enjoys a prominent place in the mathematics classroom. We do not suggest that lessons focus solely on vocabulary, rather that teachers make vocabulary instruction an integral part of teaching (Murray 2004). In building a discourse community, teachers need to use appropriate mathematics language and expect students to do the same.

Issues Related to Mathematics Symbols

The symbols of mathematics are critical components of mathematics text. In fact, the symbols of mathematics are used in different ways, reflecting their functions within the language of mathematics. Rubenstein and Thompson (2001) identify six uses of symbols:

- to name a concept, such as $\triangle ABC$

- to state a relationship, such as *less than* ($<$) as in $4 < 8$

- to indicate an operation with a single input, such as the exponent (^{2}) as in 3^2

- to indicate an operation with two or more inputs, such as division ($\div$) as in $50 \div 4$

- to represent an abbreviation for words or units, such as degrees ($°$) as in $45°$

- to indicate grouping and implied operations, such as the use of parentheses as in $5(3x + 2)$ or the fraction bar as in $\frac{3x+2}{5}$.

R E F L E C T

- Which of the six uses of symbols identified above correspond to punctuation? Which uses generate mathematical phrases and not sentences?

- In which category would you place each of the following symbols: $\frac{3}{4}$, $\perp$, %?

- Think about the first time you saw each of the following symbols: $|3|$ or $m \parallel p$. How did you first "read" them to yourself?

To draw an analogy to everyday language, symbols used to name concepts are like nouns in the language of mathematics. Relationships, such as *is equal to* ($=$), are like verbs; a written relationship forms a complete mathematical sentence.

Mathematics symbols pose a number of unique challenges in terms of communication. For instance, there is no grapheme-phoneme connection (symbol-sound connection) inherent in a symbol to cue the reader on how the symbol is verbalized; instead, the verbalization must be taught. When students see a new English word, they can use their knowledge of phonics to pronounce the word, sometimes recognizing the word as one they have previously heard. However, when students see a new symbol, even one as simple as + or $\triangle$, they have no way to verbalize it until someone, the teacher or a peer, provides the accepted pronunciation.

Because mathematics sentences may contain both vocabulary and symbols, it is not sufficient for teachers to focus only on vocabulary. We also need to attend to symbols. The issues raised by symbols are different from those raised by vocabulary. Rubenstein and Thompson (2001) identified the following challenges when addressing symbols:

1. Verbalizing symbols poses at least two challenges not faced when verbalizing vocabulary.

a. Several words may be needed to verbalize a specific symbol. (e.g., ≠ is verbalized as *is not equal to*.)

b. A given symbol can be verbalized in multiple ways. (e.g., $a + b$ can be verbalized as *a plus b, the sum of a and b, a increased by b, b more than a.*)

c. Sentences with symbols cannot always be read from left to right. (e.g., trace the pattern your eye follows in reading the sentence $\frac{x^3+2}{15} \geq 60$).

2. To read symbols with understanding, students must consider the following.

a. A given symbol can have several different meanings depending on the context. (*The prime symbol ' can mean feet or minutes in the middle grades and the derivative in advanced courses. Primes are also used to label vertices in transformed geometric figures.*)

b. The same concept can be represented with several different symbols. (*Division can be represented with a bar in a fraction, with the symbol ÷, or with the notation $a\overline{)b}$.*)

c. An expression may contain an implicit symbol that is critical for understanding. (*In each of 54, $5\frac{1}{2}$, and 5x, two symbols are placed next to each other. In 54, the implicit understanding is place value for 50 + 4, in $5\frac{1}{2}$ the implicit operation is addition as $5 + \frac{1}{2}$, but in 5x the implicit symbol is multiplication as $5 \cdot x$. Are students aware of these differences?*)

d. Where a symbol is placed influences its meaning. (e.g., *The placement of the point in 4.2 and 4 · 2 results in two meanings—four and two-tenths and four times two, respectively.*)

3. The process of writing symbols often highlights misconceptions.

a. Students write run-on sentences. (*To simplify 15 − 4 + 5, students incorrectly write 15 − 4 = 11 + 5 = 16. That is, students fail to realize that the equals sign means the two sides must name the same amount.*)

b. Students fail to make implicit symbols explicit when rewriting symbols for technology use. ($\frac{125+250}{12+13}$ *must be entered into a calculator as (125 + 250) ÷ (12 + 13), using ( ) to make the grouping implied by the fraction bar explicit.*)

Issues Related to Graphs and Tables

In many ways, graphs and tables are a cross between vocabulary and symbols. That is, graphs and tables often contain symbols as well as mathematics vocabulary. Therefore, to understand graphs and tables, students must be able to address issues of symbols, issues of vocabulary, and issues specific to them. Shuard and Rothery (1984) classify graphics in three ways:

• *Decorative graphics* help make the page appealing. These graphics are not instructional but make the reading attractive. Students can ignore these graphics without loss of meaning.

- *Related but nonessential graphics* reiterate information contained in the exposition or narrative text.

R E F L E C T

- Refer again to the sample lesson in the appendix. Find two graphics in the lesson and classify them according to one of the three categories listed here.

- *Essential graphics* are charts, figures, diagrams, or other visuals that contain information that is not repeated in the exposition. All of the information must be read from the graphic in order to connect with the exposition and make sense of the material. For instance, the graphic in Figure 3.5 shows the meaning of slope for the equation $y = 3x + 2$; assuming that this information is not repeated in the exposition, this figure would represent an essential graphic.

When mathematics students read a graph or table, they must first attend to the title that provides insight about the information in the table or graph. On a graph, students also read and interpret the labels on the axes and the scale or intervals used on each axis. For a table, students attend to the labels for the rows and columns of the table. If an axis or a column heading says *dollars (in thousands)*, students need to recognize that the number associated with a tick mark of 5 is $5,000. When they try to determine the value associated with each tick mark on the axis, students have to consider the interval between each tick mark and understand that the interval is consistent on the axis. Failure to pay attention to the units or the intervals results in a misinterpretation of the information in the graph or table.

With all graphs, students should first read and interpret the elements, but the next reading steps vary based on the graph type. In particular, the type of display influences how students should read the graph and what information they should attempt to obtain from it. In trend graphs (refer to Figure 3.6), students must attend to the slope of the segments in the graph and interpret what the slope means with respect to both the horizontal and vertical coordinates. Trend graphs are usually best interpreted when observed from left to right in keeping with their chronological nature. For example, to make sense of the graph in Figure 3.6, students need to read the title (Student Enrollment at Johnson Middle School), recognize that the tick marks on the vertical axis represent the number of students and increment by 50, and realize that the tick marks on

FIG. 3.5
Figure illustrating the meaning of slope for y = 3x + 2

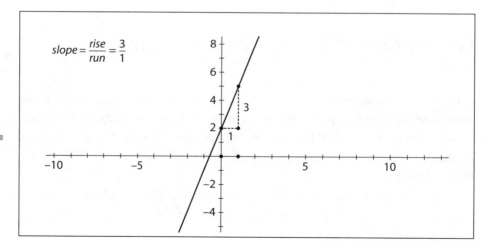

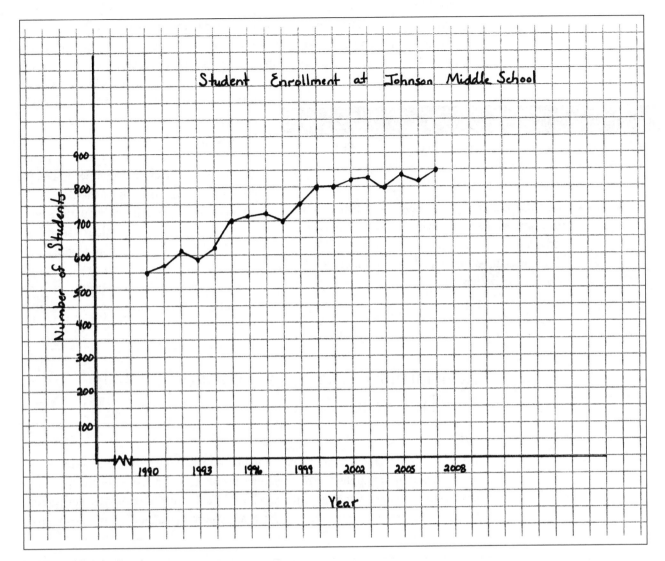

FIG. 3.6
A sample graph showing trends

the horizontal axis represent years and increment by 1. But, students also have to realize that the graph shows trends in enrollment over time. The generally positive slope of the graph indicates a trend of increasing enrollment. An analysis of the horizontal and vertical coordinates of each year's enrollment shows that enrollment has increased by about 300 students in less than 20 years, with the largest single increase occurring between 1994 and 1995. An excerpt of nonfiction text communicates a relatively small amount of information, but the information and relationships communicated by this one graph is much greater.

Other graph types require different reading strategies and eye movements. To read a bar graph, students first understand that they are used with categorical data and then assess what category is represented by each bar. They make multiple comparisons among bar heights, using the vertical axis coordinates in order to understand the relationships that are presented. The student's eyes may travel from left to right and right to left in multiple iterations to comprehend the data.

Circle graphs present a single whole composed of one or more mutually exclusive categories. The reading process requires students to view the graph holistically to determine which categories are represented by the various size sectors of the circle. The student's focus (e.g., large sectors, small sectors, or differences between sector sizes) is determined by the context and the purpose for reading.

Box-and-whisker plots provide a visual display of a data set in a manner that captures the several features of the data (e.g., the median, upper and lower quartiles, and minimum and maximum values), as in Figure 3.7. A holistic view gives students a sense of the spread of the data; for detailed information, each major point must be assessed according to its coordinate on the horizontal axis.

REFLECT

- Consider bar graphs, circle graphs, and box-and-whisker plots. Identify one data set that would be appropriately displayed by each type of graph.
- Some students think that the only numbers to be listed on an axis are the numbers they need to graph. So, they make equally spaced marks on an axis and label the marks 5, 15, 40, 75, 100. What misconceptions might such a student hold? What instructional approaches might you consider to help this student?

Readability Formulas Applied to Mathematics Text

We end this chapter with a brief discussion about readability formulas and some cautions when they are applied to mathematics text. Readability formulas are applied to texts in an attempt to determine a reading level for a text (e.g., sixth grade, tenth grade) by considering features germane to a text. Many common readability formulas, such as

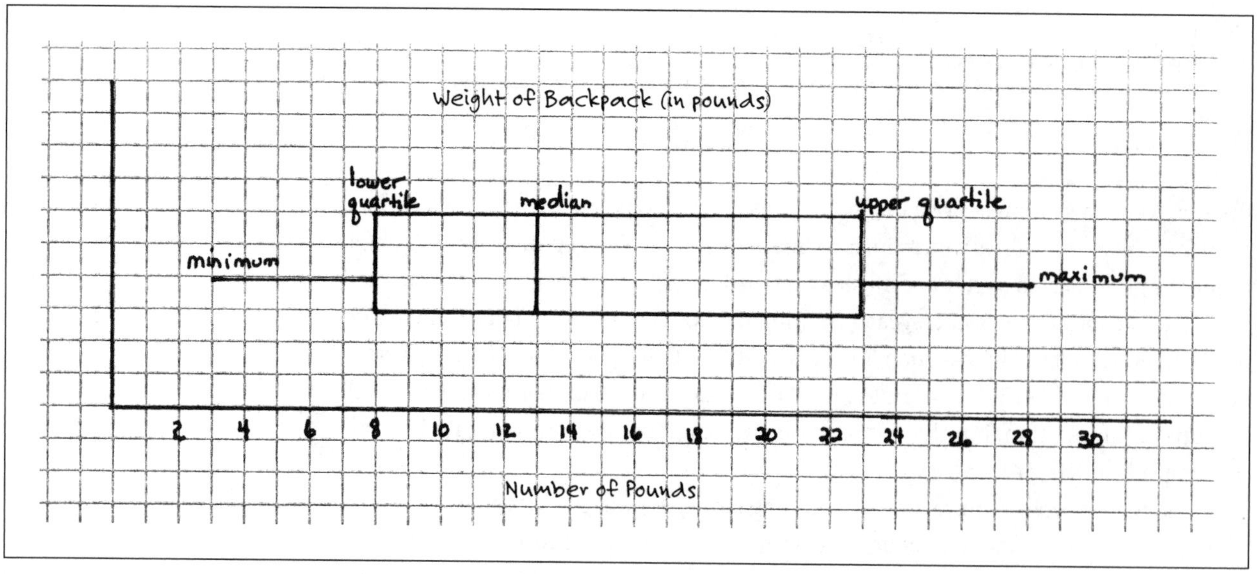

FIG. 3.7
A box-and-whisker plot

the Fry Graph (Fry 1977), are based on a connection between the number of sentences and the number of syllables. For instance, to apply the Fry readability formula, one randomly selects three 100-word passages and determines the average number of sentences and the average number of syllables in these three passages. The results are plotted on a graph that identifies the approximate grade level. Other readability formulas sometimes count the number of words with three or more syllables and consider such words as raising the reading level.

These formulas have limited applicability to mathematics. Many common words that students have used for quite some time (e.g., *quadrilateral, perpendicular, rectangle*) are considered difficult because of their number of syllables. In fact, words with three or more syllables are often considered long words in such formulas; words like triangle or rectangle fall into this category. In mathematics, sometimes phrases with one or more one-syllable words, such as *at most* or *if-then*, are more conceptually demanding than words such as *rectangle*.

In addition to the problem with syllables, the common readability formulas do not attend to symbols or to the movement from words to symbols and back to words that is common in mathematics text. If students cannot understand basic symbols in mathematics, they are likely to have trouble reading mathematics text, regardless of the grade level assigned by some formula more appropriately applied to nontechnical text.

R E F L E C T

- Identify at least two words in each of the major content strands that have three or more syllables. Which of these would you consider to be hard for your students?

- Do your students have more difficulty with short or long words in mathematics?

Summary

This chapter highlights a number of important issues related to the components of mathematics language, namely its vocabulary, symbolism, and graphing. As teachers, we need to help students address these issues if they are going to become fluent with mathematics language. The goal is not to convert mathematics class to English class, but to make mathematical language and communication with that language a natural part of mathematics teaching and learning. In the remainder of this book, we introduce a variety of practices that can be readily incorporated into mathematics lessons to make mathematical literacy a natural part of teaching.

Expand Your Understanding

1. Consider the following mathematics symbols often found in middle grades textbooks. Place each of the symbols into the appropriate category of use as identified by Rubenstein and Thompson (2001).

a. ≠

b. – (as in –3)

c. – (as in 8 – 5)

d. ()

e. >

f. ∠TRY

g. × (as in 4 × 5)

h. $

i. $\sqrt{}$ as in $\sqrt{9}$

2. Consider each of the following sample responses to one of the words from the list used by the teachers in Miller's study. To what extent would you consider the response acceptable? Provide a rationale for your thinking.

   a. Sum is the answer to an addition problem.

   b. The diameter of a circle is a line that goes across the circle.

   c. The remainder is what's left over when you subtract.

   d. The median of a set of numbers is the middle number.

Connect to Practice

3. Consider students with diverse English language proficiencies (e.g., English language learners or English speakers with limited language proficiency).

   a. Identify ten words that are used differently in the mathematics classroom than in the context of normal everyday conversation (e.g., the word *mean*). What might you do to help students make sense of the various uses of words?

   b. Identify five words that these students may find difficult to pronounce. What might you do to help them understand and say these words?

   c. Identify five words that may have different meanings depending on how they are used within a sentence (e.g., the word *more*). What do the identified words suggest about the mathematics language skills that students need to experience?

4. Give some of Miller's twenty mathematics terms to a group of middle grades students and ask them to describe them with words, examples, diagrams, or symbols. How did the performance of these students compare to the performance of the students in Miller's sample?

5. Select a page from your middle grades mathematics text. Classify each of the sentences on the page as containing only words, containing words and symbols, or containing only symbols. Find the percentage of each type of sentence. What do your findings suggest about difficulties students might have with the text?

6. Choose a mathematics word that you know is difficult for your students. What entries would you put for this term if you were entering it into your personal mathematics dictionary? Compare your entries with those of one of your peers.

7. Your first-year algebra students have been using graphing calculators. In a lesson on graphing quadratic equations, students graph $y = x^2$ on their graphing calculator. What information from the calculator would you want students to include with the graph when they sketch it on paper?

8. Find several graphs in a daily newspaper or magazine that would be appropriate to use in a middle grades classroom.

   a. What elements on the graph must students understand to interpret the graph appropriately?

   b. What aspects of the graph might lead to misinterpretation?

9. Choose a chapter in a middle grades mathematics textbook.

   a. Make note of the types of mathematics sentences in the book (i.e., only words, a combination of words and symbols, or only symbols). Which types of sentences predominate in the narrative text? Which predominate in the examples?

   b. Identify the symbols introduced in the chapter. Categorize the symbols according to the six categories identified by Rubenstein and Thompson (2001).

   c. Identify the vocabulary introduced in the chapter. Into which of the categories identified by Thompson and Rubenstein (2000) might you place each vocabulary term? (Note: some terms might fit into more than one category.)

10. Create and use a Mathematics Textbook Survey for your middle grades mathematics text. Identify issues that arose from using the inventory.

11. Select a few pages from your middle grades mathematics text.

    a. Which of the five types of mathematics text identified by Shuard and Rothery (see page 22) are prominent in your text?

    b. Look at the graphics on these pages. Classify the graphics as decorative, related but nonessential, or essential (see pages 31–32).

Learning from Theoretical Perspectives

[In supporting mathematics learning through process over product], the teacher's role changes from transmitting information and seeking predetermined responses to co-participating with students in activities that promote meaningful learning.
—Howard Smith, "Peirce's Sign and Mathematics Education"

The three chapters in this section provided a theoretical perspective on issues underlying meaning making in mathematics. Semiotics is a lens through which to consider how students give and receive meaning in any discipline, and in particular, in mathematics. To help students make sense of mathematics, we suggested we view students as *mathematics language learners*. Such a view encourages teachers to immerse students in a language-rich learning environment in order to help them become mathematically literate and fluent in the language of mathematics. That is, we need to help our students learn to listen to mathematics conversations from the teacher and their peers and to read, write, and speak mathematics on their own. As students share their emerging understandings of mathematical concepts, they clarify their thinking for themselves and give their teachers insight into their thinking so that instruction can be designed to further their understanding.

Just as ordinary English, or any language, is a sign system with vocabulary, grammar, syntax, and conventions of use, mathematics is also a sign system with its own elements of use (e.g., vocabulary, symbols, graphical representations, mathematical relationships). In order to help students make sense of mathematics and become successful learners, we need to help them connect these elements in ways that enable them to construct knowledge on their own.

Classrooms in which communication in all its forms is a natural expectation do not occur by chance. The development of such classrooms occurs as teachers design instructional activities in which students are expected to communicate mathematically and are supported in their efforts. Students need respectful and supportive classroom environments that allow them to share and justify their thinking and provide feedback to their peers in ways that are nonthreatening. The challenge of creating such classrooms is worth the effort as students strengthen their ability to make sense of mathematics.

The chapters in this section presented the theoretical foundation to support the development of a language-rich classroom. In the next section of this book, we shift our focus to illustrate how such classrooms might be constructed. Section 2 contains four extended vignettes that show different aspects of classrooms in which communication is the norm. Then, Section 3 builds on those vignettes to highlight a variety of practices across the literacy spectrum. The expectation is not that teachers will use all of the practices identified in this book in every class. Instead, the goal is to share instructional practices that may be used on a regular basis to help students make sense of mathematics.

Connect to Practice

1. Think about the theoretical issues raised in the three chapters of this section. What insights did these issues offer about any difficulties your students might experience in mathematics?

2. Select a chapter or a unit from the latter part of your middle grades mathematics textbook. The content in these chapters should contain content that is new for your students, or is revisited in a new way, and thus, may contain features that are not as evident in chapters that focus primarily on review. Survey the lessons and question sets in the selected chapter.

   a. What instructional approaches to the content suggest that the authors have written from a semiotic perspective? What instructional approaches might hinder meaning making by students?

   b. To what extent do the lessons and exercises facilitate instruction designed to create a classroom environment in which communication is an integral part of instruction?

   c. What instructional approaches do the authors take to help students comprehend and internalize new vocabulary or symbols introduced in the chapter?

   d. Based on your survey of the lessons and questions, what additional support beyond the textbook will you need to provide to help your students make sense of mathematics?

3. Based on the theoretical perspectives of these three chapters, what are you particularly interested in learning as you read the remainder of this book?

Classroom Environments to Facilitate Meaning Making

Teachers establish and nurture an environment conducive to learning mathematics through the decisions they make, the conversations they orchestrate, and the physical setting they create. Teachers' actions are what encourage students to think, question, solve problems, and discuss their ideas, strategies, and solutions. . . . If students are to learn to make conjectures, experiment with various approaches to solving problems, construct mathematical arguments and respond to others' arguments, then creating an environment that fosters these kinds of activities is essential.

—NCTM, *Principles and Standards for School Mathematics*

In the first section of this book, we provided a rationale and theoretical foundation for building classrooms in which students are expected to communicate mathematically. Because we consider all students *mathematics language learners*, we believe in instruction that focuses on classroom discourse and mathematical language development.

Our goal is not to encourage students to rely solely on one of these communication areas (i.e., sign systems or literacies). Rather, we hope that students are able to employ an appropriate repertoire of sign systems. We envision classrooms in which students, like mathematicians, puzzle over challenging problems, use a variety of ideas for solutions, work collaboratively to develop meanings, debate with one another until the truth surfaces, and convince one another of justifiable ideas. Classrooms that embody this vision of instruction are referred to as discourse communities (NCTM 1991) or math-talk communities (Hufferd-Ackles, Fuson, and Sherin 2004). Developing such classrooms is challenging, but worth the effort because we learn what our students are thinking.

In this section, we provide vignettes to illustrate how classroom discourse may facilitate the development of students' use of multiple semiotic systems, or literacies (e.g., language, mathematical signs, gestures, speaking, listening, reading, and writing) as a normal part of classroom instructional practices. The vignettes are built on practices in our own classrooms, and also in classrooms with teachers who allow us to work with their students, or observe their instruction. In each vignette, we consider student discourse or student work and critique how that discourse or work demonstrates students' attempts to make sense of mathematics and teachers' attempts to support that learning.

To develop discourse, there must first be a worthwhile mathematical task or problem that is significant and debatable to discuss (NCTM 1991). According to the *Professional Standards for Teaching Mathematics*, worthwhile tasks

- are based on sound and significant mathematics;

- engage students' intellect;

- develop students' mathematical understandings and skills;

- stimulate students to make connections and develop a coherent framework for mathematical ideas;

- [include] problem formulation, problem solving, and mathematical reasoning; and

- promote the development of all students' dispositions to do mathematics. (25)

Smith and Stein (1998) refined the characterization of worthwhile tasks so that such tasks also

- require complex thinking (a predicted well-rehearsed approach is not available);

- require students to explore and understand mathematical processes, concepts, and relationships;

- demand self-monitoring of one's own cognitive processes; and

- require cognitive effort.

Worthwhile mathematics tasks require students to focus on the mathematics inherent in the problem.

As teachers, we need to consider the nature of the mathematics tasks that we use in instruction. Do our tasks expect students to demonstrate understanding of mathematics or simply to find an answer to a problem? Do our tasks focus on the development of conceptual understanding or only on the development of procedural skills?

In addition to the nature of tasks, we also need to consider the number of tasks that we expect students to complete. What might students gain by spending more time on one (or a few) worthwhile tasks than on many simple tasks? Issues related to the nature and numbers of tasks influence the development of a mathematics discourse community.

We base the vignettes on the following assumptions about teaching and learning that are evident in a discourse community or math-talk environment:

- The classroom environment and culture facilitate meaning making. Students have opportunities to work collaboratively within a community of mathematics meaning makers.

- Communication (small group, whole class) is essential in the mathematics classroom. Students are encouraged to participate in discussions as a means of negotiating meaning and making sense of mathematics. Classroom discourse and interaction help students focus on concept development as well as on the meanings and interpretations they ascribe to those concepts. "The teacher uses her knowledge to structure the lessons to be taught and the teaching strategies . . . to engage students in dialogue to facilitate their thinking strategies, their interpretations, and their ways of communicating" (Saenz-Ludlow 2006, 194).

- Classroom activities are often structured so that students attempt to make sense of and represent a mathematics task or problem on their own first. Then, students are encouraged to compare representations with a small group of peers in which they explain and justify their solutions to others. Finally, the group is expected to reach consensus and present its findings, interpretations, and ideas to the larger classroom community.

- Teachers recognize the need to develop students' communication strategies and conscientiously plan and incorporate meaning-making practices on a regular basis. They proactively assess students' communication needs and actively seek appropriate methods to enhance students' skills and experiences.

In the chapters that follow, we present four instructional approaches that facilitate meaning making in the classroom. We selected these approaches to exemplify practices that may be used flexibly for students of different ability levels across a variety of mathematical content and a variety of pedagogical stances (i.e., teacher-directed or student-centered classrooms). The vignettes in these chapters incorporate the use of worthwhile mathematical tasks as part of instructional practice. Each of the vignettes provides a detailed look at a particular practice as it is implemented in a classroom setting. In the vignette in Chapter 4, the teacher is using curriculum materials that naturally engage students in talking about mathematics. In contrast, the vignette in Chapter 6 illustrates one practice that can be used to engage students in making sense of mathematics when curriculum materials do not naturally contain opportunities for discourse. As you read the vignettes, we encourage you to reflect on the instructional approach and the nature of the task. How do they facilitate students' learning and provide the teacher access to students' understanding? How do students interact with their peers and the teacher? Envision the learning environment, and then, contemplate how the teacher guides students in making meaning for themselves. We also encourage you to think about how you might take the illustrated activity or practice into your own classroom to effect improvement in students' mathematical literacy.

Each chapter is structured with the following sections:

- *Overview*—A brief summary of the approach, how the approach supports students in becoming mathematical meaning makers, and when this activity or practice might be used most effectively

- *Vignette*—A window into how the practice might be enacted in a middle grades classroom

- *Learning from Student Work*—Examples of student work with analysis of the responses

- *Reflecting on Use of the Practice*—How the practice naturally integrates meaning making and authentic assessment into the teaching-learning process with suggestions for teachers on how to implement the practice in their own classrooms

- *The Lesson Evolves*—How the approach might be adapted for initial classroom implementation, as well as how the approach might evolve.

In the following table, we highlight the purpose or focus of each chapter. We believe the chapters illustrate good practices because they denote learning frameworks that promote students' active involvement, critical thinking, and collaborative inquiry.

Chapter	Title	Instructional Objective	Purpose/Focus
4	*Toward a Discourse Community*	To engage students in demonstrating understanding through oral communication	Students make their thinking public as they share and debate ideas with peers and work together to explore mathematical concepts.
5	*Zoom In– Zoom Out*	To engage students in reading mathematics with understanding	Students are encouraged to become independent meaning makers of mathematics as they learn to use a process that helps them make sense of real-life contextual problems.
6	*Multiple Representations Charts*	To engage students in writing about their mathematical understanding	Students develop their vocabulary knowledge and mathematical understanding of concepts as they engage in writing to describe, explain, and make connections among mathematical terms, symbols, concepts, and procedures.
7	*You Be the Judge*	To engage students in evaluating written work so that they learn to communicate their own understanding more effectively	Students evaluate peers' written work to determine characteristics of quality responses so that they are better able to monitor the quality of their own written responses.

CHAPTER 4

Toward a Discourse Community

To support classroom discourse effectively, teachers must build a community in which students will feel free to express their ideas.
—NCTM, *Principles and Standards for School Mathematics*

Overview

Hufferd-Ackles, Fuson, and Sherin (2004) identified attributes central to students' learning of mathematics in ways that challenge and support their development of meaningful concepts, processes, and language. The researchers observed an effective elementary mathematics teacher and identified the following components of a *math-talk community* that the teacher and her students were developing as they progressed from a traditional classroom toward one robust with student thinking.

- *Questioning*: Teacher questions less exclusively; students increasingly participate as questioners.

- *Explaining mathematical thinking*: Students increase the frequency with which they explain their mathematical ideas.

- *Source of mathematical ideas*: Teacher is less the source of all mathematics ideas; students increasingly influence the direction of lessons.

- *Responsibility for learning*: Students assume greater responsibility for the learning and evaluation of others and themselves. Mathematical meaningfulness becomes the criterion for evaluation.

For each of these four components, the researchers described four different levels through which the students and teacher moved over the course of a year: (1) the teacher directs instruction with brief responses from students (traditional class); (2) the teacher begins to focus on students' mathematical thinking but the teacher is still central to the math-talk community; (3) the teacher models and helps students develop new roles as the student-to-student talk increases; (4) the teacher monitors activity but is now more peripheral to the math-talk community (88–90). Thus, students increasingly engage in discourse as they work together to construct meaning in mathematics. The development of the math-talk community was facilitated by use of a reasoning and problem-based curriculum.

Vignette

To assist our thinking, we visit an eighth-grade mathematics class of at-risk students in a working-class community around the middle of the school year. The class is taught by Ms. Ross, who is currently in her eighth year of teaching. Ms. Ross' dream is to light fires of mathematical interest and excitement in her students and support them in a deep understanding of mathematics. At the beginning of every year, she shows and discusses the movie *Stand and Deliver* (Menendez and Musca 1988) to help her students see that academic success in mathematics is possible, but takes hard work.

Ms. Ross' classroom is arranged so that students sit in clusters of four facing the center or front of the room. (See Figure 4.1 for an illustration of the seating arrangement.) This arrangement resulted from an evolution in Ms. Ross' thinking. Previous seating arrangements included traditional rows facing front, paired rows, groups of four facing one another, and now groups of four where one pair must turn around for the team to converse. A document camera at the front of the room provides a venue where student work is magnified for all to see. Although there is a screen, Ms. Ross often projects on the whiteboard so additional writing can be included in an image. Ms. Ross regularly uses a timer with a soft alarm that reminds her and her students when time allotted for some task is over.

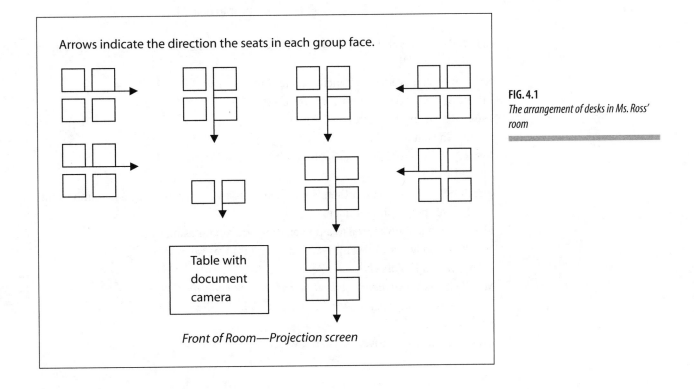

Arrows indicate the direction the seats in each group face.

Table with document camera

Front of Room—Projection screen

FIG. 4.1
The arrangement of desks in Ms. Ross' room

Ms. Ross and her students use *Connected Mathematics Project 2* (*CMP2*) (Lappan et al. 2006), which is designed to implement the recommendations from the National Council of Teachers of Mathematics; the curriculum incorporates active learning as students work together to make sense of important mathematics. Students have graphing calculators available that also produce tables of values. They previously spent considerable time studying linear functions, including contexts that produce them, tables and graphs associated with them, characteristics of graphs such as the starting value and the rate of change, and how all of these connect to equations for linear functions. Students are now in the second investigation of a unit on exponential growth. They have studied several contexts for exponential growth, have developed tables and graphs for them, and are beginning to develop equations.

On the day prior to the dialogue here, students completed *CMP2* Lesson 2.2, entitled "Growing Mold." As part of that lesson, they read about middle grades students who conducted a mold growth experiment and modeled their results with the exponential equation $m = 50(3^d)$. From the book they learned that the variable m represents the area of the mold in square millimeters and the variable d represents the number of days.

The current lesson began with students answering questions about the mold growth situation that Ms. Ross had written and displayed on the whiteboard. Students worked in *think-pair-share* mode (McTighe and Lyman 1988), meaning they thought independently first (*think*), shared their thinking with a partner (*pair*), and finally talked to another partnership or the entire class (*share*). The students are now engaged in a whole-class discussion on the mold experiment. (The prompts originally presented on the whiteboard appear in italics.)

REFLECT

As you read the dialogue and consider the information about the classroom, think about the following:

- What teacher and student actions support students' mathematical thinking?

- What evidence is there in the dialogue that the four components of a math-talk community are being developed?

MS. ROSS: So what did you think, *how does the amount of mold change from one day to the next?* [Q1]

SAM: It tripled every day. It increased rapidly.

MS. ROSS: How do you know it is tripling?

DAN: It's the growth factor.

LYNN: The paper told us.

MS. ROSS: Where? What part tells you it is tripling?

LISA: Times by 3.

MS. ROSS: I am not sure others could hear you and everyone's ideas are important. Please speak a little louder.

LISA: When it shows three to a power, then you are timesing by 3.

MS. ROSS: Jody, could you understand what Lisa was saying?

JODY: [*nods affirmatively*]

MS. ROSS: *What similar growth situations have we studied?* [Q2]

DAN: Ghost Lake. [*an exponential situation studied earlier*]

MS. ROSS: How?

DAN: First it wasn't covered. Then it was.

MS. ROSS: Is it similar to any other?

SAM: Growth factor.

MS. ROSS: What situation has a growth factor?

SAM: $r = 2^{n-1}$.

MS. ROSS: What does that refer to?

SAM: The rubles. [*Students had earlier studied exponential growth in the classic chessboard problem where rubles are doubled on each successive square.*]

MS. ROSS: *Explain what each part of the equation tells you about the growth of mold.* [Q3]

ANGELA: How much it goes up by.

MS. ROSS: Elaborate. Or get someone at your table to elaborate. Would you come up and show us? [*There is hesitation by students. No one volunteers.*] Let's take a look at the equation.

KIM: *m* equals 50 times 3 *d*. [*Teacher writes m = 50(3d).*]

MAX: No, to the power of *d*.

MS. ROSS: [*corrects symbolization*] $m = 50(3^d)$.

JAN: It starts at 50 and goes up by 3.

MS. ROSS: What does the 50 tell you?

TIM: The *y*-intercept.

MS. ROSS: Where did you look for that?

TIM: I used the calculator. I put the equation in. I looked at the table. (See Figure 4.2.) When $x = 0$, $y = 50$. So 3 is the growth factor. The *d* is the days.

MS. ROSS: How did the table help you? . . . Because that might help others who are confused. [*focuses students to share their strategies with other students*]

TIM: When *x* was 0, *y* was 50. That's where it starts off.

MS. ROSS: What about *m* and *d*, the other parts?

DAN: *m* is the mold. When it starts. No, 50 is where it starts.

MS. ROSS: What does *m* tell you?

KATE: The area of the mold in square units.

MS. ROSS: And *d*?

MANY STUDENTS: Days.

MS. ROSS: *Suppose there was 25 mm² of mold to start and it grew in the same way. What would change in the equation and in the graph?* [Q4]

RUBY: Ones with 25 are half those with 50. [*The student is looking at the values on her calculator shown in Figure 4.3 and seems to mean that cutting the initial mold value in half cuts all remaining mold values in half.*]

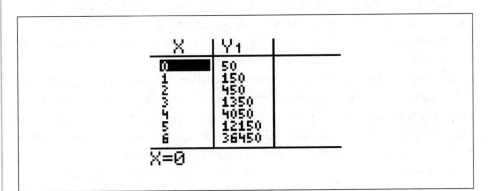

FIG. 4.2
Table of values for mold experiment when initial amount is 50 mm²

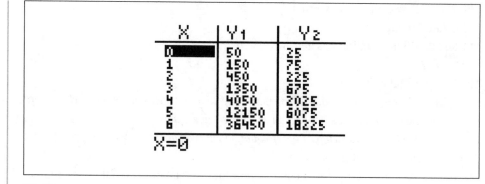

FIG. 4.3
Table of values for mold experiment with initial amounts of 50 mm² (Y_1) and 25 mm² (Y_2)

MS. ROSS: Can you show us on the calculator? Why did you put 25 where 50 was? Why not where 3 is?

RUBY: The growth factor goes in parentheses.

LORI: It never said 25. [*does not make the connection between the change in the problem statement and the impact on the values*]

MS. ROSS: Ruby, replay for us what you were saying in your group. You said something about how the table grew.

RUBY: You see for the first one 25 and 50. So 25 is half as big as 50. [*reads off values from the table in Figure 4.3*]

MS. ROSS: If the *y*-intercept is half, will the table always be half?

MS. ROSS: I see Ruby has lots to contribute today! What about others?

MS. ROSS: We will see more of this later. [*The class goes on to another part of the lesson.*]

R E F L E C T

- What did Ms. Ross learn from her dialogue with students?
- What suggestions do you have for Ms. Ross as she works to develop a classroom environment in which students regularly share their mathematical understanding with others?

Learning from Students' Work with Discourse

A rich curriculum provides a strong basis for building a discourse community. Ideally, we would like students to present their thinking about problems they are trying to solve and have other students question, challenge, and debate what is offered. Ms. Ross is fortunate that her district has adopted a curriculum that supports student construction of meaning in mathematics.

Student engagement and debate often ensue when there is something controversial to discuss. The dialogue we overheard in the vignette followed small-group work the previous day when many hurdles were overcome. There is not much left to debate when many students seem comfortable with the material. Several students appear to be able to interpret the formula for the situation and recognize that it is similar to other scenarios studied earlier. Some students have fluency with the graphing calculator, use of tables, and meanings of the values in the table.

Reflecting on Use of the Practice

What dimensions of this classroom environment support students making sense of mathematics? First, having a thinking-based curriculum helps. Students are regularly confronted with challenging problems in contexts and are asked to relate tables, graphs, equations, and situations so that the symbols and relationships are meaningful. Other scholars, for example Smith and Stein (1998), would say that students are working every day on *worthwhile mathematical tasks*.

Second, the furniture arrangement is conducive to promoting student talk and collaboration. Ms. Ross has reached a compromise from groups of four facing one another (a format she would like to use but has previously found precipitates too much socializing) to groups of four in which the natural format is pairs until she gives a signal for students to work in teams. Ms. Ross regularly reevaluates how well the floor plan works to engage students in mathematics.

Third, Ms. Ross frequently uses the *Think-Pair-Share* format (McTighe and Lyman 1988) that works with this furniture arrangement. In general, when students work initially in small groups they have a place to rehearse ideas so that they may be less uncomfortable sharing them with the full class. We discuss more details about the use of cooperative learning to support students' language development in Chapter 10.

Fourth, Ms. Ross asks many questions. She rarely if ever *tells* students. She constantly expects that they supply the mathematical thinking. The major questions (shown in italics in the dialogue) ask students to focus on rate of change, comparisons to other situations, interpreting each element of the equation, and considering what would happen if one value in the equation were altered (Q1–4, respectively). Asking higher-level cognitive questions contributes to students' meaning-making opportunities.

Fifth, Ms. Ross tries to use and build on student responses. Even when Lynn says, "The paper told us," Ms. Ross asks, "Where? What part tells you it is tripling?" When she asks for a similar situation and Sam gives an equation instead, Ms. Ross asks for the associated situation. She tries to use students' responses in whatever form they arise. She also listens to their small-group work and tries to use that, as well, as a resource for teaching (e.g., interaction with Ruby about her group's work).

Ms. Ross focuses students on building meanings. She wants them to decode the symbols in the mold growth equation to make meaning of each variable, not only what each symbol means but how it appears in a table or graph. She quizzes students about changing values or thinking about the operation associated with a value or a variable. She tries to help students recognize that sharing reasoning, and not just answers, can be a resource for others (e.g., her interaction with Tim).

Ms. Ross also incorporates some relatively simple actions into her instruction, but actions that are vital to building a discourse community. She asks Lisa to speak up to reinforce the importance of listening carefully to each other. She asks Jody if she understands what Lisa is saying to help students learn to self-assess and monitor their understanding. Ms. Ross also tries to help students realize that their thinking, whether insightful or incomplete, can be a basis for others' thinking and learning. She continues to help them understand the value of everyone's participation. She tries to make private discussions part of the public conversation (when she asks Ruby to share work from her group). Ms. Ross recognizes that getting students to share their thinking is a bit scary and it is part of her daily effort to help students understand the value of their participation for the entire community.

The Lesson Evolves

By her own account, Ms. Ross is making progress toward a math-talk community, but has not yet brought her class to where she would like them to be. Consider the math-talk community components mentioned at the beginning of the chapter. Regarding questioning, Ms. Ross is still the questioner. Her reluctant learners have not yet garnered the courage to ask a question either of the teacher or another student. Regarding explaining, Ms. Ross wants students to explain, but struggles to get them to elaborate. Regarding the source of mathematical ideas, Ms. Ross is making better progress because the mathematical ideas arise from the tasks and problems the students work in the *CMP2* curriculum; Ms. Ross is definitely not standing in front of the classroom explaining the concepts. Regarding responsibility for learning, until students give more input into the discussions, it is hard to know how they evaluate what makes sense to them.

Eventually, Ms. Ross wants to remove herself from center stage so that students are the center of the class. She would like to pose intermittent questions and not be the only question poser. The document camera in her classroom can help by offering a place for students to present their emergent thinking. Students might be encouraged to be more courageous and present their work themselves at the front of the room.

Ironically, it may be that Ms. Ross asks too many questions. Fewer questions that are a bit more open might produce more detailed student responses, resulting in other students elaborating on or questioning the response. More open and challenging questions might provide a basis for listeners to prepare questions to help them understand what a presenter says. Ms. Ross might ask students to return to their small groups, as needed, to process together an idea that some, but not all, the students in the room understand. Clearly, her efforts to help students recognize the importance of their engagement with the mathematics and their willingness to share their thinking will continue to support her and her students' progress toward building a discourse community.

The document camera is a helpful tool because it facilitates the sharing of work that students generate in their small groups. It eliminates wasting time when students rewrite their work on the board. On the negative side, only one document at a time can be viewed. In Japan, and in many Eastern European countries, teachers use the blackboard much more than in the United States, where an overhead projector or a document camera is preferred (Stigler and Hiebert 1999). Japanese teachers use the blackboard for different purposes: to provide a record of the problems, solution methods, and principles that are discussed during the lesson and as a place where different solutions can be compared (Yoshida 2005). The use of the blackboard or whiteboard might be reconsidered.

Mathematical understanding does not develop in lockstep fashion. There are steps forward and steps back. Insights and misconceptions evolve and overtake one another as clarity emerges. When we are honest and recognize that learning is a human and imprecise process, we recognize that classrooms need to view missteps as natural. Students need to understand this process, too; by talking together and being challenged, students come to understand that diverse ideas clarify and deepen their understanding. Building communities in which students understand and assume these new roles requires planning, initiation, and ongoing attention. Just like our students, we, too, need to collaborate in achieving this goal.

Expand Your Understanding

1. Suppose Ms. Ross taught a traditional curriculum in which teachers typically show students how to do mathematical procedures. Compare and contrast building a math-talk community in that environment rather than the environment described in this chapter.

2. The Hufferd-Ackles, Fuson, and Sherin (2004) article cited at the beginning of the chapter details a third-grade classroom, but the framework the article provides has implications for teaching at all levels. Obtain a copy of the article, "Describing Levels and Components of a Math-Talk Learning Community," and read the framework.

   a. Consider one of the four components and study the attributes of both teacher and students for the four levels. Where on the spectrum would you place Ms. Ross, based on the scenario and dialogue provided in the vignette? Justify your response. (The four levels are briefly described in the overview to this chapter, page 44.)

   b. What suggestions could you make to help Ms. Ross move to a higher level?

3. Read the chapter "Teaching to Establish a Classroom Culture" in *Teaching Problems and the Problems of Teaching* by Magdalene Lampert (2001, 51–100). What steps does Lampert take on Day 1 to initiate students into the culture of a community of learners? How does she see her role in this work continuing throughout the year?

Connect to Practice

4. The overview to this chapter describes four components of a math-talk community identified by Hufferd-Ackles, Fuson, and Sherin and briefly outlines four levels related to the components.

   a. Where do you see your classroom with respect to each of the four components?

   b. What actions would be reasonable for you to take to move your classroom to the next level on one or two of the components?

5. According to the *Professional Teaching Standards* (NCTM 1991), teachers need to orchestrate classroom discourse by making decisions about how and when to guide students. Consider the following thoughts that a teacher may have in response to students' utterances during mathematics instruction:

- Student provides an accurate response.
  - What questions do I ask to extend this student's thinking?
  - How can I help students make appropriate connections?
- Student response is mathematically inaccurate.
  - Do I simply acknowledge the incorrectness of the statement and move on, or do I ask questions to help this student and other students recognize the error?
  - What questions would help this and other students recognize the error presented in this statement?
  - What hints can I or should I provide to help move these students in the right direction?
- Teacher does not understand what the student is trying to say.
  - How can I help this student to clarify his or her thinking?
  - I don't understand. Perhaps another student can translate for me.
  - The answer is correct, but I'm not sure if the strategy described is mathematically appropriate.
  - a. Which of these reactions have you experienced?
  - b. What other reactions would you add to the list?
  - c. What do these reactions suggest about the importance of a teacher's listening ability?

6. Find a colleague who would like to join you in moving your two classrooms to a higher math-talk community level.

   a. Read and discuss the article by Hufferd-Ackles, Fuson, and Sherin (2004).

   b. Choose one or two of the components. Observe in each other's classes and focus on that component. Talk together about ways to raise the component to the next level.

7. What do you perceive to be your greatest challenges in working toward a discourse or math-talk community as illustrated in the vignette in this chapter?

CHAPTER 5

Zoom In–Zoom Out

USING READING COMPREHENSION TO ENHANCE PROBLEM-SOLVING SKILLS

The essence of problem solving is knowing what to do when confronted with unfamiliar problems. Teachers can help students become reflective problem solvers by frequently and openly discussing with them the critical aspects of the problem-solving process . . . .

—NCTM, *Principles and Standards for School Mathematics*

Overview

Contextualized problems (i.e., word problems) are an important part of mathematics instruction. Contextualized problems help students see how the mathematics they are learning might be used in the real world. The concrete nature of word problems has the potential to make mathematics less abstract by providing applications of the usefulness of concepts so that mathematics does not seem so abstract. However, many students struggle with mathematics word problems because they struggle with making sense of the problems they read. They have difficulty comprehending the situation in the problem and determining what information is given, what other information is needed, and what is being asked. Teachers can help by integrating reading comprehension strategies into the mathematics classroom.

Zoom In–Zoom Out adapts the zooming features of online navigational searches to the mathematics classroom. For instance, when using online technology to make sense of a map or travel route, we often begin with a large map that provides an overall view of where we are headed. However, to understand how to get from one location to another, we often need to zoom in on the map to see the route in greater detail. After viewing the details, we zoom back out to place the details in a larger context before embarking on the journey.

Likewise, in solving mathematics problems, we need to obtain an overall view of the problem, move to a close-up view to examine the details of the problem, and then zoom out again with a holistic view that makes sense of the details within the full context of the problem to understand what the problem asks. All of this happens before we actually solve the problem.

When Pólya (1957) wrote his groundbreaking work on problem solving in the 1950s, he listed four steps: understand the problem, devise a plan for obtaining a solution, implement the plan, and look back to determine if the answer makes sense in response to the question. *Zoom In–Zoom Out* focuses on all four steps of Pólya's process by helping students understand the information in the problem, determine a solution, and then compare the solution to the problem conditions.

With *Zoom In–Zoom Out*, students first read and make sense of a problem. Then, they collaborate with a peer to discuss the meaning they gleaned from the text. This initial discussion gives students a forum for sharing their holistic understanding of the problem, to identify what they know and don't know, and to compare, contrast, and reconcile their understandings. Next, the teacher brings the class together to *Zoom In* and helps the class analyze the information in the problem by making sense of the vocabulary, symbols, phrases, sentences, and numbers associated with it. *Zooming In* encourages students to self-check their independent and pair work as they made sense of the problem. Students who understood the problem are validated; those who had difficulty have opportunities to clarify their thinking. *Zoom In–Zoom Out* continues as students *Zoom Out* to understand the overall goal of the problem and to solve it. The goal of this phase is to help students make sense of the problem statement based on the information provided in it. To help students become independent problem solvers, they need opportunities to work on the problems on their own with as little teacher input as possible. *Zoom In–Zoom Out* concludes as students share their solution strategies with their peers and write about their preferred strategy.

Zoom In–Zoom Out provides opportunities for students to engage in meaningful and natural conversation about the mathematics in contextualized problems by working in both small and whole-class groups. This instructional approach is most effective with problems that lend themselves to multiple solution strategies.

Vignette

The following vignette from Ms. Sharp's seventh-grade mathematics classroom paints a picture of *Zoom In–Zoom Out* in action.

As part of her math lesson, Ms. Sharp gave each student a copy of the following problem.

Day Care Center Problem

You have been hired by a day care agency to fence in an area to be used for a playground. You have been provided with 60 feet of fencing (in 4-foot sections) and a 4-foot gate. How can you put up the fence so the children have the maximum amount of space in which to play?

- Try several different shapes that can be made with the fencing and calculate their areas.

- Include pictures of these shapes, drawing them roughly to scale.

- In addition, write a brief summary that describes which shape you think will have the largest area and why.

In prior classes, students had studied area and perimeter of quadrilaterals. Ms. Sharp decided to use the Day Care Center Problem with her students because it provided opportunities for them to use these concepts without explicitly naming them.

For the first phase of the *Zoom In–Zoom Out* activity, Ms. Sharp planned to use a *think-pair-share* process (McTighe and Lyman 1988) as follows (also see Chapter 4). She directed students to read the problem silently and think about the information in the problem while she circulated to keep students on task. After she determined that all students had read the problem, she engaged them in sharing with a peer.

> ### R E F L E C T
>
> As you read the vignette, think about these issues:
>
> - In what ways does this instructional practice support students' mathematical communication?
>
> - How can this practice help students of different reading abilities, including English language learners, comprehend a word problem?
>
> - Solve the Day Care Center Problem yourself. Think about the different strategies and approaches students might take, as well as potential hurdles they might face.

MS. SHARP: Each of you has read the problem on your own. It is okay if you did not understand all of it, but I am sure that you made sense of some of it. To help you better understand the problem, I am going to give you a few minutes to work with a partner to see if both of you interpreted the information the same way. One of you will talk first while the other listens. Then you will trade roles and repeat the process. When it is your turn to share, tell your partner what you think the problem says. When it is your turn to listen, your job is to make sure you understand what your partner thinks the problem says. After both partners have shared, talk about all the ways you agreed and disagreed. We will not solve the problem at this point. We will just work on understanding what is given and what is asked.

During peer sharing, Ms. Sharp noticed that one pair of students was struggling so she invited another pair who grasped the problem to work with them. As the students worked, she walked around the room to gain insights into the students' thinking. After a few minutes, she pulled the class together to engage in the *Zoom In* phase in which students focus on the details of the problem and the information it contains.

MS. SHARP: While you were working, I noticed that a few of you made different assumptions about what the problem says or asks. So, I want to take some time to make sure that we all understand the problem. Let's start from the beginning. What information is provided in the problem?

[*Several students raise their hands.*]

DAWN: 60 feet.

MS. SHARP: What about the 60 feet?

DAWN: It's the amount of fencing.

[*Ms. Sharp writes this information on the board.*]

MS. SHARP: What else do you know about the fence? Jared?

JARED: It's in 4-feet sections.

MS. SHARP: Why is that important?

ZACH: 'Cause you have to use it in sections.

[*She adds that information to the board.*]

MS. SHARP: Okay. Is there anything else we need to consider?

[*Some of the students begin to reread the problem, and Alyssa raises her hand.*]

ALYSSA: There's a gate.

[*Ms. Sharp adds this information to the board.*]

MS. SHARP: What are you going to do with the gate?

MIKE: It's part of the fence.

ALYSSA: No, it's not. The fence is attached to it.

MS. SHARP: Is there any more important information we need to know before we can solve the problem?

JUDY: No.

MS. SHARP: Let's see with a show of thumbs whether you agree that we have found all of the important information in the problem; thumbs up if you agree, thumbs down if you disagree, thumbs in the middle if you are unsure.

[*All students show thumbs up.*]

At this point, Ms. Sharp knew that her students recognized they had gleaned all of the important information from the problem. Now she moved to the *Zoom Out* phase in which students look at the big picture of the purpose of the problem and what it asks.

MS. SHARP: Now that we have all the important information, we need to know what to do with the information. What does the problem ask?

JOHNNY: Make a playground.

MS. SHARP: Does the problem tell us anything special about the playground that we are constructing?

TYLER: We want a large space for kids to play.

MS. SHARP: How did you figure out that we were looking for a large space? What in the problem told you we wanted a large space?

TYLER: We want maximum amount of space.

MS. SHARP: Tyler, can you read the sentence where you found that?

TYLER: [*reading from the problem*] "How can you put up the fence so the children have the maximum amount of space?"

MS. SHARP: [*to the class*] So, what does *maximum* mean?

ASHLEY: Biggest amount.

MS. SHARP: Yes, the problem did say that we want the maximum or the largest amount of space possible. Does amount of space relate to anything that we have studied recently?

MICHELLE: Area.

MS. SHARP: What do you mean?

MICHELLE: Area is the amount of space inside a shape.

MS. SHARP: Why do you think they gave you information about the fence?

ASHLEY: It goes around the playground.

MS. SHARP: Does this remind you of a math concept we studied?

TRAVIS: Perimeter??

MS. SHARP: Travis is not sure. What do you think? [*directs to the other students*]

JOHNNY: Perimeter because perimeter is the length along the outside.

MS. SHARP: Very good, so what perimeter do we have to work with?

ALYSSA: 60.

MS. SHARP: Is that all?

JOHNNY: There's a gate.

MS. SHARP: Will the gate be considered part of the perimeter? Tell your partner what you think. [*She gives students a minute to discuss the role of the gate with a peer, allowing all students to share their thinking.*]

MS. SHARP: What do you think, Casey?

CASEY: The gate is part of the fence so the total perimeter is 64.

MS. SHARP: [*to the class*] Do you agree or disagree, thumbs up or thumbs down? [*The majority of the class agrees.*]

MS. SHARP: So far, we know that we have a perimeter of 64 feet and that we need to find the maximum space or area. Working in pairs, I want you to figure out how to find the maximum space. How does the problem tell you to get started?

PAUL: Draw some pictures.

MS. SHARP: Do you think it is a good idea to just draw one and stop?

MEI: No.

MS. SHARP: Why not?

ALYSSA: It might not be the biggest one.

MS. SHARP: After you think you have found the biggest or maximum area, what else do you have to do?

JARED: Write how we figured it out.

Once the students clearly understood the goal of the problem, Ms. Sharp gave them time to solve the problem in pairs. As students worked, Ms. Sharp circulated around the room to identify several pairs of students who used different strategies. She asked them to record their solutions on the board and to prepare to explain their thinking. When all pairs had completed their work, Ms. Sharp asked the selected pairs to share their strategies with the class, and to show and talk through their solutions. When all of the selected pairs had presented their ideas, Ms. Sharp led a whole-class discussion evaluating and jointly revising, and then discussing the advantages of each unique strategy. She concluded the lesson by explaining a journal assignment in which her students would choose their preferred strategy and explain why they preferred it.

R E F L E C T

- If students had struggled with the *Zoom In* or *Zoom Out* phases, what are some questions you might use, or hints you could offer that would guide students without removing their opportunity for thinking?

- What can you determine about each student's understanding of the goal of the problem from their written solutions?

- What information do the solutions provide about students' reading comprehension as it relates to this particular contextualized problem?

- Two of the students' samples (Tyler's and Alyssa's) do not reflect a correct solution. To what extent does their work demonstrate errors in making sense of the problem?

- How could the work of Tyler and Alyssa guide your lesson planning for future instruction? What concepts or processes would you attempt to remediate for each student?

Learning from Student Work

Let's look at three samples of student work followed by some observations we made about students' understandings and misconceptions (Figures 5.1, 5.2, and 5.3). Review the samples and reflect on how the student solutions to this problem provide evidence of students' levels of meaning making or lack thereof. In addition, consider the insights teachers gain from reviewing students' explanations that can help in making future instructional decisions, including the use of *Zoom In–Zoom Out* with other problems.

Following are some observations we made about the sample student responses.

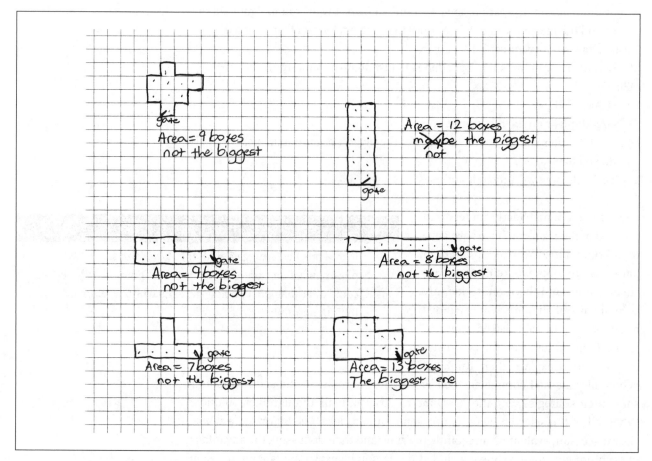

FIG. 5.1
Tyler's work on the Day Care Center Problem

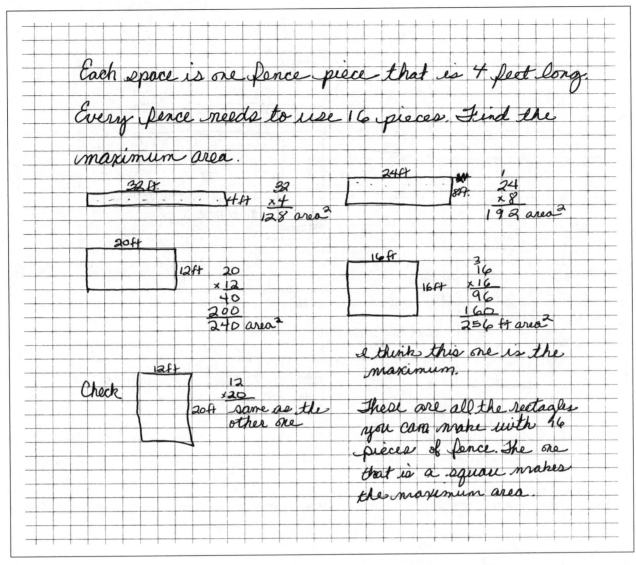

FIG. 5.2
Mei's work on the Day Care Center Problem

Tyler

Tyler's work (Figure 5.1) suggests that he understands the concepts of area and perimeter and the goal to find the maximum area. However, he does not include the scale or the dimensions on his drawings, so the person reading his solution (i.e., the teacher or a peer) is left to infer that each shape has a perimeter of 64 feet. If the length of each side of a square on the underlying graph paper is 4 feet, then all but one shape has a perimeter of 64 feet; the shape with area of 8 boxes has a perimeter of 72 feet, which may be simply a careless error.

In addition, Tyler reports area as the number of boxes rather than an actual area in square feet. Because Tyler uses a random approach to find a solution, he makes an incorrect conclusion. The shape that encloses 13 boxes does reflect the largest area of the shapes on his page, but Tyler failed to find all possible shapes with perimeter of 64 feet. The work suggests that Tyler may benefit from future instruction that focuses on using a more systematic approach to problem solving.

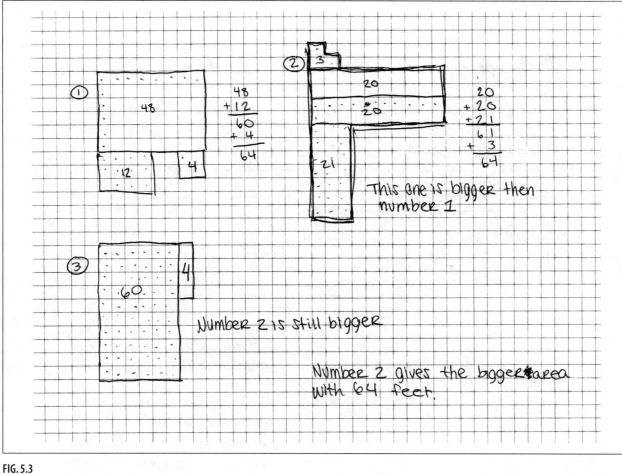

FIG. 5.3
Alyssa's work on the Day Care Center Problem

Mei

Mei (Figure 5.2) clearly understands perimeter and area, and systematically created rectangular shapes using 16 fence pieces each 4 feet long. Her response does contain a couple of minor errors. The figure with dimensions labeled 32 feet by 4 feet has a perimeter of 72 feet; however, given that all the other figures have the correct perimeter, this error might be viewed as a minor arithmetic error or due to inattention. The computation of the area of the 24' × 8' rectangle is numerically correct, although the regrouping above the 2 may suggest a potential error. Throughout, Mei used area[2] rather than square feet to label the unit of area. Nevertheless, we believe these errors are minor and do not negate Mei's conceptual understanding of the problem.

The introductory writing, the rectangle used to check the answer, and the student's written conclusion all indicate conceptual understanding. Mei may benefit from instruction that discusses appropriate units for area. Notice that Mei focused only on rectangular shapes while Tyler did not. The problem itself did not specify a rectangular playground. However, classroom instruction that compares the designs used by Mei and Tyler within the context of the problem may be beneficial if it encourages students

Alyssa

Alyssa's response (Figure 5.3) shows that she has confused perimeter and area. The goal was to build a fence using 64 feet of perimeter, but Alyssa created different configurations of 64 squares of area. Her conclusion might be based on shape 2 appearing to be larger than the other two, or perhaps she was comparing perimeters.

Alyssa also does not label the dimensions of her shapes, again leading to potential errors or misunderstandings. In Tyler's and Mei's work, each square on the graph paper has a side length of 4 feet. Even though Tyler did not label his dimensions, a side length of 4 feet can be inferred because all but one figure has the required perimeter; the manner in which Mei labels the dimensions indicates that she used a scale of 4 feet for each square side length on the graph paper. However, given the area measures on Alyssa's work, it appears that each side length on the graph paper must have a dimension of 1 foot; thus, for the first shape she obtains an area of 48 from an 8′ × 6′ rectangle. Alyssa's response shows Ms. Sharp the depth of her misunderstandings and where to focus future instruction: on meanings of area and perimeter.

The written responses of the students provide added information to Ms. Sharp about how students interpreted the discussion from the *Zoom In–Zoom Out* strategy to obtain a solution. Although students appeared to comprehend the meaning of the problem from the small-group and whole-class discussions, some students still were not able to transfer their understandings from the discussion to an approach that would yield a solution. However, her students' extended written work provides much more insight to Ms. Sharp about their meaning making than a single figure drawn to answer the question. That insight can guide her to design additional tasks to help move students forward in their mathematics learning.

Reflecting on the Use of *Zoom In–Zoom Out*

Zoom In–Zoom Out supports students' independent mathematics meaning-making attempts, and offers opportunities for students to communicate in small groups and in whole-class discussions to clarify their understandings. Teachers who observe and participate in *Zoom In–Zoom Out* can informally assess their students' understanding of mathematical concepts, processes, and vocabulary. The vignette illustrates how vocabulary instruction (perimeter, area, maximum) can be a natural part of the lesson. The terms *perimeter* and *area* were critical vocabulary words for the unit. During her observation of the pair work, Ms. Sharp discovered that several of her English language learners struggled with the meaning of the word *maximum*. Therefore, during the *Zoom In* phase, she clarified the meaning of this term which was critical to a successful solution.

The problem in this lesson was rich enough to engage students from diverse backgrounds. *Zoom In–Zoom Out* provided multiple opportunities for students to make meaning, share their thinking, clarify their understanding, share their results, and consider alternative methods to approach the problem. Discovering and valuing multiple approaches to a single problem helps students add to their problem-solving repertoire and shifts the focus of the problem-solving process away from simply getting the right answer to making meaning. (Although the vignette does not discuss the sharing and comparing of different solution approaches to the problem, this is a natural continuation of the vignette.) The journal writing helps students think about their own problem-solving style, reflect on the relative value of multiple solution paths, and communicate their mathematical thinking in writing.

The *Zoom In–Zoom Out* instructional approach uses the following processes and guidelines:

- Engage students in a *think-pair-share* activity (McTighe and Lyman 1988).
  - Give students an opportunity to read a given problem independently and think about what the problem means.
  - Have students take turns sharing what they understand about the problem while partners listen. (The goal is to give each student an opportunity to share his or her own thinking.)
  - Have partners discuss similarities and differences and arrive at a consensus of what they think the problem means.
- *Zoom In*
  - Guide the class as the students analyze the information in the problem needed to understand it. During this phase, help students discern the difference between important and extraneous information. This process also provides students an opportunity to identify and clarify the meaning of both common and mathematical vocabulary.
- *Zoom Out*
  - Ask partners to identify what the problem says, what mathematics is needed to solve the problem, and what approaches might be used to solve the problem (e.g., drawing a picture, creating a graph or table, writing a paragraph); if necessary, lead the whole class in a discussion of the process described for partners. Let an array of possibilities arise so students have plenty to consider as they solve the problem.
- Solve
  - Provide opportunities for students to work with peers to solve the task and construct a written explanation of the process they used.
- Group share
  - Provide opportunities for students to illustrate different problem-solving approaches and to share the results of their work with their peers in a whole-class setting. The purpose of this phase is to provide all students with opportunities to recognize and value different methods that could be used to solve the problem and to analyze the effectiveness and efficiency of different approaches. Teachers may want to begin with a partial solution so the whole class can work together to continue with that particular line

of thinking. This final stage corresponds to Pólya's looking back from a solution to the question; the vignette stops before this discussion occurs.

The Lesson Evolves

Zoom In–Zoom Out can be implemented gradually as students take increasingly more responsibility for the phases. When the strategy is introduced in the beginning of the school year, a teacher could herself model thinking aloud to solve a problem and intersperse such thinking with pair and whole-class discussions to help students grasp the work of the phases. In this first introduction, the sample problem should be slightly below students' ability level, so the focus can be on understanding the process rather than struggling with the mathematics. In the vignette, the teacher guided the students through each of the phases, but allowed them to work together to make meaning. In a subsequent implementation of the strategy, the teacher could challenge students to solve a more complex question related to the same problem and give them greater independence in the phases of the process. For example, the following question could be an extension of the Day Care Center Problem:

> Imagine that the fencing is flexible, and can be made to bend. What shape would have the greatest area and why? (Danielson 1997)

In time, as students become accustomed to using *Zoom In–Zoom Out*, the teacher may gradually release control and allow students to complete all of the phases with a peer. The ultimate goal is for students to become independent problem solvers who are confident in their ability to read a problem, uncover the important information, identify the goal (or question), and solve the problem using multiple representations.

Expand Your Understanding

1. There is an assumption in the Day Care Center Problem by many of the students (and possibly the teacher) that the playground needs to be rectangular. There are actually other possible solutions with greater areas.

   a. Suppose the fencing were flexible, as proposed in the extension problem. Then what shape would produce the greatest area?

b. Suppose, as the original problem suggests, that the fencing is limited to the 15 4-foot rigid sections and the 4-foot rigid gate. If we "think outside the box" and imagine shapes besides rectangles, then what shape could make the largest area? What would that area be?

c. What aspects of the problem or how it was introduced might have limited the majority of the students to think in terms of rectangles? What does your analysis suggest for your own teaching?

2. All of the sample student responses are done on graph paper. How might this "tool" influence students' approaches to the problem?

Connect to Practice

3. Refer back to the three sample student responses in this chapter. What instruction would you provide for each student to address any misconceptions evident in their responses?

4. Look through your middle grades mathematics textbook. Find one or more problems that would be appropriate to use with the *Zoom In–Zoom Out* strategy.

   a. What issues would you expect your students to have with the information in the problem?

   b. Identify any vocabulary that you will need to ensure that your students understand in order to be successful with the problem.

   c. What concepts do students need to understand in order to solve the problem? What difficulties do you expect students to have in obtaining a solution?

4. Try the Day Care Center Problem with your middle grades students. Compare their responses and discussion about the problem with those in the vignette. Identify any similarities and differences between your students' responses and the student responses in the vignette.

CHAPTER 6

Multiple Representations Charts to Enhance Conceptual Understanding

When students' learning experiences are structured in such a way that connections and associations are made among different representations of new ideas, learning becomes more meaningful and useful because of the connected network of ideas so created.
—Mal Shield and Kevan Swinson, "The Link Sheet"

Overview

When students write about mathematics, they make their understandings and insights visible not only to themselves but to others, including their teacher and peers. The process of writing helps students synthesize their thinking and reveals when understanding is robust or fragile. Rose (1989) indicates, "writing down mathematical concepts, processes, and applications in order to inform, explain, or report invites students to record their understanding through written language, a process that improves fluency" (17). As we indicated in the section introduction and illustrated in the Chapter 4 vignette, some curriculum materials are designed so that communication among students is naturally encouraged. However, even if teachers use curriculum materials in which expectations for written communication (specifically reading and writing) are not evident, teachers can engage their students in writing about mathematics on a regular basis. In this chapter, we illustrate one practice that encourages writing; we present additional practices in Chapter 12.

Multiple Representations (Multi-Rep) Charts help students develop their conceptual understanding of mathematical ideas through writing by providing an opportunity for them to describe, explain, and make connections among mathematical terms, symbols, concepts, and procedures. That is, students' writing demonstrates the extent to which they make sense of mathematics concepts and draw connections among symbols, words, and diagrams. Students' written work provides information to teachers that can guide further instruction and helps students recognize that there are many ways to view and use mathematics concepts.

Mathematical Example	Real-Life Example
Visual Example	Explanation in Words

FIG. 6.1
Blank Multiple Representations Chart *(adapted from Shield and Swinson 1996)*

To begin *Multi-Rep*, students fold a sheet of paper into fourths and label the sections (or cells) as Mathematics Example, Real-Life Example, Visual Example, and Explanation in Words (see Figure 6.1). For a given topic, students write an entry in each of the four sections to demonstrate their understanding of the concept or procedure. The mathematics example should be a symbolic representation of the concept; the visual example should be a diagram or picture that illustrates the concept in a meaningful way. The explanation in words should be a sentence or two that demonstrates basic understanding of the concept. A real-life example might be a situation or word problem in which the concept would be used in the real world. Small-group or whole-class sharing of responses encourages students to consider multiple approaches and representations of the concept, potentially deepening their own understanding of the mathematics concept.

Vignette

The vignette that follows portrays Mr. Evans' sixth-grade classroom as he models and discusses fraction concepts with his students. The vignette also illustrates how *Multi-Rep* can be implemented in a whole-class setting and in a situation in which the teacher directs the instruction.

REFLECT

As you read the vignette, think about these issues:

- What are some benefits of having students share their ideas about the development of their *Multi-Rep* chart?

- What might you learn about your students' successes and struggles with meaning making by reviewing their *Multi-Rep* charts?

At the beginning of a fraction computation unit, Mr. Evans asked his students to complete a pretest he copied from his curriculum guide. He was familiar with the scope and sequence of his students' mathematics curriculum from the previous year and he knew they had studied fraction computation in depth. He hoped the pretest results would help guide his instructional planning on fractions. The pretest showed that many of his students were not able to complete fraction addition or subtraction problems accurately, but the test's multiple-choice format did not provide the depth of information he needed to pinpoint the source of students' errors or misconceptions. In addition, he could not gauge whether his students had a strong conceptual understanding of fractions and fraction computation or whether they were relying on rote computational steps.

Another teacher recommended using *Multi-Rep* charts. Mr. Evans was intrigued with the potential of the charts to enable his students to demonstrate their knowledge of important vocabulary and symbols and to make connections among different aspects of fractions. In addition, he had been trying to include more writing in his classroom and thought he might be able to use *Multi-Rep* charts regularly with a variety of content topics to engage students in writing. As his students worked to complete the *Multi-Rep* chart on fraction concepts, he expected to gain insights into his students' conceptual knowledge. He thought that if he identified the gaps in his students' knowledge about fractions, he could better plan his instruction.

MR. EVANS: The pretest you took yesterday showed we have a lot of work to do before everybody is confident and competent in fraction computation. We're going to start by reviewing what fractions mean, what they look like, and some of the ways we use fractions in our everyday lives. I want to try something new called a *Multi-Rep*. That's short for *Multiple Representations Chart*. I want everybody to take out a piece of paper and fold it into fourths. See, you're already using fractions. Label each of the four sections like the example on the overhead (see Figure 6.1). In the top left section write Mathematics Example. In the top right section write Real-Life Example. The bottom left is for a Visual Example, and the bottom right section is for your Explanation in Words.

Mr. Evans circulated around the room as he gave instructions. He assisted students who needed help and redirected those who were off task. When all students had labeled their *Multi-Rep* charts, he continued with the lesson.

MR. EVANS: For the Mathematics Example section, you need to choose a fraction that you want to work with for the whole chart and write it in the section.
[*He pauses while students write.*]
MR. EVANS: Now we're ready for the Real-Life Example. Think about the fraction you wrote in your first section, and then discuss with your neighbor some of the ways you might see or use the fraction when you're not in school. It might help to think about the things you and your families do every day. After you and your partner share, choose your favorite example and write it in the top right box.
[*Mr. Evans circulates around the room during the sharing time and comments on some of the good examples he hears.*]
MR. EVANS: Let's move now to the bottom left section of our *Multi-Rep* chart, Visual Example. This is where you will draw a picture of your fraction.
ROBIN: How do you draw one-half of an hour?
MR. EVANS: Think about the clock and how the minute hand changes in a half hour. That's a tough one, so it's okay if your picture isn't the same as your real-life example, as long as it still fits your fraction.

Mr. Evans circulated as students drew their pictures. He helped those who struggled to get started, and asked students who had completed their work to help others who had questions. As he circulated, he distributed markers and transparencies of blank

Multi-Rep charts to several students for them to duplicate their charts to share with the class on the overhead projector. He was careful to select charts with drawings that represented a variety of fraction models: area (the fraction names part of a whole object); set (the fraction names part of a group of objects); and length (the fraction names a portion of the length of an object).

MR. EVANS: We are almost done with our *Multi-Rep* chart and I have seen a lot of great ideas and pictures. The final section is where you explain your visual and math examples in your own words. Use appropriate math vocabulary in your explanation.

When his students had finished, Mr. Evans gave them an opportunity to share and discuss their work in small groups. Then, he led a whole-class discussion in which students shared their thinking with the entire class.

MR. EVANS: You all worked hard on your *Multi-Rep* charts and they show a lot of good math thinking. I'd like a few of you to share your work with the rest of the class. If you had trouble with one of the sections, you may get some ideas from what others did. Also, pay attention to all the different fractions, pictures, and real-life examples. Will someone share with the class the fraction they chose?

LILY: Two-thirds.

EVAN: Three-fourths.

MR. EVANS: Two-thirds and three-fourths are great examples. [*Because he wants to assess his students' conceptual understanding of fractions, he decides to probe their responses before proceeding further.*] Before we go on, let's talk about what fractions mean. What is two-thirds?

ANDREW: Two out of three parts.

MR. EVANS: That's a good start. What does the three tell us?

PARKER: The bottom number.

MR. EVANS: Yes, does anybody remember the name for the bottom number?

ANNE: Denominator.

MR. EVANS: Thanks, Anne. How does the denominator of three help us know how big the fraction is?

JAMAAL: It's how many parts are in a whole.

MR. EVANS: If there are three parts in a whole, what does the two in the numerator tell us?

MARGARET: We have two parts.

MR. EVANS: You're both right! If I have two-thirds of a pie, that means I have two parts and there are three parts in the whole. What if the pie was cut into three pieces, one big one and two small ones, and I have the two small pieces, do I still have two-thirds of the pie?

MIKE: No.

GARY: The pieces need to be the same size.

MR. EVANS: Here's a brainteaser for you. How can you give someone two of three pieces of a pie, but only half of the pie?

MIKE: What if I cut the pie in half and then cut your half in half. It's two of three pieces but only really half.

MR. EVANS: What would have to be true about the pieces for it to be fair?

GARY: The pieces have to be the same size.

MR. EVANS: I definitely think we're onto something important. Let's see what real-life examples of fractions you wrote. Who is willing to share their example? José?

JOSÉ: 25 cents is one-quarter of a dollar.

MR. EVANS: Good one! Kathryn?

KATHRYN: I did three-fourths of a yard of ribbon.

MR. EVANS: That's an interesting example because your fraction is part of a length of something. Who else will share their example? Robin?

ROBIN: I practice the piano a half hour every day.

MR. EVANS: These are all excellent real-life examples of fractions. I gave some of you transparencies. I want you to show your picture of a fraction. Everyone should check to see if they agree that the picture shows the fraction. Remember what we discovered earlier, that all the pieces need to be the same size.

Mr. Evans was pleased with the work his students did. He collected the *Multi-Rep* charts for display on the bulletin board.

MR. EVANS: You all did a great job on these charts. For tonight's homework, I want you to do another *Multi-Rep* chart, but this one will be on fraction addition. I have a blank chart that you can use for a template. We'll share everybody's ideas tomorrow so make sure you get yours done. Do a challenging problem, but one you can explain.

Learning from Student Work

Consider the following sample *Multi-Rep* charts dealing with three different aspects of fractions and their operations (see Figures 6.2, 6.3, and 6.4).

Following are some observations we made about the student responses in the *Multi-Rep* charts.

Lily

Lily shows understanding of ideas about three-fourths (Figure 6.2). Although Lily's visual example shows the rectangle divided into four congruent parts, the explanation in words does not emphasize that all four of the parts must represent the same area or portion of the rectangle. This is an important aspect of fraction meaning that a teacher might want to emphasize in instruction because many students just look at the number of parts into which a whole is divided and do not consider whether or not those parts represent the same fractional part of the

> ## REFLECT
>
> As you review the sample charts, think about how you would answer the following:
>
> - What do these responses suggest in terms of each student's understanding of fractions and their operations? Note that not all of the sample responses in the charts are mathematically correct.
>
> - *Multi-Rep* requires students to demonstrate understanding in various representations. What might you learn about your students' understanding from this writing activity that you couldn't learn from skill-based tasks or traditional word problems?

FIG. 6.2
Lily's Multi-Rep *chart on fraction meaning*

FRACTIONS

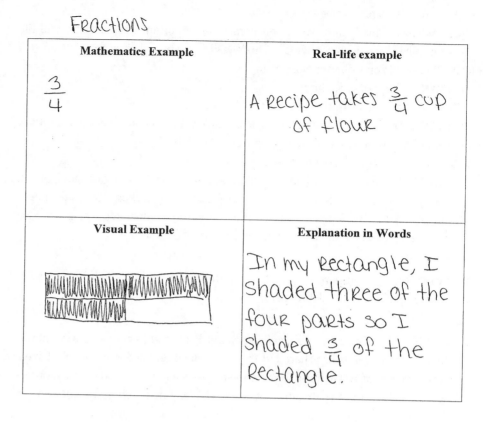

Mathematics Example	Real-life example
$\dfrac{3}{4}$	A recipe takes $\dfrac{3}{4}$ cup of flour
Visual Example	**Explanation in Words**
	In my rectangle, I shaded three of the four parts so I shaded $\dfrac{3}{4}$ of the rectangle.

FIG. 6.3
Elijah's Multi-Rep *chart on fraction addition*

fraction addition

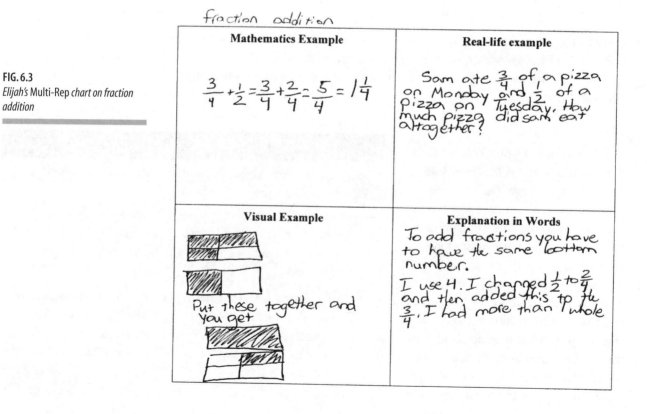

Mathematics Example	Real-life example
$\dfrac{3}{4} + \dfrac{1}{2} = \dfrac{3}{4} + \dfrac{2}{4} = \dfrac{5}{4} = 1\dfrac{1}{4}$	Sam ate $\dfrac{3}{4}$ of a pizza on Monday and $\dfrac{1}{2}$ of a pizza on Tuesday. How much pizza did Sam eat altogether?
Visual Example	**Explanation in Words**
Put these together and you get	To add fractions you have to have the same bottom number. I use 4. I changed $\dfrac{1}{2}$ to $\dfrac{2}{4}$ and then added this to the $\dfrac{3}{4}$. I had more than 1 whole

Fraction Multiplication

Mathematics Example	Real-life example
$\dfrac{3}{4} \times \dfrac{3}{5} = \dfrac{9}{20}$	Carlie had $\frac{3}{4}$ package of cookies. She gave $\frac{3}{5}$ away. How much does she have left
Visual Example	**Explanation in Words**
?	To multiply fractions, I think you multiply the numerators together and multiply the denominators together.

FIG. 6.4
Andrew's Multi-Rep chart on fraction multiplication

unit. Lily might be asked to draw a visual representation of several other fractions to determine whether her visual models always display equal-size parts, even if she fails to note that distinction in her explanation.

Elijah

Elijah (Figure 6.3) demonstrates the ability to add $\frac{3}{4}$ and $\frac{1}{2}$. However, the real-life example contains some difficulties. Although the overall context is one that results in addition, it is not clear from the wording of the problem whether Sam is eating one pizza or two. If there is only one pizza, then there is a fundamental error because Sam cannot eat more than one pizza. Notice that this contextual difficulty is not one that arises when dealing with whole numbers. If there were two pizzas and Sam ate $\frac{3}{4}$ of one and $\frac{1}{2}$ of the other, then there needs to be a note that both pizzas were the same size; otherwise, it makes no sense to add them together. Students need to pay attention to the size of the unit when operating with fractions, even though this was not an issue when operating with whole numbers.

The visual example illustrates the problem and the answer, but not the solution process. We don't know whether Elijah obtained a common denominator before adding. He may have just put the $\frac{1}{2}$ from the second rectangle with the shaded half of the first rectangle and noted that $\frac{1}{4}$ was left over. There is nothing wrong with this approach. In fact, in a class this diagram could be the basis for a discussion of different strategies to add fractions and for determining which strategy is the most appropriate in a given situation. Students who decompose $\frac{3}{4}$ into $\frac{1}{2}$ and $\frac{1}{4}$ demonstrate flexibility in thinking that we want them to have.

In his explanation, Elijah referred to the common denominator as the bottom number. Is this just a case of a student using informal language? Does he know the standard mathematics vocabulary? Mr. Evans might analyze his instructional practices and reflect on whether or not he has been using the correct mathematical terminology himself. As teachers, if we fail to use appropriate mathematics vocabulary and only use informal language, then students cannot be expected to develop fluency with formal mathematics terminology.

If we are concerned that students will not understand the use of the term *denominator*, then we might use both *denominator* and *bottom number* in conjunction until our students become comfortable with the mathematical term. For English language learners, it is also important to write the term so that students can connect the word as they hear it with the written visual form.

Andrew

Andrew's response suggests a fragile understanding of fraction multiplication or simply a procedural understanding (Figure 6.4). Andrew appears to be able to multiply two fractions together symbolically, in this case $\frac{3}{4}$ and $\frac{3}{5}$. This ability is supported with his explanation in words, although the language suggests that he may not be completely sure about the process to use. However, Andrew is unable to create a visual representation for his procedure.

There are major difficulties with the real-life example. Although one could have $\frac{3}{4}$ of a package of cookies, it is not clear what $\frac{3}{5}$ references. Is it $\frac{3}{5}$ of the package or $\frac{3}{5}$ of the $\frac{3}{4}$? This is an important distinction. As written, the story is represented symbolically as $\frac{3}{4} - (\frac{3}{5} \times \frac{3}{4})$. That is, the problem and question suggest the student may be thinking about subtraction, particularly with the use of the phrases *gave away* and *have left*. Thus, it is not clear whether Andrew is able to identify situations in which multiplication is the required operation. Asking students to write their own word problems gives teachers insights that are not possible when students only solve given problems. If students are not able to write problems on their own for the correct operation, will they recognize the correct operation when they are asked to solve problems by the teacher?

Andrew's *Multi-Rep* chart suggests limited understanding of fraction multiplication. His understanding appears to be procedural in nature. So, Mr. Evans needs to design mathematics tasks that help him develop conceptual understanding of fraction multiplication from various perspectives (e.g., visual as well as practical).

Reflecting on the Use of *Multiple Representations* Charts

One benefit of the *Multi-Rep* charts is it individualizes instruction because students can engage in the activity at various levels of understanding. Ideally, students should be able to convey meaning in all four sections of the chart. However, even those students who struggle with the writing-intensive portions of the chart should be able to address the more symbolic or visual portions. As students share their responses to the different sections with their peers, they learn from each other and broaden their own thinking about a concept.

The *Multi-Rep* chart reinforces the importance of understanding mathematics from multiple perspectives or representations. The vignette illustrates how requiring students to think of a real-life example of their chosen fraction helped them relate the concept to something familiar (money, time, crafts). The examples students provided in the whole-class discussion also give opportunities for Mr. Evans to assess their understanding informally. Students who are only able to provide a mathematical example, but who cannot give an everyday example for the concept or who cannot explain the concept in words, may lack the in-depth understanding that is desired. The different representations of the concept required by the *Multi-Rep* chart give teachers insight into what aspects of a concept may need more instructional focus in the classroom.

Writing is one aspect of mathematical literacy in which we need to engage students on a regular basis. The use of *Multi-Rep* charts is one means to that end. The charts can be used with any curriculum and instructional approach (e.g., teacher-directed or student-centered). Use of the charts demonstrates the power of writing in the mathematics class for both students and teachers.

To use *Multiple Representations* charts, you might consider these guidelines and processes:

- Select a mathematical concept, vocabulary word, symbol, or procedure as the topic of the *Multi-Rep* chart.
- Have students fold a sheet of paper into fourths and label the sections Mathematics Example, Real-Life Example, Visual Example, and Explanation in Words.
- Guide students (whole class, small groups, pairs, or individually) to complete each of the sections.
- Provide opportunities for students to share their completed work in small groups or with the whole class.
- Use student work as a means of assessing understanding and to support instructional planning.

> ### REFLECT
>
> - What section of the *Multi-Rep* chart do you think will be the most difficult for your students to complete?
> - What approaches can you use to help students communicate their Explanation in Words clearly and completely?
> - Think about the conceptual understanding required by each section. How might you address students' difficulties with each section through questioning or other meaningful experiences?

The Lesson Evolves

How might you get started with such a writing activity in your classroom? You might start by modeling the completion of some *Multi-Rep* charts as a whole-class activity with students, helping to provide appropriate responses. Notice that multiple responses can be accepted for each section to reinforce the idea that multiple answers are acceptable. This work with the entire class can help students begin to think about what constitutes an acceptable written, verbal, or visual response.

Then, you might have students work on *Multi-Rep* charts in small groups, placing their solutions on chart paper or an overhead transparency to share with the rest of the class. If all groups complete a chart on the same topic, students can see different solutions during the sharing phase. Students can also provide constructive feedback to responses shared with the class. Depending on the teacher's philosophy, groups might revise their work after sharing and getting feedback from peers.

Eventually, students can complete *Multi-Rep* charts independently, perhaps as a homework problem (replacing several computational problems), or as a test question to provide an overall assessment of students' understanding of the concept. As students make additional connections, they can be encouraged to expand their chart to include non-examples, words or explanations in their first language, word origins for related vocabulary, or some multiple literacy creative work (e.g., a poem, rap, or song) that demonstrates meaning of the concept.

Expand Your Understanding

1. Identify at least one concept from every major content strand (number sense and operations, geometry, measurement, algebra, data analysis and probability) for which the *Multi-Rep* chart would be effective.

2. a. Create your own *Multi-Rep* chart on the meaning of a fraction, fraction addition, or fraction multiplication. Reflect on your thought processes as you worked on the entry in each section.

   b. Describe the level of understanding of a concept that is required to complete each section as well as how each entry demonstrates your understanding of the concept.

Connect to Practice

3. How might you modify the *Multi-Rep* chart for use in your own classroom? What issues or concerns do you have about using this writing activity?

4. Refer back to the three sample student responses in this chapter.

   a. What written comments would you provide each student in response to their Explanation in Words? How does their choice of words convey the confidence they have in their understanding?

   b. Compare and contrast what response you should plan for students who cannot provide a suitable Real-Life Example versus students who cannot provide a reasonable Visual Example.

5. Try *Multi-Rep* charts with one of your middle grades classes using a concept that you believe your students should be able to understand. Compare and contrast your students' responses to the charts with the responses of the students in the vignette.

6. Mr. Evans allowed students to choose their own fraction or additions for doing their *Multi-Rep* charts.

a. What do you learn from a student's fraction choice for their work on meanings (e.g., $\frac{1}{2}$ versus $\frac{3}{4}$ versus $\frac{3}{5}$ versus $\frac{7}{12}$)?

b. What are different fraction addition problems students might propose? What different information would you gather from different choices?

c. What are benefits and liabilities of having students choose their own items for the *Multi-Rep* charts?

CHAPTER 7

You Be the Judge

ENGAGING STUDENTS IN THE ASSESSMENT PROCESS

It is now well-accepted that the ability to assess one's own work is an important element in most forms of learning and that it is an ability which must be cultivated if learners are to engage effectively in lifelong learning.
—David Boud, "The Role of Self-Assessment in Student Grading"

Overview

Students' abilities to assess their knowledge and identify skills they need to improve are valuable *self-regulatory strategies* (van Kraayenoord and Paris 1997). Student self-assessment also provides teachers with useful evaluation data (Charles, Lester, and O'Daffer 1987). In its *Assessment Standards for School Mathematics* (1995), the National Council of Teachers of Mathematics (NCTM) states students' self-assessment serves to increase their confidence in their ability to do mathematics, and helps them become more independent learners (meaning makers). In addition, research has demonstrated that self-assessment leads to improved performance in mathematics (Hassmen and Hunt 1994; Koivula, Hassmen, and Hunt 2001).

When students are expected to communicate mathematically, particularly in written form, they need feedback about their responses. Writing in mathematics is a non-typical activity for many students and they are often unclear about what they should write. It is natural for teachers to take time at the beginning of a year (with refreshers throughout the year) to help students learn how to evaluate their own and their peers' responses. They need to learn how to differentiate a model response from a minimally acceptable response from an unacceptable response. As students become capable of critiquing the responses of others, they learn how to improve their own responses so that readers know exactly what they mean and are not left to infer understanding. Learning to communicate effectively and critique the communication of others is an essential part of being mathematically literate.

You Be the Judge is one approach to enhance students' abilities to self-assess their work by providing an opportunity for students to assess peers' solutions to a performance task. Holistic rubrics, such as the one presented in Figure 7.1, provide a set of criteria that students can use to critique their own and other students' work.

Rubrics are most commonly used to critique performance tasks and problems that require students to communicate their understanding. When a consistent rubric is applied across numerous tasks at the same time or over time, student growth and understanding of complex processes can be compared and contrasted. When the same overall rubric is used across tasks, performance across those tasks can be compared on the same scale to determine whether students achieve at the same level regardless of content or whether they perform better on some content strands than on others. A word of caution: rubric scores are not the same as partial credit scores and should not be converted to percentage scores to determine students' grades. In the rubric in Figure 7.1, a score of 3 is considered successful and a score of 2 indicates substantial progress toward a solution. It is unlikely that you would want to assign grades of C (75 percent) and F (50 percent), respectively, to these scores.

When students assess their peers' work with the same rubrics teachers use to assess their work, students understand the process and are better prepared to rise to the teacher's expectations. When they examine the quality of work produced by their peers, they become sensitized to both effective and ineffective problem-solving methods and solution presentations. In order to assign scores to others' work and to justify the scoring decisions, students must discern how well each solver understood the problem, the appropriateness of the solution method, and the solver's ability to convey his or her understanding and thought processes on paper. As students practice the assessor role, they teach themselves what it takes to be an effective problem solver and communicator, and how to be accurate in their own self-assessment.

In preparation for using *You Be the Judge*, teachers should collect student work on a performance task, select a few papers at different levels, and mask students' names. Then, as students engage in *You Be the Judge*, teachers should review

REFLECT

- What concerns do you have about implementing this type of activity in your classroom?

Successful Responses

4   Solution is complete; the response is a model response.

3   Student works out a reasonable solution, but minor errors occur in notation or form. Any errors are clerical in nature rather than conceptual.

Unsuccessful Responses

2   Response is in the proper direction and displays some substance. The response may demonstrate a chain of reasoning. However, the student makes major errors that are conceptual in nature.

1   Student makes some initial progress but reaches an early impasse.

0   Work is meaningless; the student makes no progress. There is nothing mathematically correct.

FIG. 7.1
A sample holistic rubric (adapted from Thompson and Senk 1993)

the scoring rubric in the context of the problem, and lead a discussion about the qualities of responses that would result in each of the scores. Students then use the rubric to determine a score for selected work and provide a written or oral justification for their scoring decisions.

Vignette

In the vignette that follows, Mr. Yin uses *You Be the Judge* with his eighth-grade algebra class in a small-group format.

Mr. Yin's algebra students are generally successful at solving linear equations. However, they often struggle to connect contextual problems and symbols. He wondered about their ability to develop a situation for a linear equation. Although he had been trying to embed more writing into his class, many of his students still struggled to write a high-quality response. So, he thought it might be useful for them to critique a number of responses; he hoped that students would then be a bit more critical of their own responses.

A few days prior to using this particular instance of *You Be the Judge*, Mr. Yin gave his two classes of algebra students the following problem.

Write Your Own Problem

Create a question about a real situation that can be answered by solving the equation

$4x + 8 = 5x + 2$

Be sure to tell what x represents.

REFLECT

Before reading further, think about one or more acceptable responses to the problem. Then, think about the following:

- What are general difficulties students might face when attempting this problem?
- What issues would you expect to surface in your own students' work on this problem?

Mr. Yin identified responses from each class that illustrated some of the difficulties he expected his students to have. He removed students' names and copied the responses, attaching pseudonyms to each paper and arranging the samples so that responses would not be used in the class with the author of the response.

Mr. Yin began the activity with directions and discussion about the rubric in a whole-class session.

MR. YIN: Today we're going to do something different. Instead of working to solve new problems, you get to play teacher and score other students' work.

ZACH: Does this count for a grade?

MR. YIN: Zach, we're doing this activity because I want everyone to learn how to tell the difference between a great response, a good response, and one that isn't so good. That way, when you do your own work, you will think more about how to write a good quality response. I thought it might be helpful for the class to critique several responses to the problem we did the other day. Then, you can look at your own response and see how you would score it and how you could improve it. I made copies of answers to the problem. The ones I am going to ask you to critique are from my other class. The names aren't on the papers, so you don't have to worry about giving your friend a bad score. Before we get started, let's talk a little about the problem you did the other day. [*puts a copy of the problem on the overhead*] Who can tell me what the problem asks?

LENA: We have to write a word problem.

MR. YIN: Yes, Lena, and can you tell me anything special about the word problem?

LENA: It has to work for the equation.

MR. YIN: What can you tell me about the equation?

TOMMY: There's x on both sides of the equals.

MR. YIN: What does that tell you about how many variables are in the equation?

TOMMY: Two.

MR. YIN: Does that mean that you will have to write a problem that has two different things that vary or change?

ERIC: No. The x is the same. So, only one thing changes.

MR. YIN: Remember that we need to define the variable so the reader will know what the x in the equation stands for. Now let's take a look at the scoring rubric that I want you to use.

Mr. Yin spent a few minutes reviewing each of the score descriptions and clarifying terms such as *impasse, initial, notation,* and so on. Then he distributed copies of four samples of student work to each student. (See Figures 7.2 through 7.5 for these samples.) Before he moved students to their small groups to critique and score the papers, he had them briefly review the samples. He then instructed the small groups to score each paper and write their score and justification on chart paper.

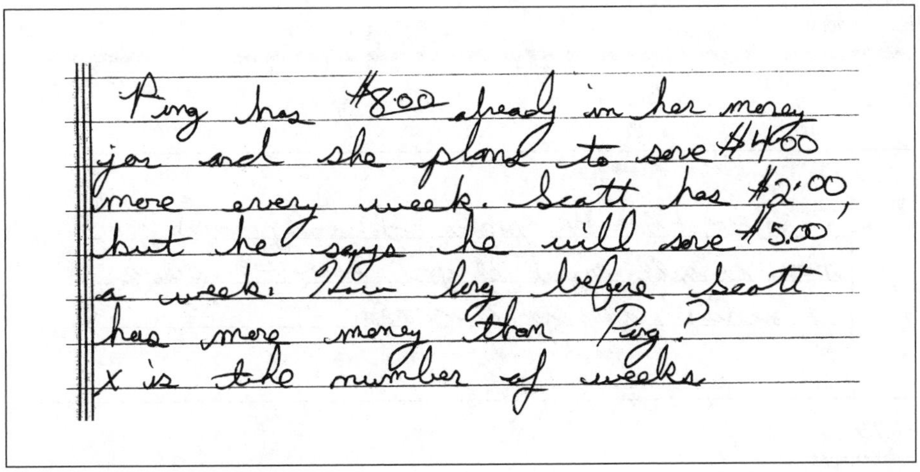
Ping has $8.00 already in her money jar and she plans to save $4.00 more every week. Scott has $2.00, but he says he will save $5.00 a week. How long before Scott has more money than Ping?
x is the number of weeks

FIG. 7.2
Miguel's response

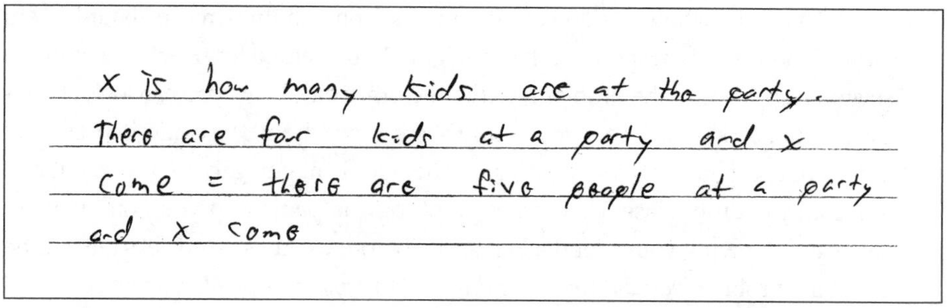

x is how many kids are at the party.
There are four kids at a party and x
come = there are five people at a party
and x come

FIG. 7.3
Zach's response

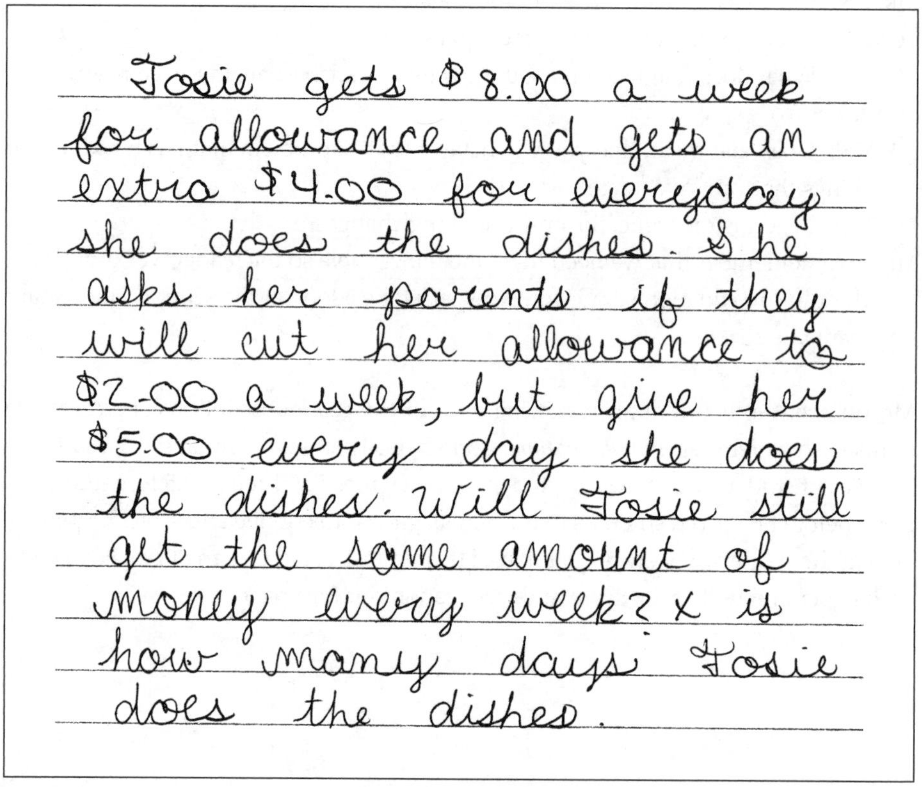

Josie gets $8.00 a week
for allowance and gets an
extra $4.00 for everyday
she does the dishes. She
asks her parents if they
will cut her allowance to
$2.00 a week, but give her
$5.00 every day she does
the dishes. Will Josie still
get the same amount of
money every week? x is
how many days Josie
does the dishes.

FIG. 7.4
Lena's response

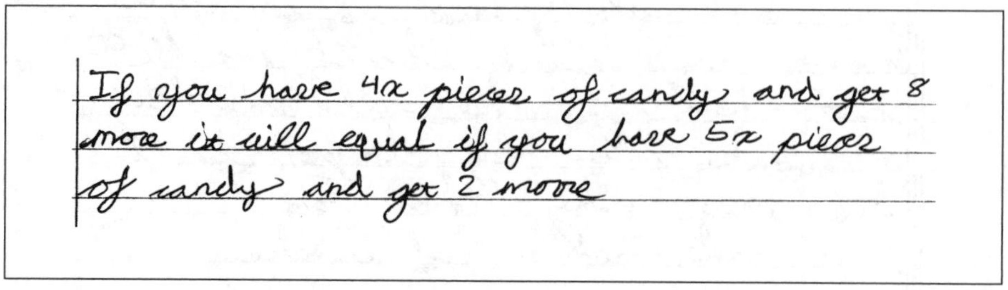

If you have 4x pieces of candy and get 8
more it will equal if you have 5x pieces
of candy and get 2 more

FIG. 7.5
Julia's response

While the students worked, Mr. Yin circulated to listen to group dialogue. Following are excerpts from conversations he overheard:

REFLECT

- Before you read the rest of the vignette, assess each response in Figures 7.2 through 7.5 using the general rubric in Figure 7.1.

Group 1—discussing Miguel's response

TIM: It's a 4. It tells what x is and all the numbers are right.

SUSAN: I think it's a 3. There's an equals not a more than sign. This person wrote "How long before Scott has more money than Ping?"

CHAN: I missed that. If it said, "How long before they have the same" it would be a 4. This person messed up a little. I still think it's pretty good. I think this is a minor error.

Group 2—discussing Zach's response

JUAN: It's a 3. It gives what x is and puts the 4 and 5 in, but they forgot about the 8 and 2.

LISA: It can't be a 3. It doesn't even make sense.

JULIA: Mr. Yin said we have to say our score and why before we decide on the group score. So, Lisa, what's your score?

LISA: I think it's 1. It says [pointing to the rubric] "student makes some initial progress." They tried to say what x was, but the rest doesn't make sense.

JULIA: I gave it 0 for meaningless. They said x was how many kids were at the party, but then they say there are four kids at a party or there are five people at a party. The equation makes you multiply the 5 and the 4 times the x and this problem doesn't have anything to do with multiplying.

Group 3—discussing Lena's response

MIGUEL: Josie's not very smart. Why would she ask her parents for less allowance?

TRACY: Maybe she likes doing dishes and wants to make more money.

MIGUEL: How can she make more money with only $2 allowance?

TRACY: I worked it out. If she does the dishes six days every week, she makes the same. If she does them less than six times she makes less, but if she does them more, then she makes more. The problem makes sense because if Josie does the dishes six days a week, both sides equal $32. They just asked the question wrong since the answer could be yes or no depending on how many days she does them.

MIGUEL: I still don't think she's very smart. Who wants to do dishes every day?

AMY: Okay, Miguel. What's your score? Does the problem make sense for the equation?

Group 4—discussing Julia's response

SHANNON: So, Linda votes a 2 because it says to start with $4x$ and add 8 equals to start with $5x$ and add 2, but we don't know what the x stands for, so it's "in the proper direction" but "makes major errors." Greg says it's a 3 because they made it equal, but they forgot to tell what x is. Chad says it's a 2 because it doesn't make sense to say "$4x$ pieces of candy." I think it gets a 2 because for a 3 it needs to be a "reasonable solution" and a 3 is successful. I like what Chad said about it not making sense. Nobody goes to the store to buy $4x$ pieces of candy.

CHAD: I say we give it a 2 because they didn't say what x was. They put x in the word problem and that doesn't make sense.

LINDA: We should add something about the part they did right, like they added the 8 to the $4x$ and made it equal to when they added 2 to the $5x$.

Mr. Yin observed the discussion as the groups assessed each of the four sample responses. He encouraged each group to share their findings for each problem and had the class vote on which group presented the strongest rationale for their score decision. He was impressed with the level of discussion, and the seriousness with which the students worked to make an appropriate scoring decision. He also noticed that to score the responses successfully, his students had to examine the problem critically, think about the role of the variable in the equation, meaningfully communicate about the mathematics, and justify their individual and group score choices. After all peer assessments were shared, Mr. Yin added comments of his own so that students would know features of the responses that he considered to be important. He also wanted to ensure that students would not be misguided by inappropriate scoring or faulty review of their work by their peers.

MR. YIN: Okay, now I'm going to give you back your answers to this problem from the other day. For homework, I want you to critique your own response using the rubric. If you need to, redo your answer and correct it. I also want you to think about what you learned by reading these sample responses that can help you write better answers on homework or test problems or even when you do those constructed response items on the state test.

The next day, Mr. Yin engaged his students in discussions about their reflections on the activity from their homework assignment.

MR. YIN: For homework last night, I asked you to think about what you learned from our activity yesterday. What do you need to do in order to write a better response? Anyone want to share?

CELINE: I don't usually write what my variable stands for.

MARK: When writing a problem, you need to write a question. Some of those papers yesterday didn't have any questions. I sometimes forget to do that.

R E F L E C T

- Does your state or district use performance assessments? If so, what challenges have students faced in being successful? How might *You Be the Judge* help students overcome those challenges?

When Mr. Yin reflected on his students' interactions with the activity, he was generally pleased that they really tried to apply the rubric conscientiously. He thought about how he could use this activity more frequently without taking an entire class period. He decided to make up some sample responses to problems and have students critique the responses as a warm-up activity once every couple of weeks. He also planned to monitor his students' writing to see if it improved as they had more opportunities to critique good and poor responses.

Learning from Student Work

Consider the four samples of student work that illustrate a range of abilities to transmediate from the symbols of algebraic equations to real-world algebraic situations: that is, to translate from the sign system of symbols to the sign system of words.

Following are some observations we made about the sample student responses.

Miguel

Miguel's scenario fits the equation $4x + 8 = 5x + 2$ with the exception of *has more money than*. The context is reasonable, and indicates an understanding of the concepts of variable and constant. The definition of the variable is also conceptually sound. A review of equations versus inequalities using real-world contexts would likely result in Miguel self-correcting his error.

We consider this response to be successful and score it a 3. We view the error of posing an inequality rather than an equation as a clerical error resulting from lack of attention to detail. Others might disagree and score this response a 2. Our decision on the score is based on our focus regarding Miguel's understanding of the role of the variable x, the rate of increase (4 or 5), and the initial values (8 or 2).

> ## R E F L E C T
>
> - Traditional approaches to teaching algebra that use the equation $4x + 8 = 5x + 2$ rarely move beyond having students solve the equation for x. What are the potential benefits of having students review their peers' attempts to make meaning from this symbolic equation?
>
> - What do these sample responses show about students' conceptual understanding of algebraic equations and mathematical symbols, and their ability to transmediate from symbols to words?
>
> - To what extent do the students who created each of these responses understand the concept of variable? Justify your response.
>
> - What questions would you ask each of these students to assist them in making their responses conceptually sound?

Zach

Zach's work shows many conceptual difficulties. Zach's definition of the variable conflicts with its use in the problem scenario. He also ignored the constants of 8 and 2 in the equation, and treated the multipliers of 4 and 5 as constants. This response clearly shows Zach's lack of understanding of algebraic equations and their symbols. We believe this response shows no reasonable progress, so we would score the response as 0.

Lena

Lena defined the variable using an appropriate context and represented the constants of 8 and 2 as fixed weekly allowances. There is some confusion in the wording of the question statement, because it does not require a solution to the equation. Rather, the question is open to a variety of answers depending on the chosen value of the variable. However, the remainder of the problem situation shows that Lena has a strong conceptual foundation in algebra, and the use of the phrase *the same* does indicate that she understands that both sides of an equation are equivalent. Remediation of Lena's difficulty may be accomplished without direct teacher intervention by simply allowing her to read the evaluation comments produced by her peers.

We give this response a score of 3. Although we believe the response is successful and demonstrates much understanding, it is not a model response because of the issue with the question statement.

Julia

Julia's context is weak. Julia failed to define the variable, and the problem situation does not reflect that she understands the role the variable plays in the equation. However, the phrases *get 8 more*, *will equal if*, and *get 2 more* are appropriate for the context and do show some understanding of parts of the equation. Notice that the context could work. For instance, $4x$ could be the number of pieces of candy if Julia takes 4 pieces from each of x baskets or x pieces are taken from each of 4 baskets. We believe Julia has made limited entry into the problem and we give her response a score of 1.

In this task, students did not have to solve the symbolic equation. In fact, we know that many students can solve equations symbolically even when they cannot construct situations that represent the equation. We believe that mathematically literate students must not only be able to solve equations symbolically, but they must also be able to construct an equation for a situation provided by the teacher and write their own situations to represent equations.

REFLECT

- If students can only solve the symbolic form of an equation, to what extent do you believe they have constructed meaning of a variable? Justify your response.

Reflecting on the Use of *You Be the Judge*

Given the increased use of performance tasks on student examinations, it is crucial for students to acquire the thinking skills necessary to produce quality responses. That is, they need to demonstrate use of mathematically sound procedures and be able to provide clear and complete explanations of their work that illustrate a thorough understanding of the concepts. The rubrics for these tasks are constructed with criteria that evaluate the nature and quality of the written response. Repeated practice in completing performance tasks surely has benefits, but students who are unfamiliar with the scoring rubrics that are used to assess their work and have no experience in identifying the qualities of model responses are at a disadvantage.

In the *Assessment Standards for School Mathematics*, NCTM recommends that teachers make assessment an open process. In this way, "everyone who is affected by the assessment of students' learning" (1995, 18) understands the process. Where rubrics are used to assess students' performance on high-stakes tests, *You Be the Judge* is an activity that provides students an opportunity to interact meaningfully with those same scoring rubrics. As the vignette shows, students can learn to evaluate responses critically against a scoring rubric, and gain a working understanding of the characteristics of quality work. Through this experience, the assessment process becomes transparent, and students are better prepared to produce model responses to constructed response tasks.

To use *You Be the Judge*, you might consider the following guidelines and processes:

- Select a performance task for which students may choose a variety of solution paths. Have students solve the problem and explain their thinking, then remove student names from their work and replace them with a code.

- Distribute student work to small, heterogeneous groups for assessment. Attempt to give each group a range of papers to assess in terms of quality.

- Familiarize students with the assessment rubric. Be sure the language is clear to them.

- Direct students to score each paper as a group and provide a written rationale for the given score. Circulate about the room and take anecdotal notes about student understandings that are evident in the small-group discussions. Provide guiding suggestions for groups who are struggling to reach agreement.

- Review peer scores and scoring rationales to add guiding comments so that students are not misguided by their peers' assessment. Redistribute the papers with the scores and your comments to their owners.

- Provide opportunities for students to discuss what they learned through the assessment process and highlight the meaningful conversations you heard while circulating. Give students with unsuccessful scores the opportunity to use the group feedback and your comments to rework the problem.

The Lesson Evolves

You Be the Judge can be effectively implemented in a variety of formats. When first introduced, the entire class can assess a student's response that is displayed with an overhead projector or with a document camera. Students should be familiar with the scoring rubric before they make any assessments, and the same general rubric should be used consistently whenever this process is used. If appropriate, teachers may want to choose a rubric that is similar to the one used to score their students' statewide achievement test. To gain the maximum benefit from using the process in a whole-class format, students should independently score a response and write a phrase or two justifying their assessment before discussing their assessment in a small group. After small-group discussion, the response can be discussed as a whole class. This method encourages all learners to think critically about the problem and the qualities of the response, to justify their thinking in writing, and then to attempt to convince their peers of the accuracy of their assessment.

As the strategy evolves in the classroom, small groups can work together to assess several samples of student work, writing their scores and justifications on chart paper to share with the class. The ultimate goal of the strategy is to improve students' ability to discern the qualities of a model response to a performance task so that they are better able to produce model responses themselves. As students progress in their familiarity with the assessment process, they can be challenged to assess their own work. Regardless of the curriculum

> **REFLECT**
>
> - How might you modify this strategy for use in your classroom?

being used, evaluating responses via rubrics is one means to engage students in worth-while tasks and to provide them an opportunity to reflect on their mathematical understanding (Wilcox and Jones 2004).

Throughout the year, teachers could occasionally have students critique a response as part of homework or a warm-up activity, with students providing an oral rationale for their score. This approach could be used to help students recognize common errors that are often found with particular concepts.

Expand Your Understanding

1. Compare your district or state rubric for performance tasks to the rubric in this chapter. What are the similarities and differences in the rubrics?

2. Investigate other rubrics from assessment projects. For instance, *Balanced Assessment* (Wilcox and Jones 2004) is an assessment system in which responses to performance tasks are scored using 4 points. Student papers might initially be split into two categories: *has it* and *doesn't have it*. On their scale, a 4 is excellent, a 3 needs minor revision that the student is able to determine for himself or herself, a 2 needs some instruction, and a 1 needs major instruction. Compare this rubric with the rubric in this chapter. What scores would you assign each of the responses in Figures 7.2 through 7.5 on this scale?

3. In this chapter, we have introduced holistic rubrics. Investigate analytic rubrics (see Charles, Lester, and O'Daffer 1987). Compare and contrast the two types of rubrics. Which rubric format do you prefer? Why?

Connect to Practice

4. Try *You Be the Judge* with your middle grades students using some performance task that is appropriate based on the content they have studied. How do your students' interactions compare to the interactions of the students in the vignette?

Developing Classroom Environments to Facilitate Meaning Making

We [mathematics teachers] need to shift toward classrooms as mathematical communities—away from classrooms as simply a collection of individuals.

—NCTM, *Professional Standards for Teaching Mathematics*

In each vignette in Chapters 4 through 7, we illustrated how classroom environments that focus on conceptual understanding provide students opportunities to work with peers to make sense of mathematics and communicate their mathematical thinking, orally and in writing. In our vignettes, students worked on worthwhile mathematical tasks individually (*Multi-Rep*), in pairs (*Zoom In–Zoom Out*), in groups (*You Be the Judge*), and engaged in whole-class discourse (*Toward a Discourse Community*). When students work individually before sharing in a small or large group, the diversity of responses increases and this diversity is desirable. When students are faced with a challenging problem, they often receive needed support by working in pairs or in small groups.

At some point in each vignette, students' work became public, either by sharing their thinking orally, or by presenting their work to others in written form. For too long, mathematical thinking has remained private, hidden, inside each of our heads, and inaccessible by those who "didn't get it." In a discourse community, participants' mathematical thinking becomes explicit and available for public response. For example, in *You Be the Judge*, student groups reviewed, critiqued, and debated the mathematical thinking of others. Engaging in such public debate has many benefits:

- productive solution paths become available for everyone to learn and adopt;
- misunderstandings, a natural part of learning, become points for conversation by everyone; and
- clarifying misconceptions, errors, or misunderstandings strengthens everyone's mathematical understanding.

A critical element in a math-talk community is tone setting. As teachers, we need to coach students to value the math-talk community format and to engage in it appropriately. For example, prior to engaging in a whole-class discussion of completed tasks we might say, "We are going to share our work now. I want everyone to try to understand what others will explain. Listening carefully to others helps us clarify ideas and extends our thinking. As you listen to others explain their thinking, I want each of you to think of a question to pose to the speaker."

Initially, we help students learn how to ask good questions by modeling them ourselves. As our math-talk community evolves, we want students to pose more of these questions. We also want to guide students to address mathematical ideas, not personalities. We support students with remarks like, "We all make mistakes. They are a natural part of learning and they are helpful. When we clarify mistakes our understanding is strengthened. Mistakes force us to think more clearly. When we see something we think may not be correct, respect the person and question the idea. If you think something is not right, you could say, 'Please explain again the part about . . . ' or 'I was thinking differently' and tell your reasoning. Sometimes when we ask someone to explain, they figure out for themselves that they need to think differently."

Orchestrating a math-talk community is hard work for teachers and students. After selecting worthwhile mathematical tasks, we need to anticipate a range of student responses so that we can think ahead about what to say or do when they arise. There is always the potential for surprises when we ask students to think openly about problems and share their work, but we increase our readiness to respond when we anticipate their responses. In addition to asking students to formulate questions or figure out someone else's thinking from their work, there are other strategies we might employ to build a math-talk community. For instance, we can ask a student who is unsure about his work or who is just getting started to share his initial understandings with the class. The entire class then has an entrée to follow a particular line of thought and work to further its development. As teachers, our challenge is to avoid providing so much scaffolding for students that we preempt their opportunity to think.

The real payoffs for working to build a math-talk community begin when students debate mathematical ideas among themselves. Then, there is evidence they are engaged, taking responsibility, and really working to build their own and others' understanding. The first time a student responds to another without teacher intervention, he or she should be praised for this move and others should be encouraged to do the same.

In sharing students' responses, it is often important to share different approaches to the task so students see different ways of conceptualizing the problem. Worthwhile tasks are particularly conducive for sharing multiple strategies. However, as teachers we need to think ahead about which strategies to share and in what order to sequence them. The goal is to help students detect similarities and differences among various approaches, evaluate how a strategy might further their own understanding, and consider the possible adoption of another student's strategy. However, we need to acknowledge that not every idea gets resolved on the day it is raised. A list of open questions can be posted to be revisited as students have more ideas to contribute.

The vignettes in the four chapters of this section illustrate that developing a classroom in which students focus on mathematical literacy is an ongoing process. Each of the teachers was still in the process of building a classroom environment in which literacy was an integral component. The vignettes also illustrate that a literacy focus is possible regardless of the extent to which the curriculum supports it. Although Ms. Ross (Chapter 4 vignette) used a curriculum that encouraged small-group discourse, the teachers in the other vignettes used curricula with less support for such approaches. Nevertheless, they were able to implement reading (Chapter 5: *Zoom In–Zoom Out*), writing (Chapter 6: *Multiple Representations Charts*), or writing with assessment (Chapter 7: *You Be the Judge*) in ways that enhanced their instruction and gave insights into their students' thinking and meaning making with mathematics. All four teachers were building math-talk communities at some level. In Section 3, we share additional strategies and practices that support meaning making and mathematical literacy.

Connect to Practice

1. In what ways do the mathematical tasks illustrated in each of the vignettes address the qualities of worthwhile tasks outlined in the introduction to this section?

2. Choose a problem from a middle grades mathematics text. Modify it as needed so that it meets the criteria for a worthwhile task.

3. What are some relationships between using a worthwhile mathematical task in the classroom and engaging students in discourse?

4. Compare and contrast the discourse illustrated in the vignettes to the discourse in your own classroom or one that you have observed.

5. In what ways do the practices and strategies illustrated in the vignettes support the development of students' conceptual understanding?

6. Identify an instructional practice you are already using or have observed. How might you adapt this practice to increase the level of discourse and a focus on conceptual development?

7. Consider the classroom environments represented in the vignettes. What effect might similar environments have on students' motivation and mathematics anxiety? How might you establish this type of environment in your classroom?

8. In classrooms in which the teacher does not emphasize discourse and collaboration, students' mathematical thinking and work are private. In mathematical discourse communities, students' thinking and work are open to sharing in a public manner. How might teachers encourage students to take risks and participate in discourse communities in a productive manner?

9. Observe one of your peers teaching a mathematics lesson or ask one of your peers to observe you. Make notes about the classroom discourse. Who is doing the talking? What is the purpose of these verbalizations? How are meanings negotiated during the lesson? What type of listening did you discern? What do students gain or lose as a result of engaging in the observed classroom discourse community?

Teaching Practices That Encourage Meaning Making

Communication about the mental realm where mathematics takes place is essential for others to gain access: both for information and for instruction. Such communication is also important as a central aid to students in formulating their own mathematical ideas.

— David Pimm, *Speaking Mathematically*

Teachers cannot directly access what a student thinks or understands. However, to support students' learning and nurture their mathematical development, we need to use instructional practices that make their thinking visible so we access and assess what they know and are able to do. Students make and give meaning through various forms of communication. In addition, students use metacognitive processes to interpret signs (e.g., words, symbols, graphs, or diagrams) and make sense of mathematical concepts, processes, and relationships.

In the chapters that follow, we advocate teaching practices that support students as they make sense of mathematics through reading, listening, speaking, writing, and grappling with mathematics concept development. Each chapter focuses on instructional practices with a particular literacy focus. Some practices are described in detail in one chapter and referenced briefly in others because many practices address multiple literacy components. We believe these practices are valuable because they encourage students to communicate mathematics as they construct mathematical meanings. However, rather than attempt to use all the practices we present in the book, we suggest teachers make judicious use of them. Specifically, we recommend that readers identify a few powerful practices within each communication mode and use them regularly, so that both teacher and student become comfortable with their use.

CHAPTER 8

Building Meanings Through Concept Development and Communication

> One of the most robust findings of research is that conceptual understanding is an important component of proficiency. . . .
> —NCTM, *Principles and Standards for School Mathematics*

Effective mathematics instruction offers students opportunities to develop conceptual as well as procedural understanding of mathematics concepts. Briefly defined, conceptual understanding refers to the ability to perceive underlying meaning of something (e.g., why putting sugar in a pie makes the pie taste sweet) while procedural understanding refers to knowledge about how to accomplish a task (e.g., following a recipe to bake a pie). Unfortunately, concept development is often confused with procedural or skill development. Consider the following excerpt of a dialogue between a teacher and his seventh-grade students during a lesson on solving linear equations. In this particular episode, the teacher is reviewing how to solve $2x - 4 = 6$.

MR. MILLER: To solve this equation, you first have to get rid of the 4. How do we get rid of the 4? [*points to Mark*]

MARK: Add four to both sides.

[*Mr. Miller writes $2x - 4 + 4 = 6 + 4$; $2x = 10$.*]

MR. MILLER: Now we have $2x = 10$. How do we get rid of the 2?

[*He waits for students to raise their hands and then calls on Sandra.*]

SANDRA: Divide by 2, so $x = 5$.

In order to design instruction that helps students make sense of mathematics, we need to understand the differences between concepts and skills. A concept is conceived in the mind; it is an abstract or generic idea generalized from particular experiences. Concepts include mental representations, images, and tangible (e.g., concrete objects) or intangible ideas (e.g., the geometric concept of *point*). Specifically,

R E F L E C T

- Does this vignette focus on skills or concepts? What concepts, if any, are students learning?

students who have conceptual understanding have an integrated perspective on mathematics ideas; they not only know how to complete procedures but they also know why those procedures work, why they are important, and when they are useful and are able to connect new ideas to concepts they have already learned (Kilpatrick, Swafford, and Findel 2001, 118). In contrast, a skill is the process of doing something, such as riding a two-wheeled bike or rollerblading on in-line skates. In the vignette, Mr. Miller focused on developing students' skills to solve an equation. The lesson focused on a series of steps to be followed in a specific manner. If Mr. Miller wanted to focus on concept development, he would have emphasized the role of the equal sign (=) and the meaning of equality, as well as how operations undo one another; this focus would help students understand the concepts behind the process. Although concepts and skills are both important in mathematics, a focus on concept development helps students make sense of mathematics and develop their mathematical literacy.

Concept development occurs in many forms through participation in varied experiences. We emphasize the need for students to engage in mathematics explorations to *make sense* of mathematics. Peer interaction is essential to this development. As students engage in social interaction, they have opportunities to reconcile their new knowledge with previously known information, thereby developing their understanding of mathematics.

Models for Mathematical Concepts

The following vignette illustrates how students can engage in making sense of mathematics as they explore concepts using concrete tools.

Ms. James, a sixth-grade mathematics teacher, was planning her unit on rational numbers. She recalled the difficulty her students had with understanding rational numbers and their operations the previous year. Although she had provided clear explanations, and carefully described the procedures for operating on fractions, many of her students continued to struggle with rational numbers and their operations. They had difficulty computing with fractions and were unable to solve application problems that involved fractions. She decided to approach the unit differently this year.

During the summer, Ms. James attended a workshop on the use of various manipulatives, including pattern blocks, to develop students' understanding of fractions. She wondered how her students might respond to the use of these manipulatives and decided to begin the unit on rational numbers with an exploration using pattern blocks. She gave students a set of pattern blocks (see Figure 8.1) and they worked in groups of three to answer the following questions:

- If the trapezoid represents the whole, what pattern block represents one-third?

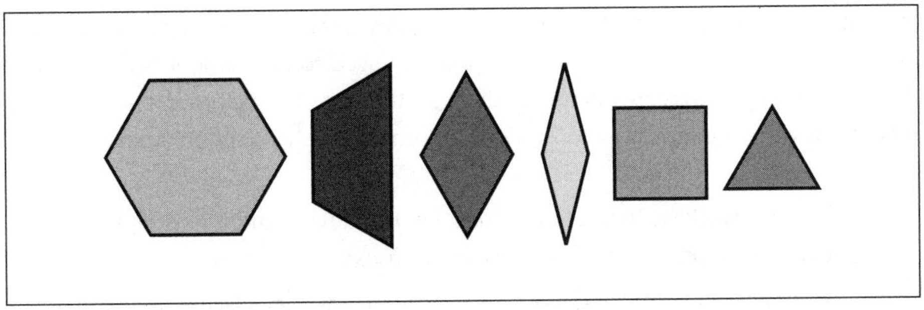

FIG. 8.1
A set of pattern blocks

- If the trapezoid represents three-halves, what pattern block represents the whole?
- If two hexagons are considered the whole, what fraction of the whole is a trapezoid?

As they worked, students used their prior knowledge of numerator and denominator to formulate various conclusions.

During the lesson, Ms. James was surprised when her students questioned their own and others' understanding. For example, when they attempted to answer the second question (If the trapezoid represents three-halves, what pattern block represents the whole?), one student said that it wasn't possible because "three-halves is not really a fraction because the top number is bigger." Another replied, "Yes, it is. It just means you have more than the whole." Given this information, another student placed three triangles on the trapezoid and said, "Three of these triangles fit into the trapezoid." As the discussion continued, students in this group determined that each triangle represents one-half; there are two halves in a whole so the answer had two equal triangles or one blue rhombus.

When everyone completed the task, Ms. James engaged students in a whole-class discussion about their findings. Students shared their answers and demonstrated how they were obtained.

After the lesson, Ms. James reflected on how much she had learned about her students' understandings when she listened carefully to them. She was surprised at their ability to figure things out by working with peers. She also was pleased with their abilities to explore a concept using manipulatives and share their reasoning with others. When students needed to test their ideas, they used the pattern blocks to check their conjectures. They discounted a presented idea, or confirmed their own notions. When given time to explore, many students were able to make sense of the meaning of fractions on their own. Therefore, Ms. James decided to extend the use of manipulatives to other lessons.

The vignette depicts the use of a particular manipulative, namely pattern blocks. Manipulatives are mathematical models (e.g., an object, picture, drawing, or diagram) that may be used to represent and make sense of mathematical concepts. Models come in various forms,

R E F L E C T

- The vignette suggests one misconception students might have when working on the task. What are some other misconceptions that might arise?

including tactile (e.g., pattern blocks), visual (e.g., pictures or diagrams), or virtual (Web-based simulations of tactile experiences) and are used to help students develop understanding of the concepts being studied. Instruction that incorporates the use of models provides opportunities for students to communicate about mathematics in the following ways:

- Students work with peers in a *discussion-rich* environment to explore mathematics ideas and to make and test conjectures.

- Students *speak about* and *listen to* mathematics as they discuss observations and findings.

- Students *read* and *write* mathematics as they record their findings and explain their solution strategies or reasoning.

Models help students make sense of mathematics because students use and interpret multiple representations for the concept through models. However, concepts are not developed simply by using models. Mathematics ideas are not inherent in models themselves. Rather, these instructional tools illustrate concepts or relationships in ways that help students consolidate their understandings. The interpretations obtained with the manipulative need to be facilitated so that students generate appropriate mathematical understandings and relationships.

Mathematics teachers typically use models to introduce concepts or develop conceptual understanding before students focus on formal procedures or strategies. Initially, students explore mathematics using prior knowledge and reach conclusions based on observations and experimentation with the tools. In the case of Ms. James' class, students extended their prior understanding about fractions to answer the questions in the lesson.

A thorough description of the different models available for mathematics instruction is beyond the scope of this chapter. (We refer the reader to a mathematics methods text for a complete discussion of many mathematics manipulatives; some possibilities are Rubenstein, Beckmann, and Thompson 2004; Van de Walle 2004.) Nevertheless, in Figure 8.2 we provide four examples to illustrate the understandings that might be developed when models are used to facilitate the teaching and learning of mathematics. For example, integer operations are sometimes difficult for middle grades students. Rather than provide students with rules to follow, Example 1 of Figure 8.2 shows how students can make sense of integer addition when they are given an opportunity to explore integer computations with two-color counters. As students model several integer problems with the counters, they can generate procedures for adding integers rather than being told a rule.

Example 2 in Figure 8.2 illustrates the use of algebra tiles to represent the multiplication of two binomials. As students use the tiles, they are able to visualize how the distributive property provides a basis to obtain a product. They might also extend their prior understanding that a rectangular region may be used to represent the product of a multiplication problem.

The model of Example 3 in Figure 8.2 illustrates the meaning of multiplication of fractions, in this case $\frac{1}{3} \times \frac{1}{3}$. A rectangle represents the unit whole or 1. Students first identify $\frac{1}{3}$ of the rectangle, illustrated by the shading of the left column. Then, students find $\frac{1}{3}$ of that shaded region, illustrated by the darker gray region. To interpret the result, the student must determine the fraction of the whole represented by $\frac{1}{3}$ of the $\frac{1}{3}$. In this case, the darker gray region represents $\frac{1}{9}$ of the rectangle.

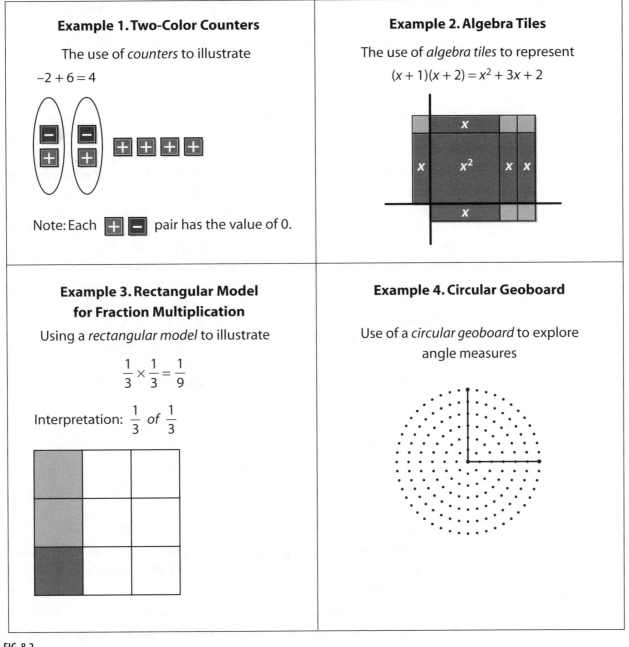

Example 1. Two-Color Counters

The use of *counters* to illustrate

$-2 + 6 = 4$

Note: Each  pair has the value of 0.

Example 2. Algebra Tiles

The use of *algebra tiles* to represent

$(x + 1)(x + 2) = x^2 + 3x + 2$

Example 3. Rectangular Model for Fraction Multiplication

Using a *rectangular model* to illustrate

$$\frac{1}{3} \times \frac{1}{3} = \frac{1}{9}$$

Interpretation: $\frac{1}{3}$ of $\frac{1}{3}$

Example 4. Circular Geoboard

Use of a *circular geoboard* to explore angle measures

FIG. 8.2
Examples of mathematics models

Example 4 of Figure 8.2 illustrates the use of a circular *geoboard* to explore angle measures. With the geoboard, students can demonstrate angles requested by the teacher, such as a right angle or an obtuse angle, and determine the measures of those angles.

As the four examples in Figure 8.2 illustrate, mathematical models enable students to visualize and investigate mathematics concepts. During explorations with the models, students reveal

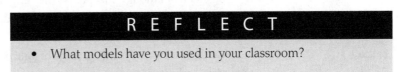

REFLECT

• What models have you used in your classroom?

their prior understandings, make and test conjectures, and justify and share their reasoning. The communication in which students engage as they explore with the models provides insights into our students' thinking that can guide further instruction.

Graphic Organizers

Graphic organizers provide another means to help students connect mathematics ideas and relate previous and new knowledge. A *graphic organizer* is a visual display that shows the organizational structure of concepts or illustrates the relationships between or among concepts; it is a communication tool to help students make sense of new ideas, compare and contrast concepts, connect ideas, and illustrate relationships among concepts. Graphic organizers exist in various forms and are titled differently, including knowledge maps, concept maps, or concept diagrams. Some organizers are specific to particular topics; others may be used across a range of topics.

Research (e.g., Boyle and Weishaar 1997; Horton, Lovitt, and Bergerud 1990; Horton et al. 1993; Kinchin 2000a, 2000b) indicates that graphic organizers support student learning. They help students:

- collect information, make interpretations, solve problems, devise plans, and become aware of how they think (Bracket 2004),
- consolidate information into a meaningful whole to connect the facts, terms, and concepts they are learning (Horton, Lovitt, and Bergerud 1990),
- relate new knowledge to existing knowledge (Kinchin 2000a, 2000b),
- strengthen vocabulary knowledge (Horton, Levitt, and Bergerud 1990; Monroe and Pendergrass 1997; Moore and Readence 1984),
- strengthen their ability to communicate information (Hyerle 1996),
- construct meaning by representing visually knowledge gained from reading or listening (Griffin, Malone, and Kameeni 1995; Heimlich and Pittelman 1986; Monroe and Pendergrass 1997), and
- remember and categorize information (Guastello, Beasley, and Sinatra 2000).

In addition, graphic organizers often pinpoint students' misconceptions. In the sections that follow, we illustrate how graphic organizers can be used to support mathematics concept development and students' mathematics language fluency by comparing and contrasting concepts and illustrating relationships among concepts.

Comparing and Contrasting Concepts: Venn Diagrams and These Are/These Are Not

Students solidify their understanding as they distinguish similarities and differences between or among concepts. As they engage in such comparisons, they determine features that are particular to a concept. In addition, misconceptions they hold about concepts often come to the fore so that students are able to clarify their understanding. Here, we discuss two ways that graphic organizers can be used to assist students as they compare and contrast concepts.

Venn diagrams show mathematical or logical relationships among different groups (i.e., sets). Specifically, a Venn diagram is a drawing in which loops represent groups of items with common properties. Concepts or values that belong in more than one set are placed where the loops overlap. When used as part of instruction, Venn diagrams help students distinguish similarities and differences between or among concepts.

The Venn diagram in Figure 8.3 illustrates the relationship among different classifications of numbers. A student can readily see that whole numbers are both integers and rational numbers. The diagram in Figure 8.4 illustrates relationships among several quadrilaterals; it shows that rhombi, squares, and rectangles are all parallelograms and that a square is both a rhombus and a rectangle.

REFLECT

- Create a Venn diagram to show the relationship between *prime numbers* and *odd numbers* for the set of natural numbers from 1 to 20. How might the creation of such a diagram help students distinguish prime numbers and odd numbers?

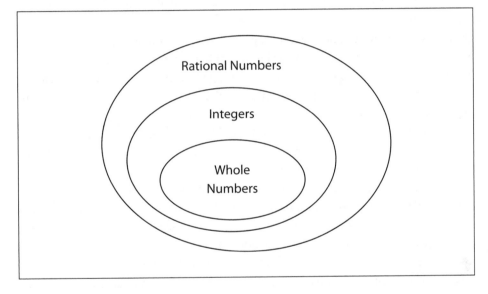

FIG. 8.3
A Venn diagram to illustrate classifications of numbers

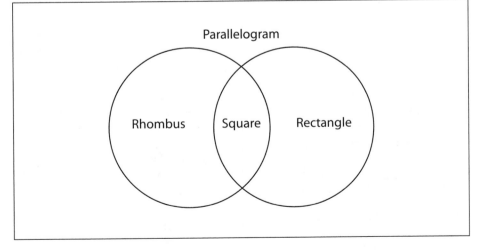

FIG. 8.4
A Venn diagram to illustrate relationships among parallelograms

While learning mathematics, middle grade students often confuse concepts, words, or symbols that appear to be closely related to each other (e.g., *parallel* and *perpendicular*; *factor* and *multiple*; the symbol for *is less than*, <, and the symbol for *is greater than*, >). A *These Are/These Are Not* chart can help students distinguish among characteristics of mathematics concepts or symbols that may or may not be related, but are often confused. The creation of this chart provides students opportunities to compare features of particular concepts by observing characteristics of objects, symbols, or representations (see Figures 8.5 and 8.6). When students examine objects listed in the *These Are* column, they can observe similarities. As students compare information across categories, they formulate conclusions about the distinguishing characteristics of the object or concept. In particular, students must discern how symbols or images differ to clarify understanding of the specific mathematical signs.

These Are/These Are Not charts help students connect mathematical understandings. When using these charts, we might start with the categories and items that do or do not fit the identified category (e.g., parallelograms and non-parallelograms). Students may conjecture items that fit either category. Then, we can provide students the opportunity to suggest where the items should be placed. For example, with the *These Are/These Are Not* chart in Figure 8.5, a student might believe that a parallelogram is any four-sided figure and draw a trapezoid to place in the *These are parallelograms* category. The teacher would let everyone know that the trapezoid actually belongs in the *These are not* category. Now students can determine how the trapezoid differs from the other quadrilaterals and use this new information to reformulate their conclusions. They know that a parallelogram is a figure with four sides, but having four sides is not a sufficient condition to determine whether a figure is a parallelogram. This process continues until students have included enough additional figures to be able to distinguish parallelograms from other figures.

Figure 8.6 shows the use of a *These Are/These Are Not* chart to investigate the role of the equal sign to represent an equation. With *These Are/These Are Not* charts, students can be encouraged to examine the role or function of symbols (e.g., equations, inequalities, and expressions) as well as words or figures.

There are many ways that teachers can use *These Are/These Are Not* charts in the classroom. Students can place new figures or symbols in the chart based on their conjectures and the teacher can indicate if the placement is appropriate. Alternatively, teachers might ask students to identify other items that belong on the chart, but the

FIG. 8.5
A These Are/These Are Not *chart for* parallelograms

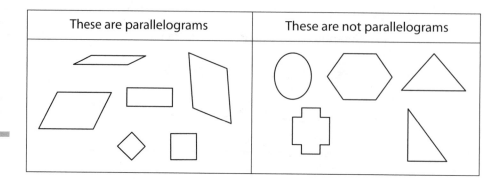

These are parallelograms	These are not parallelograms

These are equations	These are not equations
$n = 3$ $3x + 5 = 7$ $3 + 4 - 1 = 5 - 2 + 3$ $y = x^2$ $A = lw$ $l = \dfrac{1}{2}w$	$x > 2$ $4 < 7$ $5 - 3$ $\dfrac{1}{2} + \dfrac{3}{4}$

FIG. 8.6
A These Are/These Are Not *chart for equations*

teacher places the item in the appropriate category. This option has less risk for the student but still has value because students have an opportunity to determine if the item is placed where they assumed it would go. Without undue attention, students can monitor their conjectures and refine their observations. Once the teacher determines that the majority of the students have a rudimentary understanding of the concept, vocabulary can be introduced and students can be encouraged to provide an explanation or definition for the concept represented by the items in the chart, orally or in writing. Then, students compare and contrast their statements for additional refinement.

R E F L E C T

- Identify two other concepts that could be explored using a *These Are/These Are Not* chart.

- How might students benefit from the completion of such charts?

Illustrating Relationships Among Concepts: Concept Maps and Semantic Feature Analysis Grids

At times, students may fail to see connections among mathematics ideas. Therefore, it is important to engage students in activities that help them see how the concepts they are studying are related. "Without connections, students must learn and remember too many isolated concepts and skills. With connections, they can build new understandings on previous knowledge" (NCTM 2000, 274). Concept maps and semantic feature analysis grids are two types of graphic organizers in which connections among concepts are made explicit.

A *concept map* includes nodes that depict mathematics concepts and links that represent relationships among the concepts. Often, the links are labeled with phrases such as *is an example of, is related to,* or *is classified by* to clarify the illustrated relationship (Baroody and Bartels 2000; Novak and Gowin 1984; Schwartz 1988). Concept maps may vary in their level of complexity depending on students' previous experiences with the content. For instance, a concept map created at the beginning of a unit might incorporate only some relationships or might have links misplaced. When that same concept map is revisited at the end of the unit, more relationships may be included and links can be checked and modified as needed. Concept maps allow students to reveal their knowledge or solidify their understanding as students illustrate how they believe key ideas are related.

Figure 8.7 contains a concept map for *powers*. The concept map contains links to show the meaning of the concept as well as related vocabulary. Notice that the vocabulary links provide insight into general vocabulary (*exponent* and *base*) as well as special vocabulary (*squares* and *cubes*).

The intent of the concept map in Figure 8.8 is to solidify understanding of a particular concept—in this case, equations. Different types of nodes radiate from the central node for *equations* to clarify the meaning of the concept, to provide examples, and to compare with other related concepts by illustrating non-examples.

Before we expect students to generate a concept map independently, we need to model its use in a whole-class setting. We might begin with a partially completed concept map and encourage students to refine and reflect on their learning by including additional properties and examples. We might create a list of phrases and examples and expect students to organize them in a way that makes sense. We can encourage students to organize concept maps in different ways based on the connections they make and compare different organizations.

Concept maps can facilitate communication in various ways. Students can use them to take notes, review learned concepts, and relate new information to information previously learned. Teachers can use them to have a class share and gather information during a brainstorming session, and to assess students' understanding and diagnose misconceptions. Thus, concept maps are a versatile tool.

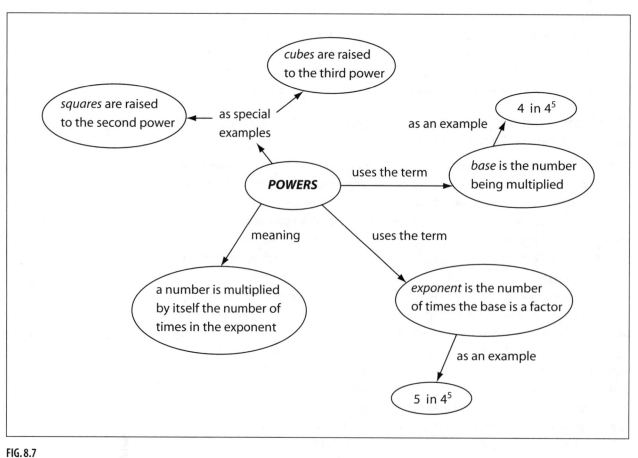

FIG. 8.7
A concept map for powers

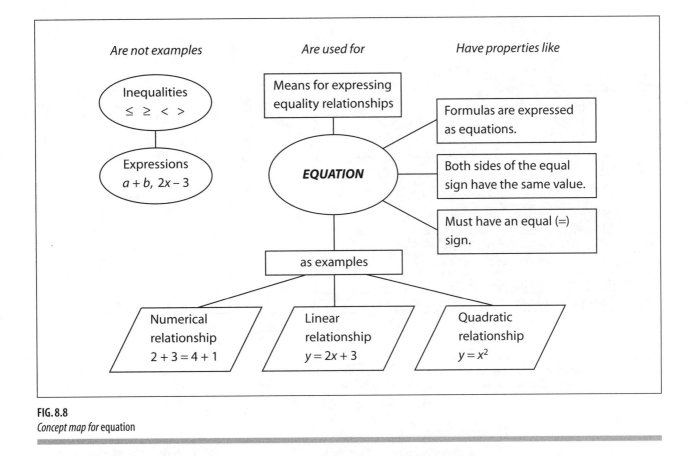

Are not examples   *Are used for*   *Have properties like*

Inequalities
≤ ≥ < >

Expressions
$a + b, 2x - 3$

Means for expressing
equality relationships

EQUATION

Formulas are expressed
as equations.

Both sides of the equal
sign have the same value.

Must have an equal (=)
sign.

as examples

Numerical
relationship
$2 + 3 = 4 + 1$

Linear
relationship
$y = 2x + 3$

Quadratic
relationship
$y = x^2$

FIG. 8.8
Concept map for equation

Semantic feature analysis grids (Baldwin, Ford, and Readence 1981; Johnson and Pearson 1984) help students examine similarities and differences among a group of concepts or ideas that differ by a few basic features. Students examine the relationships among concepts by comparing them across common categories. To create a semantic feature analysis grid, students create a grid with a set of related concepts listed down the left and the features or properties listed across the top (or vice versa). Students then mark the cells of the grid to indicate that a concept is associated with a particular feature. As students complete the grid, they examine characteristics of related concepts; the systematic strategy of the grid enables them to compare and contrast characteristics and draw conclusions about particular concepts.

Figure 8.9 shows a grid that represents an analysis of different types of data displays. The different types of data displays are written across the top and the properties of the displays are listed on the left. As students complete the grid, they determine the appropriateness of particular displays for different types of data or different communication goals.

R E F L E C T

- Create a concept map for the central theme of *area*. Identify appropriate nodes that clarify the meaning of area, provide examples of area, and demonstrate relationships among areas of different polygons.

- Create a concept map that illustrates relationships among real numbers, rational numbers, whole numbers, natural numbers, integers, and irrational numbers. Compare your concept map to the Venn diagram illustrated in Figure 8.3. Aside from the number of sets involved, what are similarities and differences between the two representations?

Property \ Data Display	Circle Graph	Pictograph	Bar Graph	Histogram	Line Plot	Box-and-Whisker Plot	Stem-and-Leaf Plot	Scatter Plot	Line Graph
used to compare data	x	x	x	x		x			
includes an x- and y-axis			x	x				x	x
involves the use of pictures or icons		x							
shows change over time									x
shows how the data cluster or group together					x	x	x	x	
shows how two sets of data are related								x	
typically involves categorical data	x	x	x						
typically involves numerical data				x	x	x	x	x	x

FIG. 8.9
A semantic feature analysis grid for data displays

Figure 8.10 shows a semantic feature analysis grid related to classifications of triangles. In addition to classifying triangles by side lengths and angles, students can determine the possible relationships that combine side lengths and angle measures. For example, the grid indicates that it is possible to have a right triangle that is isosceles or scalene but it is not possible to have a right-angled equilateral triangle.

A semantic feature analysis grid may be constructed by individuals, in small groups, or as part of a whole-class discussion. Prior to instruction, a teacher might engage students in a discussion of particular concepts to determine students' prior knowledge. During instruction, students can complete a grid as a record of their observations. After instruction, a completed grid can be used to assess how well students understood the topic under discussion.

The grid itself may be generated by the teacher or by students. On *student-generated grids*, a category (i.e., classification of triangles) is identified but the terms and properties (i.e., side lengths and angle measures) may be omitted. Students can be asked to share as many concepts as possible that fit into that category and identify features that will be explored. Once the grid is developed, students have an opportunity to determine whether each concept has the features that have been listed. During this process, students may identify other features or concepts to examine and add them to the list.

A *teacher-generated grid* is similar to the student-generated grids, but the concepts and properties are identified in advance to address topics that have been, or will be studied. The teacher may invite students to add new terms and features to the grid. Again, students have time to examine or explore the properties in order to complete the grid. Once students have completed a student-generated or teacher-generated grid, they may share observations, debate areas of disagreement, reach consensus about particular features, and share other features they believe should have been included.

By Sides / By Angles	Equilateral (three congruent sides)	Isosceles (two congruent sides)	Scalene (no congruent sides)
Right		X	X
Obtuse		X	X
Acute	X	X	X

FIG. 8.10
A semantic feature analysis grid for classification of triangles

A Summary of Graphic Organizers

The graphic organizers described in this chapter represent only a sample of the types of organizers available for use. As we have discussed throughout this section, we can use graphic organizers in various stages of the learning cycle. At the beginning of a topic of study, they can be used as advanced organizers to introduce new concepts. During instruction, graphic organizers can be used to build understanding. At the conclusion of a unit of study, they can serve as a post-organizer. Initially, students are introduced to particular graphic organizers; later they can be encouraged to generate others independently to make sense of new knowledge. In early experiences with graphic organizers, we need to model the use of a particular organizer to help students understand the benefits that it provides, to introduce the purpose and specific form of the organizer, and to use the organizer with both familiar and new material. After several graphic organizers have been introduced, students should compare and contrast the uses of various graphic organizers so they understand when one type of organizer might be more useful than another. Students should have many opportunities to select for themselves an appropriate organizer for a particular learning goal.

Students can be encouraged to develop graphic organizers as *note-taking devices* to help them make sense of mathematics and to assist them as they study. Graphic organizers can also be used as *environmental print* to decorate and enhance the mathematics classroom. These permanent or interchangeable displays provide visual representations that are resources for students as they work and grapple with new information.

Concept Development Through Body Motion

Students of mathematics learn in a variety of ways (Gardner 1983). Many middle grades students thirst for movement and some learn best through the kinesthetic realm (Griss 1994). It can be beneficial to use movement and have students physically model shapes of graphs, geometric forms, and relationships. Figure 8.11 contains examples from four topics that illustrate how body motions might be used to solidify students' understanding of mathematics concepts and help them connect mathematics language with physical activity.

- Suppose a teacher asks a group of students to arrange themselves in order according to their heights. How might she help students use their result to formalize their understanding of concepts such as mode, range, and median?

- In what other ways might body motions be used to develop or revisit mathematics concepts?

These kinesthetic activities help make some mathematical phenomena concrete for some students. Movement activities are good as brief closing activities or as in-class breaks when students have been seated for a long time. In addition, as students move their bodies to illustrate mathematical ideas or concepts, we have a chance to assess their understanding and identify misconceptions.

Algebraic Graph Aerobics

Stand. Pretend your body is the y-axis.

- Show the x-axis. (Arms outstretched horizontally.)
- Show $y = x$. (Right arm up at 45° angle to body, left arm down at 45°.)
- Show $y = x + 1$. (Hold arms as with $y = x$ but stand on tiptoes.)
- Show $y = 2x$.
- Show $y = -x$.
- Show $y = -2x$.
- Show $y = |x|$.
- Show $y = x^2$.

Slope Aerobics

Stand and use your arms to show the following.

- Show a line with a positive slope.
- Show a line with zero slope.
- Show a line with undefined slope. (How can you distinguish 0 slope and undefined slope?)
- Show a line with a slope of 2.
- Show a line with a slope of –1.
- Show a shape where the slope is changing.
- Show a shape where the slope is unchanging. (Any line!)

Geometry Aerobics

- Use your arms and show parallel lines.
- Show parallel lines that are not horizontal.
- Show perpendicular lines.
- Show an acute angle.
- Show an obtuse angle.
- Show a straight angle.
- Show skew lines.
- Show a 45° angle.
- Show a 135° angle.
- Show a 170° angle.
- Show your neighbor an angle. Your neighbor should estimate its measure.

Human Box Plot

Have students arrange themselves in order by height.

- Raise your hand if your height is the median.
- Raise your hand if your height is at the 25th percentile.
- Raise your hand if your height is at the 75th percentile.
- Raise your hand if your height is at or between the 25th and 75th percentiles. (This is the "box" in the box plot. What percent of the group does the box represent?)
- Raise your hand if your height is below the 25th or above the 75th percentile. (These are the "whiskers" in the box plot.)
- Who is in the upper quartile?

FIG. 8.11
Ideas for math aerobics

Summary

Collectively, the instructional approaches described in this chapter represent methods to help students make meaning in the mathematics classroom through visual and verbal representations and body movements. As students focus on concept development, they have opportunities to use the language and symbolism of mathematics and work toward building their mathematical literacy and fluency with the mathematics sign system.

Expand Your Understanding

1. Many resources for teachers (e.g., lesson plans, virtual manipulatives, applets) exist on the Web. Even if manipulatives are not available in the classroom, students can interact with manipulatives in a virtual manner. Investigate pattern blocks or other manipulatives at the National Library of Virtual Manipulatives (NLVM) (http://nlvm.usu.edu/en/nav/vlibrary.html) or the Illuminations website of the National Council of Teachers of Mathematics (http://illuminations.nctm.org). Also, investigate some of the activities at these sites, particularly ones that encourage communication.

2. Choose a mathematics concept and create a concept map for that concept (e.g., polygons, volume, measures of central tendencies).

3. a. How might a semantic feature analysis grid be used to explore various features of a quadrilateral?

   b. Create a semantic feature analysis grid to examine the following properties of quadrilaterals: angles, sides, diagonals, symmetry.

4. Compare and contrast the graphic organizers described in this chapter.

Connect to Practice

5. Try one of the activities described at the NLVM site or the Illuminations website with a middle grades mathematics student. How did the student interact with the activity? What did you learn by talking with the student as he or she completed the activity?

6. Consider your mathematics curriculum. What topics could you have your students examine by using a semantic feature analysis grid? Create a grid that includes both the categories and properties.

7. With your class, create a concept map for a topic that you have already studied or are in the process of studying. What challenges did your students have? What did you learn about your students' ability to communicate their understanding of the concept?

8. Review your middle grades mathematics curriculum.

a. Identify at least two different opportunities to engage students in kinesthetic activities (math aerobics).

b. Try at least one kinesthetic activity with your students. Describe how your students reacted to the activity.

CHAPTER 9

Building Meanings Through Language Development

The investigation of the meaning of words is the beginning of education.
—Antisthenes, c. 445–365 BC

Learning the terms of mathematics need not be a burden. Words are a natural part of human activity; they have histories, relations to one another, and connections to the real world. Students can appreciate language and value its role in supporting communication and understanding when they are engaged in inventing, visualizing, and studying the history, uses, and connections of words.
—Rheta N. Rubenstein, "Strategies to Support the Learning of the Language of Mathematics"

Language is the medium of teaching and learning in the classroom. Teachers and students use language to pose questions, explain their thinking, compare strategies, and provide justifications for their reasoning. We teach with language and we assess students' learning with language. We listen to students' efforts to express mathematical thinking and we read their mathematical writings. Language is central to meaning making in mathematics learning.

Like learners of any language, mathematics students face a number of challenges when learning the elements of the language system. As described in Chapter 3, the vocabulary of mathematics often creates particular difficulties for students:

- Some words in everyday language have different meanings in English and mathematics (e.g., the word *plane*).
- Some words have meaning solely in mathematics (e.g., *parallelogram*).
- Some words have comparable meanings in English and mathematics but the mathematics meaning is more precise (e.g., *similar*).
- Some words have multiple meanings within mathematics (e.g., *square*).
- Some words are learned in pairs that are commonly confused (e.g., *numerator* and *denominator*, *factor* and *multiple*, *radius* and *diameter*).

As teachers of mathematics, our job is to help students meet the challenges of mathematics language. How can we guide students to take ownership and gain fluency with the language of mathematics? How can we help them make sense of multisyllabic words? How can we help them compare and contrast the use of words in everyday English with the use of those words in mathematics? How can we support their understanding of meanings of terms in ways that make sense to them and are not just formal definitions? This chapter suggests practices that address these issues.

Daily Practices

There are several practices that can easily become a natural part of our daily, ongoing classroom instruction. Consider first how we often attach formal language to concepts. Mathematicians typically begin chapters in advanced mathematics books with definitions of new terms, then theorems (i.e., statements of truth) are stated and proved about these newly defined terms. This approach makes sense when the goal is to develop a deductive system in which axioms or postulates (statements assumed to be true) lead to definitions, which lead to new knowledge (theorems or statements to be proved). But, this deductive approach is not the way most mathematicians originally determined what might make a good definition. Rather, they first explored ideas connected to the topic and looked for relationships. Later they determined that a set of assumptions and definitions might make a good starting point. For example, the Euclidean geometry that students often study in school starts with assumptions of undefined terms (e.g., *point, line, plane*) and a set of postulates. Then theorems are proved based on those undefined terms and postulates. However, before Euclid organized geometric knowledge into the deductive system that we know today, ancient mathematicians explored figures and looked for connections.

As middle grades teachers, we need to approach vocabulary development in ways that make sense to learners. In middle grades instruction, it often makes more sense for learners to have terminology introduced *after* an idea has been explored rather than to start with the terminology. This enables students to focus on concepts so that language is later attached to ideas that are familiar. Think about the vignette in Chapter 1 in which Ms. Greenwood had students explore stem-and-leaf plots before they attached the name to the display.

As another example, consider the following brief vignette.

Mr. Bernstein wanted his students to explore ideas related to square roots. He wanted to help his students develop a solid conceptual understanding and he wanted them to have a visual model of a square root. He decided to start by having his students work on the following task with a partner:

Use base ten flats (100 square centimeters) to create another square flat whose area is 400 square centimeters.

His students had previously studied area of squares so they easily built a square with dimensions 20 centimeters by 20 centimeters. He then encouraged his students to find square flats with areas of 900 and 1600 square centimeters. Students quickly used flats to build squares with dimensions 30 centimeters and 40 centimeters on a side, respectively.

Mr. Bernstein then challenged his students to build a square with an area close to 200 square centimeters. Based on the previous squares they had built, students realized they needed to determine a number which when multiplied by itself is 200. When they couldn't build the square with base ten blocks, he suggested that they try to draw the figure on graph paper. With this small hint, his students were able to estimate the length of the side of the square needed to enclose an area of 200 square centimeters. He encouraged his students to repeat the task to find square flats with other areas, such as 300, 500, or 800 square centimeters.

When he brought the class back together, most of the students understood the underlying concept of the task (i.e., to find a number which when squared produces some other number). He then introduced the term *square root* to describe the length of the side of the square with the given area.

The vignette illustrates a useful practice in the classroom—*allow language to follow concept development*.

A second regular practice when introducing new terms is to *pronounce the word clearly, spell it, write it, use the word in a sentence*, and *engage students in these processes*. We should not assume students hear a word and connect it to the written word we intend. For example, one teacher reported hearing *Pythagorean theorem* as a child; but he thought the teacher had a lisp and meant to say *serum*. He was so distracted by his assumption of the teacher's error that he could not focus on the mathematics the teacher was addressing. In another instance, one of our colleagues used the phrase *row by column* to describe an interpretation for multiplication; her college student heard this phrase as *robot column*. Both examples reinforce our need as teachers to ensure that students hear new terms correctly, read the terms in a complete sentence, and pronounce them for themselves.

Fluency in the language of mathematics, like fluency in any spoken language, requires many opportunities to use the language, even with halting efforts. Unlike English, which students use in and out of school, students rarely use the language of mathematics outside of the mathematics classroom. We suggest two additional daily practices to support mathematics language development: make our classrooms language intense and help students find ways to use mathematics language outside of class.

REFLECT

- Recall an incident in your own learning in which not seeing a word in print or hearing it carefully pronounced led to some confusion. How was your understanding of the concept influenced?

- What are some words that your students sometimes hear or say incorrectly?

- What do you suppose students think or say to themselves when they encounter a symbol that they don't know how to pronounce?

As indicated, we need to *make the mathematics language experience within our classrooms intense*. All students need immersion into the language of mathematics. Having students work in groups provides opportunities for all students to use mathematics language. While students work in groups, teachers have a chance to monitor conversations, listen for language use (both appropriate and inappropriate), and make instructional decisions about what issues to bring to the entire class. Students can be asked to support their peers in language learning, for example, double-checking each other when they use words like *factor* and *multiple*. As students share a variety of solutions to problems and publicly question one another (with teacher support and guidance), they have many opportunities to address language issues.

Another ongoing practice to intensify mathematics language experiences is to *find ways students can use mathematical language outside of school* as part of instruction. For instance, we can assign homework that requires students to explain to someone else how and why they solved a problem as they did. When students explain a problem or process to their parents, they help their parents understand the nature of the mathematics they are studying. But more important, they have another chance to select and use appropriate mathematical terms and phrases. We can also have students listen for mathematics language in media and conversations outside of school and capture those in a section of their notebook or for a class bulletin board, perhaps providing credit for students who share such conversations with the rest of the class.

A final ongoing practice we mention is one illustrated in the vignette in Chapter 3. We can reserve space on a bulletin board or wall for a *word* or *sentence wall* so that new terms are prominently displayed with images or definitions to remind students of their meanings. Students might make their own *personal glossaries* or *word walls* (Murray 2004; Richards 2005; Toumasis 1995) to help them clarify and own new terms and to provide a way to take the word wall home with them. (Recall the sample dictionary entries for *prime number* and *equation* from Chapter 3.)

Personal dictionaries can be constructed in several ways. Students can have one or more pieces of paper in a notebook for each letter of the alphabet. As they encounter a new word or phrase, they can write a definition in their own words, indicate the symbol used for the term if applicable, draw a diagram if appropriate, provide one or more examples and indicate why each is an example, and provide one or more non-examples and indicate why each is a non-example. Students might write entries on index cards with a hole punched in the upper corner so they can be hooked on a ring. Murray (2004) has students write words on a folder that has been partitioned into sections for each letter of the alphabet. In addition to the entries for their personal dictionaries, students can write entries on large newsprint pages that can be posted on a word or sentence wall and referenced throughout the year.

Word Origins, Prefixes, and Suffixes

Technical words, such as *hypotenuse, perpendicular, polynomial,* or *isosceles,* are found only in mathematics (i.e., they are discipline specific) and seem foreign to many students. Particularly for terms that are not everyday English words, the origins or etymological roots of a word may assist students to make sense of the meaning. When they research word origins, students may find connections to words they know that help them make sense of the new term. For example, *hypotenuse* comes from the Greek words *hypo-* meaning "under" and *teinein* meaning "to stretch." In a right triangle, the hypotenuse (see Figure 9.1) is the side that "stretches" from one leg to the other "under" the right angle (assuming you draw it that way!).

Another example to illustrate the benefit of word origins is *perpendicular,* as in lines making a right angle (square corner). *Perpendicular* comes from a root meaning "plumb line," a line hanging with a weight at one end; *per* means "through" and *pend* means "to hang." When a plumb line hangs down, it creates a line perpendicular to the earth (see Figure 9.2). Students can be reminded of related English words with *pend* as one of their roots. A *pendant* hangs on one's neck. A *dependent* is a child who "hangs" onto a parent or guardian for support.

Figure 9.3 contains samples of word origins across content strands that indicate the potential of word origins to help middle grades students make sense of vocabulary.

In general, making links to related English words helps build meaning and enhances overall language development. Steven Schwartzman's book, *The Words of Mathematics*

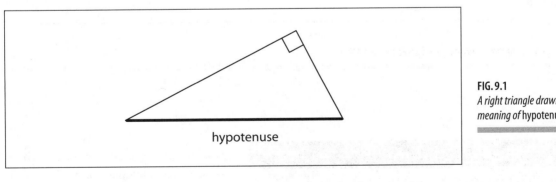

FIG. 9.1
A right triangle drawn to illustrate the meaning of hypotenuse

FIG. 9.2
A drawing to illustrate the meaning of perpendicular

Term and Word Origin Root	Other Related Words
Percent • *per:* for each • *cent:* 100	century centennial centipede centigram
circumference • *circum:* around or bend around • *ferre:* to bring or carry	circumnavigate circumlocution circumspect circumscribe circumvent
acute • *acute:* sharp or pointed	acute vision acupuncture acrobat
coordinate • *co:* together with • *ordinate:* a straight row	cooperate cooperative coincide
graph • *graphein:* to write, to scratch	telegraph autograph graphology graphics
reciprocal • *re:* back • *pro:* forward	reciprocity reciprocate

FIG. 9.3
Sample word origins for mathematical terms (adapted from Rubenstein 2000)

REFLECT

- Consider the origins for *reciprocal*. In what ways do the meanings of *re* and *pro* connect to how the numerator and denominator interact in a reciprocal?

- Write down as many words as you can that contain the prefix, *tri-*. What common meaning do all these words share?

- The suffix *-meter* means measure. List at least five words from middle grades mathematics that have *meter* as a root or suffix.

(1994), is an excellent source for teachers to learn etymologies of mathematics terms. Alternatively, good dictionaries often provide word origins.

In addition to the roots or origins of words, there are many common prefixes and suffixes students need to know. For example, a student who knows that *bi-* means *two* has a head start on understanding the meaning of *binomial* or *bisect*. Likewise, a student who knows that *equi-* means *equal* should be able to suggest possible meanings for *equilateral, equiangular,* or *equivalent.*

When teachers appropriately integrate word roots, prefixes, or suffixes into their instruction, they help students make sense of the meanings of words. However, our goal is for students to become independent word sleuths themselves. We want to look for opportunities when new terms are introduced and select students (i.e., the "Word Sleuths Team" for that unit) to research the origin of the word. They can create a poster with the word, show links to its origins (root, prefix, suffix) and, as appropriate, draw a diagram that illustrates how that meaning became attached to that word. Teachers can invite students to explain their poster to the class and to post it on the class' word wall.

Venn Diagrams

Language is a particular challenge to students when words are used in both everyday English and mathematics (i.e., special vocabulary), but with a more technical meaning in mathematics. For example, as indicated in Chapter 3, *similar* is one such word. In this case we

R E F L E C T

- What are some mathematics terms that also occur as everyday English words?

want students to recognize that there is a specialized mathematical meaning and it has more details than the general everyday English meaning of *similar*. One way to help students attend to these distinctions is to invite them to create Venn diagrams to demonstrate how the same word is used in English and in mathematics. Venn diagrams may be used in conjunction with the Word Origins strategy; often origins of some root in the word provide a link that shows what the two uses have in common. Venn diagrams may be enhanced by notes or comments that detail the distinctions between the two words.

Figure 9.4 illustrates a Venn diagram for the word *similar*, showing both the distinct English and mathematical meanings as well as the sense that is shared by the two uses. A statement of distinctions between the terms accompanies the Venn diagram.

Some words, like *prime*, seem to have totally different meanings in mathematics and everyday English. But, when the origin of the word is known, commonalities emerge. Figure 9.5 demonstrates how a Venn diagram may help clarify the meanings in English and mathematics.

There are instances in which a mathematics term has different meanings in different content strands of mathematics. Venn diagrams may also be helpful here. Figures 9.6 and 9.7 for *square* and *range*, respectively, illustrate how Venn diagrams may be beneficial when words have more than one mathematics meaning.

As teachers, we may provide Venn diagrams to help students appreciate the nuances of language or may develop them together as a class. However, we want students to generate their own diagrams as necessary. These diagrams may become contributions to a word or sentence wall or a personal language glossary or dictionary (as described in Chapter 3 and earlier in this chapter). The diagrams can be a source of continued attention as students gain fluency with these distinctions.

FIG. 9.4

Venn diagram for similar

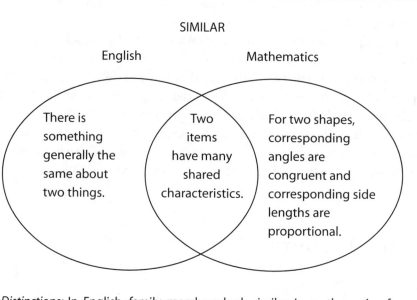

SIMILAR

English   Mathematics

There is something generally the same about two things.

Two items have many shared characteristics.

For two shapes, corresponding angles are congruent and corresponding side lengths are proportional.

Distinctions: In English, family members look similar. In mathematics, for shapes to be similar, one must be an exact enlargement or shrink of the other, like copies of the same document made on a copy machine.

FIG. 9.5

Venn diagram for prime

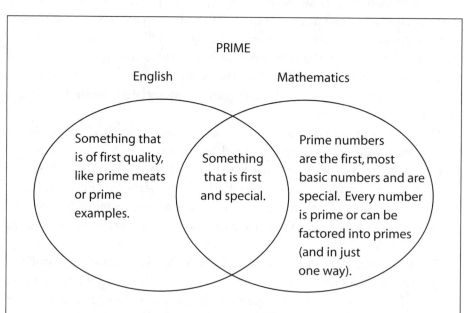

PRIME

English   Mathematics

Something that is of first quality, like prime meats or prime examples.

Something that is first and special.

Prime numbers are the first, most basic numbers and are special. Every number is prime or can be factored into primes (and in just one way).

Distinctions: In English, *prime* is used in many situations to indicate highest or first quality. In mathematics, when any natural number is factored (represented as a multiplication) into the smallest possible natural numbers, those basics into which it eventually falls are prime numbers (i.e., 2, 3, 5, 7, 11, 13, ...). Primes are the building blocks (in terms of multiplication) of other numbers. Prime numbers have exactly two distinct factors: the number itself and 1.

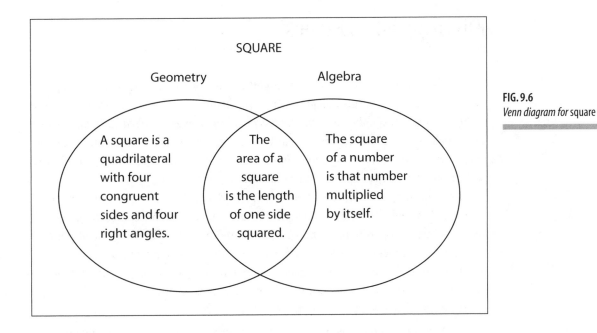

FIG. 9.6
Venn diagram for square

SQUARE

Geometry

Algebra

A square is a quadrilateral with four congruent sides and four right angles.

The area of a square is the length of one side squared.

The square of a number is that number multiplied by itself.

English language learners (ELLs) in particular may benefit from Venn diagrams. Often, ELLs first encounter a word (e.g., *similar* or *prime*) in its non-technical setting. As teachers, we need to help students compare and contrast the everyday meaning and the less familiar mathematical meaning. In their glossaries or notes, ELL students may also include the word or words from their first language that correspond to the English and mathematical meanings.

R E F L E C T

- Modify the Venn diagram for *square* to create a diagram for *cube*.

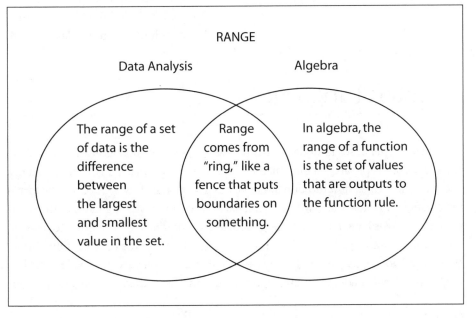

FIG. 9.7
Venn diagram for range

RANGE

Data Analysis

Algebra

The range of a set of data is the difference between the largest and smallest value in the set.

Range comes from "ring," like a fence that puts boundaries on something.

In algebra, the range of a function is the set of values that are outputs to the function rule.

Distinguished Pairs

Certain pairs of words usually learned together create another language challenge for students. Examples include *numerator* and *denominator*, *radius* and *diameter*, *factor* and *multiple*, *solve* and *simplify*, *equation* and *expression*, or even *hundreds* and *hundredths*. Other pairs include homonyms or near homonyms (*pi* and *pie*, *intersect* and *intercept*), words with and without modifiers (*bisector* versus *perpendicular bisector*), or phrases with related terms (*factor list* versus *prime factorization*).

Distinguished Pairs is an activity that helps students clarify the differences by helping them find commonalities and distinctions between commonly confused word pairs. Teachers may assign different groups of students to study different difficult pairs, to focus on the distinctions between them, and to create a skit, poster, verse, Web page, or other device to dramatize what each term means and how they are different. An artifact that can serve as a reminder may be posted on the word wall.

Here are examples of distinctions students may make.

- *Numerator* and *denominator* are the two terms in a fraction. *Denominator* comes from *name* (like "nominate"). It tells the name or unit of a fraction, like fourths.

  Numerator comes from *number*. It tells the number of units there are of the denominator, like 3 in $\frac{3}{4}$ tells there are three of those things called fourths.

- *Factor* and *multiple* both have to do with multiplication. A *factor* is a number being multiplied. Factors of 12 are 1, 2, 3, 4, 6, and 12. Factors make products just like factories make products. A *multiple* is a number you get after multiplying something by some whole number. So the multiples of 12 are 12, 24, 36, 48, 60, . . . and come from 1×12, 2×12, 3×12, 4×12, and so on. A number has a multitude of multiples.

> ## REFLECT
>
> - When asked to simplify $2(x - 5)$, some students write $2x - 10$ and then continue to "solve" to obtain $x = 5$. How does confusion between *solve* and *simplify* contribute to this misconception?
>
> - Write a sample distinction for *equation* and *expression*.

Invented Language

Despite the belief of some students that mathematics exists and has always existed independent of people and culture, mathematics, like music, visual art, writing systems, and other human communication systems, has a human history. Part of that history is the creation of words and symbols as a means to communicate the ideas of the discipline. As the word origins section suggested, terms were created or selected to relate to other words (often Greek or Latin) with meanings relevant to the concept. Oftentimes, students do not appreciate this history because they are not a part of its evolution. How might we engage students in language activities that help them understand and appreciate the thinking behind the naming of various concepts? For example, *triangle* is a shape with three (*tri-*) angles. Any one of us might have created this word, but someone else got there first! One teaching approach is to look for opportunities in which students can invent their own language.

Interestingly, the invented language strategy is easiest to use with either young or advanced (college) mathematics students. Young students may not already know formal mathematical terminology and college students may first encounter new concepts with specialized vocabulary (*group, ring, field, vector,* etc.). Middle grades students may already have heard much of the special vocabulary of mathematics. However, teachers can be alert for opportunities that encourage students to create their own informal terms.

The first vignette below illustrates one method that encourages invented language—suppress the technical terminology until students have had their own chance to suggest words. The second vignette illustrates that once the seed for invented language is planted, students may spontaneously suggest vocabulary terms.

David Whitin (1995), a mathematics educator with an interest in language, described an experience in which students explored all the rectangles that could be created with different specific numbers of square tiles (see Figure 9.8). Essentially, they were finding factorizations of the number of tiles. When students analyzed the results for many different numbers of square tiles, they concluded that some numbers made only long narrow rectangles. Other numbers made a variety of rectangles, including those that were closer to squares. The students were asked to name the two categories to distinguish the two types of numbers. Some students suggested calling the groups *sidewalk numbers* and *patio numbers,* respectively. This invented language provided an important image for the more formal terms, prime numbers and composite numbers, respectively, that were introduced later.

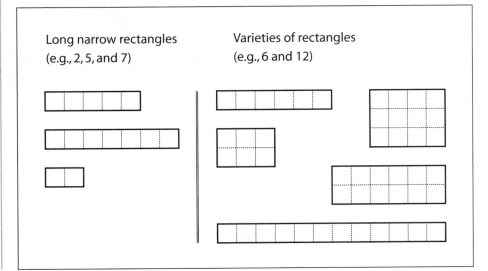

Long narrow rectangles
(e.g., 2, 5, and 7)

Varieties of rectangles
(e.g., 6 and 12)

FIG. 9.8
Rectangles made with different numbers of square tiles

In geometry a group of high school students had learned that a midpoint divides a segment into two congruent parts. They later encountered an angle bisector that divides an angle into two congruent parts. One student wondered why they couldn't call the angle bisector a *midray*; this was a simpler term (fewer syllables) and it echoed directly the analogous concept between segments and angles. The students adopted this term. Later in the course when the students were asked to identify the points in space equidistant from two parallel planes, they chorused *midplane*. The teacher was surprised. She had been thinking instead of a plane parallel to the other two and located halfway between them. The students' spontaneous generation of another analogous term indicated their comfort with the *mid-* prefix and their easy identification of another meaningful use of it.

When we have students invent names for technical terms, at some point we need to introduce the standard term to students so they are able to communicate mathematically with individuals outside their class. Related to the sidewalk and patio numbers in the vignette, we might explain, "When mathematicians first thought about these numbers, they, too, noticed differences in the shapes of the rectangles they make. Some numbers have just one multiplication (one times the number itself), while others have many multiplications. Those with one multiplication, our 'sidewalk numbers,' are called 'prime.' Our 'patio numbers' are called 'composite.'" This would also be a good time to integrate word origins. Students might have a portion of their personal glossary in which they include both their informal, invented language and the formal, technical term.

Symbols, too, are communication tools that have human histories. As with language, the strategy of invention can be applied to symbols. We don't often think of symbolism as fair territory for invention, but it can be. For example, one of the authors of this book had a teacher who used the symbol in Figure 9.9 to mean *bisect*. (It is a 2 with a slash through it to suggest "cut in two.") It was only as an adult that she realized the teacher had invented this symbol!

Just as with vocabulary, many symbols have already been invented. But, occasionally you may find an opportunity to invite students to invent symbols. Although we can say two figures are similar and can use $\triangle ABC \sim \triangle DEF$ to denote the figures are similar, we do not have ways within diagrams to indicate that this relationship exists or that particular lengths are proportional. This lack of notation within similar figures contrasts with conventions we have to indicate that corresponding parts of figures are congruent or parallel. Perhaps a student would like to invent symbols for these needs as they arise.

FIG. 9.9
An invented symbol to mean bisect

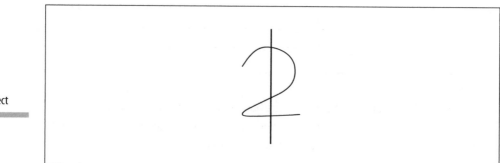

When students invent language, they realize that all the formal terms they are expected to learn are inventions of people who created those terms because there was a need for them. Language is a human endeavor and it evolves as needs arise. This message needs to be shared when students engage in language or symbol invention. Certainly, people who create computer software regularly invent symbols (icons or buttons). Think about the use of :) at the end of an email message to mean *smile* or the use of UR on a text message on a cell phone to mean *you are*. Our students, too, can be inventors of new terms or symbols as new needs arise. A major benefit of invented terms or symbols is that students make sense of mathematics *in their own terms*.

Literature Connections

Middle grades students typically enjoy having a story read to them. There are many quality children's literature books that engage students and that can help them make sense of mathematics vocabulary. For instance, *The Greedy Triangle* (Burns 1994) is a story of a triangle who becomes tired of his life and believes life would be better if he had one more side and one more angle. Therefore, he visits a shapeshifter and becomes a quadrilateral. This process continues with the shape converting into a pentagon, hexagon, heptagon, and so on. The story, together with pictures and connections to real-life contexts where the shape occurs, provides an appealing introduction or review of important geometry terms and helps students identify mathematics outside the classroom.

Figure 9.10 contains a list of several children's literature books that we have found can help introduce language or concepts, either through engaging stories or through interesting pictures. When we introduce concepts or vocabulary through literature, we often start a lesson by brainstorming about the content to activate students' prior knowledge. We then read the story aloud in its entirety, pausing only to allow students to predict upcoming events. The act of predicting allows students to focus their attention on reasoning, patterns, and problem solving while adjusting their personal schemata to fit the story. To take full advantage of the motivating influence of literature, we first read the story with a focus on enjoyment; we withhold the dissection of the story's mathematics until a second pass through the story (Hunsader 2004).

Teachers and students can also create their own stories to share with the class and with younger students. We find that reading literature to the class provides a common foundation on which we can build our lesson. The content of the story helps students make sense of the mathematics in a nonthreatening manner. The illustrations in children's literature that are associated with the language can be particularly helpful for English language learners. When students see the written term, hear it spoken, and view a picture of the term, they are able to make connections to learn the term effectively.

Book	Synopsis
Anno, Masaichiro and Mitsumasa Anno. 1983. *Anno's Mysterious Multiplying Jar.* New York: Philomel Books.	A jar contains an island with two countries. Each country contains three mountains. Each mountain contains four walled kingdoms. The patterns continue until there are 10! of them. Through the book, students learn the meaning and symbols for factorial (!).
Burns, Marilyn. 1994. *The Greedy Triangle.* New York: Scholastic.	A triangle is unhappy with its life and changes into other polygonal shapes. Problems arise when the shape becomes a circle. Eventually, the shape returns to a triangle.
Christaldi, Kathryn. 1996. *Even Steven and Odd Todd.* New York: Scholastic.	Steven only likes even things and Todd only likes odd things. The book can help students understand these concepts.
Crosbie, Michael J. 1993. *Architecture Shapes.* New York: John Wiley & Sons.	Geometry shapes and vocabulary are introduced through architectural pictures.
Ellis, Julie. 2004. *What's Your Angle, Pythagoras?* Watertown, MA: Charlesbridge.	A brief biography of Pythagoras includes an introduction of the Pythagorean theorem, with pictures to illustrate the concept underlying the theorem.
Hoban, Tana. 1974. *circles, triangles, and squares.* New York: Simon & Schuster.	Photographs of real-world objects introduce these shapes.
McCallum, Ann. 2006. *Beanstalk: The Measure of a Giant.* Watertown, MA: Charlesbridge.	In this take on the familiar Jack and the Beanstalk tale, the focus is on aspects of ratio as Jack compares himself to a giant boy named Ray.
McMillan, Bruce. 1991. *Eating Fractions.* New York: Scholastic.	Pictures show food cut into various fractional parts.

FIG. 9.10
Sample children's literature books to introduce mathematics language or symbols

Book	Synopsis
Neuschwander, Cindy. n.d. *Sir Cumference and the Dragon of Pi:* *A Math Adventure.* Watertown, MA: Charlesbridge.	Sir Cumference must determine the meaning of pi to save his father.
Neuschwander, Cindy. 1997. *Sir Cumference and the First Round Table:* *A Math Adventure.* Watertown, MA: Charlesbridge.	Sir Cumference helps develop a round table for the knights and invents the terms *radius* and *diameter* to describe the characteristics of a circle.
Neuschwander, Cindy. 2004. *Sir Cumference and the Great* *Knight of Angleland.* Watertown, MA: Charlesbridge.	Sir Cumference learns about angles on his adventure.
Neuschwander, Cindy. 2006. *Sir Cumference and the Isle of Immeter.* Watertown, MA: Charlesbridge.	Area and perimeter are introduced as the characters try to solve a riddle.
Pallotta, Jerry. 2002. *Apple Fractions.* New York: Scholastic.	Different types of apples cut in various ways introduce fractions.
Schwartz, David M. 1998. *G Is for Googol: A Math Alphabet Book.* Berkeley, CA: Tricycle Press.	Mathematics terms are related to letters of the alphabet.
Stevens, Janet. 1999. *Cook-a-Doodle-Doo!* San Diego: Harcourt Brace.	A modern spin is given to the tale of the Little Red Hen. The book provides a humorous account of misconceptions in language while the characters make a strawberry shortcake from a recipe.
Sundby, Scott. 2000. *Cut Down to Size at High Noon:* *A Math Adventure.* Watertown, MA: Charlesbridge Publishing.	Concepts related to ratios and scale drawings are introduced through a story about hairstyles in the Wild West.

FIG. 9.10
Continued

Summary

As teachers, we need to heighten our sensitivity and that of our students to the language of mathematics. We need to be aware of when and how new terms are introduced. We need to be alert to terms that appear in everyday English and help students make distinctions between the uses of the term in English and mathematics, and where possible, see the source of the commonalities and differences. We need to make our mathematics classes language intensive to develop mathematics language learners.

Expand Your Understanding

1. Think of several mathematics terms at the middle grades level important in each of the following content strands. For a few of the words, identify issues that might make the terms a challenge for middle grades students to learn.
    - Number and operations
    - Geometry
    - Measurement
    - Patterns and algebra
    - Data analysis and probability

2. a. Identify some confusing pairs of words from each of the content strands in question 1.

    b. For a pair of related words, describe how you might dramatize for students the differences between them.

    c. Create a poster or computer graphic to help clarify the distinctions between a commonly confused pair of words.

3. Research the etymological roots of a few words in each content strand that are of interest to you.

4. Review your mathematics textbook (or a textbook in another discipline). Determine whether terms tend to be introduced before or after concept development.

5. For a word that has both a mathematical meaning and a less technical meaning in English, create a Venn diagram to clarify the meanings that the words have in common. Identify the distinctions between the words.

6. Compare and contrast *Distinguished Pairs* with the *These Are/These Are Not* charts from Chapter 8. When might you choose to use each one?

7. Identify some other children's or adolescent literature that has a mathematics aspect and can be used to help students understand mathematics language or concepts.

Connect to Practice

8. Reflect on the strategies introduced in this chapter. Which ones do you feel confident using? Explain.

9. What strategies do you already use to support students' mathematics language acquisition and fluency? In what ways are these strategies helpful?

10. Consider each of the following vocabulary challenges experienced by a middle grades student. What might be the source of the difficulty for the student? How might you help the student address the challenge?

   a. A student thought a *mixed number* was a reciprocal because the two parts were mixed up.

   b. A student thought an *expression* was how your face looked.

   c. Some students thought an *inequality* was a false equality.

   d. Some students thought the *difference* between 29 and 92 was that one is larger than the other.

11. Before being introduced to formal terms, one class invented terms for the median of the lower half of the data (first quartile or 25th percentile): small median, little median, or junior median.

   a. How might these invented terms support students' sense-making efforts?

   b. What might be comparable invented terms for the third quartile or 75th percentile?

12. Many students need to have visual images of concepts to help them make sense of the concept. Suppose your students struggled to find the total of 16 items whose *average* price was $1.14. How might you help students visualize an average?

13. Preview the curriculum materials that your students will study in the next few weeks.

   a. What terminology will students confront?

   b. What practices might you use to support their language development?

14. Listen closely to students over the next week and identify instances in written or oral work where students might benefit from support in language development.

   a. Discuss these instances with colleagues.

   b. What strategies might you use to help these students address their difficulties with language?

15. Work with a colleague to plan some language development strategies for a unit in the future. Implement your plan and evaluate its effectiveness.

CHAPTER 10

Building Meanings Through Speaking and Listening

> Whether working in small or large groups, [students] should be the audience for one another's comments . . . they should speak to one another, aiming to convince or to question their peers.
> —NCTM, *Professional Standards for Teaching Mathematics*

Using mathematics language fluently and effectively includes the abilities to listen and speak about mathematics. This chapter focuses on practices that encourage students to listen and speak to the teacher as well as to their peers in low-risk environments.

Cooperative Learning Practices

One effective practice that promotes listening and speaking in mathematics classrooms is to have students work with a partner or in small groups. Cooperative learning multiplies significantly the opportunity all students have to express their thinking orally and to listen to, understand, and question the thinking of others. Research has documented the social, psychological, and cognitive benefits of students learning to support each other in cooperative groups (Johnson and Johnson 1990a, 1990b; Kagan 1992; Slavin 1983). The key ideas underlying cooperative learning are positive interdependence and individual accountability. Positive interdependence means that tasks are structured so that students benefit from collaboration; the tasks are cognitively demanding to encourage students to work together to understand the problem. If the problem is too easy, students have no reason to discuss the problem with peers. Individual accountability means that, in the end, each student is responsible for his or her own learning. Each student in the group should understand the task well enough to speak for the entire group. No group member should be able to hide behind other members of the group.

For cooperative learning to work as intended, teachers need to support students in addressing social skills, including: (1) how to share time, space, and materials; (2) how to debate an idea respectfully rather than confrontationally; and (3) how to evaluate cooperative efforts. Many resources are available to help teachers learn more about aspects of cooperative learning: forming teams, building team spirit, motivating cooperation, and building social skills (e.g., Davidson 1990; Kagan 1992). Cooperative learning has myriad formats. Here, we briefly describe a few that we believe are particularly applicable to mathematics.

Think-Pair-Share

Think-pair-share (McTighe and Lyman 1988) is an uncomplicated activity for students and teachers to use as an introduction to cooperative learning. This was the cooperative learning strategy used by the teacher in the vignette in Chapter 4. Students first *think* quietly and independently about a problem or question for the allotted time, possibly writing ideas or the beginning of a solution. This *think* time is designed to give each student an opportunity to have something to contribute in later conversations, or to at least have a question that can be asked of their peers. Personal think time invests each learner in the solution process and increases the likelihood that a diversity of strategies will emerge when students begin to share with peers.

Then, each student partners (i.e., *pairs*) with another student to share ideas, question each other, and reconcile understandings related to the context or the content of the problem. Students may also share their ideas about how to complete the task or solve the problem. When differences of opinions occur, students should try to convince each other of the validity of their selected approaches based on the mathematics inherent in the problem. Pair time gives students an opportunity to share their ideas in a risk-free context because the rest of the class need not know if their initial thinking was correct or incorrect, complete or incomplete. In addition, pair time gives students a chance to test their ideas and build confidence prior to sharing information in a larger setting. By observing the work of student pairs, the teacher is able to assess students' understandings, redirect students who are confused, and identify different approaches students have used.

Finally, there is an opportunity for discussion (i.e., *share*) in a larger group, either with another pair or the entire class. Verbalizing our ideas, even just to one other person, helps clarify our own thinking, identify missteps, consolidate ideas, and strengthen our understanding. Speaking to one partner is safe. When the larger group discussion occurs, a student can say, "We thought . . ." rather than "I thought . . ." so that the focus remains on ideas rather than on individuals. As teachers, we can direct students to consider similarities and differences among their responses, and help students increase their flexibility in using varied problem-solving strategies.

Think-pair-share is applicable in a variety of situations. It is good to use whenever a substantive question is posed, as a means to learn what students already know about a topic, and for review. At a simpler level, *think-pair-share* can be used whenever we see puzzled faces around the room. We can ask each student to try individually to clarify the point of confusion and then share their thinking with a partner. This strategy gives us an opportunity to listen to student conversations and hear how students are thinking about the question under discussion so that we are prepared to guide a follow-up group discussion.

REFLECT

- To ensure that students use their time wisely, many teachers limit the amount of time for the think or pair phases of *think-pair-share*, sometimes using a timer to keep track of the allotted time. Why might teachers want to specify the amount of time for students to work individually or in pairs?

Roundtable

Roundtable (Kagan 1992) is another introductory cooperative learning format. Students use one sheet of paper for their group. In turn, each student writes one response to a given prompt, says it aloud, and then passes the paper to the next person. Students continue to make one contribution at a time and circulate the paper among the group members until time is called. Group members may ask for clarification of a response but cannot critique others' responses. *Roundtable* can be used to create an anticipatory set for a lesson, to check for acquisition of information, or for review. We illustrate the potential for *Roundtable* in the following vignette.

Ms. Cray is planning a lesson for her sixth-grade students on parallelograms. She knows they studied various quadrilaterals last year but is unsure about their knowledge of the properties. Therefore, she decided to have students work in groups using the *Roundtable* cooperative learning activity. She gave the groups the prompt, *What are properties of a parallelogram?* She collected the responses from the six groups in her class and reviewed them to plan her lesson. Ms. Cray realized that her students knew quite a bit about parallelograms, but concluded they have some misconceptions that she needs to address.

Figure 10.1 includes the responses from one group. (Each property is from a different group member as the paper circulated twice among the four members.)

R E F L E C T

- The misconception, "It doesn't have any right angles," can hinder students' ability to deal with class inclusion concepts (i.e., all rectangles are parallelograms). How might having advance knowledge of this misconception influence how you would plan a lesson on properties of parallelograms?

> There are four sides.
>
> There are four angles.
>
> Opposite sides have the same length.
>
> The angles add up to 360°.
>
> It looks like a slanted rectangle.
>
> It doesn't have any right angles.
>
> Opposite sides are parallel.
>
> It looks like those tan pieces in our pattern blocks.

FIG. 10.1

Sample group responses for What are properties of a parallelogram?

Middle grades students come to our classes having already been exposed to many mathematics topics. As the vignette illustrates, we can learn much about what our students already know as they engage in the *Roundtable* activity, and we can use that knowledge to anticipate potential difficulties and design our instruction accordingly. To be effective, the prompts used with *Roundtable* need to address concepts for which multiple statements can be written. Here are some additional prompts that address middle grades mathematics content.

- What are properties of a rectangle?
- What are factorizations for 72?
- What other measures are equivalent to 120 mm?
- What are patterns in the multiplication table?
- What are some differences between a circle graph and a bar graph?
- What are some features of the graph of $y = 3x + 12$?

Co-op

A more complex cooperative learning format is *Co-op* (Davidson 1990) in which different groups have related but independent tasks that are later shared. For example, different groups might solve different but related problems. Then each group shares its findings and a class discussion compares what is similar and different among the solutions. Consider the following brief vignette.

Mr. Wade's algebra class is working on linear functions. He decided to use *Co-op* so that the class can look at several problems in a relatively short amount of time. He used the following four problems, with each group completing just one problem. Each group had a piece of newsprint and was expected to make a table of values for the problem, graph the data, write an equation for the problem, identify important features of the function, and relate the features to the context of the problem. After each group had worked on the problem, the group presented its work to the class and then posted the newsprint on the board. Then, Mr. Wade planned to have the class compare and contrast the functions represented on the newsprint pages.

Problem 1: Sam has $50 in the bank. He deposits $5 each week and does not withdraw any money. How much will he have in his account in w weeks?

Problem 2: Alejandra spends $10 each week attending movies. How much will she spend in w weeks?

Problem 3: Roxanne has $50. She spends $2 each week on snacks. How much will she have left after w weeks?

Problem 4: Howard has $200. He spends $20 each week for lunch. How much does he have left after w weeks?

After the groups presented their work, Mr. Wade engaged the class in a discussion about the similarities in the problems. His students made the following comments:

TYLER: The graphs for 1 and 2 increase but the graphs for 3 and 4 decrease.

ALLYNDRETH: Some graphs slant more than others.

JOSHUA: The graphs cross the vertical axis at the amount that the person had at the beginning, like Sam's graph crosses at 50 and Howard's crosses at 200.

DYLAN: The slope is the same as the amount each person gets or spends each week.

R E F L E C T

- Reflect on benefits of the *Co-op* strategy in Mr. Wade's class as evident in the vignette. What opportunities for speaking and listening were provided? How did these opportunities help students make sense of the mathematics of the lesson?

SARA: Every equation has w times a number.

LYNNE: The number multiplied by w is the amount each person gets or spends each week.

TINISHA: All equations have a number added at the end except for Alejandra.

Mr. Wade used the students' comments to discuss the slope-intercept form of linear functions. The equation format arose from students' observations and discussions about the problem. When Mr. Wade gave a quiz on the concept a few days later, he was pleased that students were able to write about a linear function and develop an equation from a context.

Jigsaw

A more complex cooperative learning format is *Jigsaw* (Davidson 1990). In this activity, each member of an original group, or home team, is assigned a different topic on which to become *expert*. The different topics are aspects of one larger concept. For example, consider the following properties of quadrilaterals: symmetries, diagonals, angles, side lengths. Each member of the home team is assigned one of the properties to investigate. Then, each team member allies with those from other teams assigned to the same topic to become an expert on that topic. For instance, team members from various groups assigned to investigate symmetries of quadrilaterals would work together to become an expert on symmetries; likewise, all those assigned to investigate diagonals (or angles or side lengths) would work together. These groups investigate their topic and rehearse presentations of what they learned. Then, the experts on this topic return to their home teams and teach other team members what they have learned about the topic.

Cooperative learning practices support students' meaning making in mathematics. When students communicate while working in cooperative groups, they clarify their own thinking, try to express to others what they mean, listen to one another, ask each other questions, and strive to understand each other's reasoning or representations. For teachers, listening to this dialogue provides much information for formative evaluation. We assess how fluent students are with mathematics language, determine what examples they use to explain their thinking, discover what potential difficulties or misconceptions exist with a concept, and ascertain what students do or do not understand.

R E F L E C T

- Reflect on opportunities for oral communication in the *Jigsaw* format.

- Compare and contrast opportunities for oral communication with *Jigsaw* and *Co-op*.

Other Practices to Encourage Language Use

Although cooperative learning practices naturally lend themselves to speaking and listening among peers, there are other practices that also provide opportunities to engage students in language use. In particular, students focus on speaking in *Silent Teacher* and *Symbol-Language Glossary*, on both speaking and listening in *Give and Take*, and on listening in *Make My Day*.

Silent Teacher

As meaning-making teachers, one of our most difficult acts is to keep quiet. Once we pose a worthwhile task for students and check their understanding of the task, we need to remain silent and let students deal with a challenge and work out the task for themselves. Being silent but observant is difficult for teachers. We wouldn't be teachers if we didn't love to explain! But often, we need to give students time and space to grapple with a rich task and use or develop language, symbols, or representations that make sense to them. Then, we can develop questions for students that build on *their* approach to the task rather than ours.

Being a *Silent Teacher* is a practice that is useful on a regular basis as a normal part of instruction. We have found it beneficial to have students read aloud the mathematical sentences and expressions that are under discussion. For example, one of the authors of this book made an interesting discovery when she had laryngitis. She had lessons written on transparencies and asked her students to read what she had written because she could not talk. However, when the students read the lessons aloud for the class she learned some of them did not know how to read several of the symbols correctly. Upon reflection, she became aware that she had done so much of the speaking herself she had provided few opportunities for students to verbalize the symbols and other mathematics vocabulary. This lack of student verbalization undermined their chances to learn.

> ### R E F L E C T
>
> - Recall an experience as a student when you were engaged with a problem and excited to be making progress, but someone gave the answer away. How did you feel? To what extent were you able or willing to continue working on the problem?

As Usiskin (1996) notes, "If a student does not know how to read mathematics out loud, it is difficult to register the mathematics because the oral language is essential for memory" (236). In Chapter 3, we described several issues that arise as students learn to express symbolic mathematics orally. Issues of verbalization can be addressed effectively if we become the *Silent Teacher*, at least on occasion.

Symbol-Language Glossary

One way to support students as they learn to pronounce mathematical symbols is to have them create and use a *Symbol-Language Glossary*. This tool not only helps students learn the meaning of a symbol, but it also indicates the correct interpretation and verbalization of the symbols and provides cautions about common errors. Figure 10.2 contains sample entries in such a glossary. Teachers can encourage English language learners to add an additional column to indicate the verbalization in their native language, thus helping build on learning that may have previously occurred in another language or country.

As part of mathematics instruction and note taking, teachers should urge students to write symbols and their verbal interpretations. Initially, we can help students identify when new items might be added to this glossary. Later, as new material is studied, we may ask students to decide for themselves when new information should be added

Symbols	Correct Interpretation or Verbalization	Common Errors
$13 > 5$	• 13 *is greater than* 5	
$13 - 5$	• 13 less 5 • 5 less than 13 • 13 decreased by 5 • 13 take away 5	• 13 less than 5 • 5 minus 13 • 13 subtracted from 5
$\dfrac{8}{9}$	• eight-*ninths* • 8 *divided by* 9 • The numerator is divided by the denominator.	• nine eights • eight nines • 9 divided by 8
$2(x + 4)$	• 2 times the *quantity* x plus 4 • 2 times the *sum* of x and 4 • The two is multiplied by both terms in parentheses, $2(x + 4) = 2x + 2(4)$.	• two times x plus 4
$\Delta A \cong \Delta B$	• Triangle A *is congruent to* triangle B.	• Triangle A equals triangle B.
$m\angle ABC = 90$	• Measure of angle ABC is 90 degrees.	

FIG. 10.2
Symbol-Language Glossary *sample entries*

R E F L E C T

• Recall a time in your own mathematics learning when symbols (maybe Greek letters) were introduced that you did not know how to pronounce. How did not being able to verbalize a symbol affect your learning?

to their list. The goal is to build independence by guiding students to recognize when they need to add information to their glossary. When students work in small groups or in a class discussion, they can refer, as needed, to their glossaries. In this way they learn to use a tool they have developed for themselves and they begin to own the information that they record.

Give and Take

Another communication practice that encourages attentive mathematical speaking and listening is *Give and Take*. Students work in pairs; one *gives* and the other *takes*. Using precise mathematical vocabulary, the *giver* verbally describes something mathematical to the *taker*. The information communicated might be a concept, a process, a geometric figure, a graph, or an algebraic statement. The taker carefully listens to the descriptions and translates them out of view of the giver into an appropriate representation of the idea, such as a sketch, a paragraph, or mathematical symbols. The taker may request that any portion of the description be repeated, but cannot ask any other questions. When finished, the students compare the idea that was orally communicated by the giver with the representation the taker created. Then, they discuss the differences between the two. Partners then switch roles and repeat the process. Note that for all applications of *Give and Take*, neither the giver nor the taker should be able to see their partner's work until the process is complete.

Give and Take can be used with multiple content topics. For instance, here are three examples:

- *geometry*: The giver can create a geometric figure out of view of a partner using geometric (pattern) blocks, Cuisenaire rods, compasses and protractors, or graph paper. The giver gives oral directions to the taker who tries to replicate the figure using only the oral directions.

- *algebra*: The giver can read an algebraic equation (e.g., two times the quantity x minus five is the same as seven times x plus two) while the taker writes the equation symbolically.

- *graphing*: The giver can describe a graph and the taker attempts to replicate it.

After students engage in *Give and Take*, they should identify any challenges they faced as the giver or taker: "What issues arose between you and your partner when doing this activity?" or, "What did you learn from early attempts that you applied to later attempts?" As students reflect on disagreements, they become sensitive to what is required in order for directions to be clear.

Students often do not recognize the value of learning precise mathematical vocabulary and the benefits of knowing and using that vocabulary. The motivational element of *Give and Take* is that only with careful, complete, and precise descriptions will the representation of the mathematical idea created by the taker match the idea communicated by the giver. As teachers we are aware that giving precise directions is not trivial. *Give and Take* challenges students and motivates them to listen carefully to every facet of their partner's verbal descriptions, helping them become better consumers of oral mathematical communication.

Give and Take provides many windows into students' mathematical thinking and language fluency. This learning strategy can be used as a diagnostic tool near the beginning of a unit to determine what students already know. It can be used as formative assessment in the midst of a unit to determine what understandings students have and what misconceptions still need to be addressed, or as a summative assessment at the end of a unit to determine what students have mastered. As teachers we can listen to hear what terms students produce, what concepts they understand or misunderstand, and what language, phrases, or concepts need attention. When we notice difficulties, we can encourage students to add terms to their personal glossaries or revise entries to address those difficulties.

REFLECT

- Think about a time when you had to fix or tell someone how to fix something technical or mechanical in your house (e.g., plumbing) and received help over the telephone. What technical terms were used that you did not know? To what extent did you struggle to explain or understand what to do?

Make My Day

Another activity that encourages students to listen carefully in the mathematics classroom is called *Make My Day*, a practice adapted from activities developed by the Florida Department of Education (1994). Teachers give students a figure, a number, or an expression written on a piece of paper large enough to be seen from several feet away. Students stand at their seat or in the front of the room and listen to clues spoken orally by the teacher. If the student's figure, number, or expression matches the clue, the student "makes the teacher's day" and steps forward.

Consider the following vignette describing this practice in a seventh-grade class.

Mr. Dylan's class had studied factors, multiples, primes, and composites for several days. He was concerned that students still had some difficulty with the vocabulary and the concepts, but he wanted to engage in some activity other than written work. He decided to use *Make My Day* with his students because it would get them out of their seats and he would be able to determine their understanding of the concepts in a non-written format.

He wrote the numbers 1, 2, 3, 4, 6, 7, 8, 10, 11, 12, 15, 20, 25, 40, 50, 75, 100 on large sheets of paper and randomly distributed them to 17 of his students. He instructed his students to arrange themselves in numerical order in the front of the room. Then he used the following clues to assess his students' understanding of the concepts they had been studying:

- If you are a factor of 12, Make My Day.
- If you are a multiple of 4, Make My Day.
- If you are a prime number, Make My Day.
- If you are an even number, Make My Day.
- If you are a composite number, Make My Day.

Mr. Dylan noticed some students had trouble responding appropriately to his oral prompts. They were not able to hear a clue and respond in a way to demonstrate their understanding. He thought about the difficulties students experienced and decided to plan instruction that focused on listening skills.

Make My Day can be used with many topics as the following list suggests:

- *integer operations*: If students have numbers, then clues could be *If you have the sum of –2 and 4, Make My Day* or *If you have the product of –3 and 5, Make My Day*.

- *geometry*: If students have figures, then clues could be *If your figure has congruent sides, Make My Day* or *If your figure is a parallelogram, Make My Day*.

- *algebra*: If students have algebraic expressions, then a clue could be *If you have the sum of a number and 3, Make My Day*.

In each case, students must listen to the clue and interpret the spoken word or phrase in order to evaluate their number, figure, or expression to determine if it meets the clue. *Make My Day* not only provides an opportunity for students to listen carefully to mathematics language, but it provides teachers with a quick assessment of their students' knowledge.

Summary

As indicated in Chapter 9, we need to make our classrooms language intensive environments if students are to develop ease and confidence with the language of mathematics. Practices that encourage students to speak and listen to mathematics provide opportunities to develop that fluency.

Expand Your Understanding

1. Learn more about the research on cooperative learning and how it supports social and emotional growth as well as cognitive growth. What aspects of the cooperative learning research would you like to incorporate into your own classroom?

2. Use the *Co-op* structure to learn more about cooperative learning structures in general. Have each member of your group investigate two or three different cooperative learning structures to share with the group.

3. Find a peer and try *Give and Take* with a geometry task in which the giver describes how to build a figure for the taker. Compare your figures and analyze any differences in your figures. How might you increase the effectiveness of your communication?

Connect to Practice

4. Think about your middle grades mathematics curriculum. Identify some symbols that your students might include in a *Symbol-Language Glossary*.

5. Integrate the use of *Give and Take* as part of one of your mathematics units and evaluate your implementation of the strategy. What did you learn about students' language fluency? What would you do differently next time?

6. Try *Make My Day* with your students for some appropriate contexts. How did your students respond?

7. Try the *Roundtable* cooperative learning format with your class with an appropriate prompt. How did your students respond? What were some of the benefits of the activity in your class? How might you improve this practice for another lesson?

8. Identify at least one middle grades mathematics topic that lends itself to the use of the *Jigsaw* cooperative learning strategy. Try this strategy with your class and evaluate its effectiveness with your students. What did you learn about their ability to make meaning of mathematics?

9. Prepare a series of mathematical expressions or sentences in symbols and ask some students to read them aloud. Identify challenges your students experienced verbalizing the expressions.

10. Listen to student interactions as they engage in a worthwhile mathematical task. What did you observe or hear that might not have been accessible in other classroom situations?

11. Make an audio recording of one of your mathematics classes and then listen to the tape.

    a. How would you evaluate your classroom discourse community?

    b. What changes, if any, would you want to make? Why?

    c. Identify two goals related to discourse that you would like to accomplish with your students.

CHAPTER 11

Building Meanings Through Reading

> . . . reading is a cognitive process. [M]eaning results from the interaction between reader and text.
> —Marjorie Lipson and Karen Wixson, *Assessment and Instruction of Reading Disability*

As indicated in Chapter 3, we as teachers want our students to make sense of mathematics and to develop abilities to learn on their own and not rely solely on the teacher for knowledge. We want to help them become independent learners who are able to apply their developing reading skills to mathematics text. In this chapter, we share practices designed to help students interact with their mathematics text with understanding. Some of these strategies are first introduced in this chapter; others have been described earlier in this book, but they are revisited through a reading perspective.

Students engage in the reading process in three significant phases (Daniels and Zemelman 2004). *Prereading* practices set the stage for reading; they give students a purpose for reading, help them develop questions to ask about the reading, and assist them in accessing prior knowledge. *During reading* practices help students make sense of what they read; these practices help them search for answers to specific questions, monitor their comprehension, make inferences, visualize concepts as appropriate, and make and test conjectures about the concepts. *Postreading* practices help students look back over the ideas they have encountered, connect personally to the text, and reflect upon knowledge gained.

We begin with a vignette before discussing specific practices for each of these phases. As you read the vignette of Mr. Howard's seventh-grade class, try to identify prereading, during reading, and postreading practices.

As part of their school improvement plan, the faculty at Jamison Middle School decided a focus for the year would be to improve students' reading abilities. Members of the faculty believed if all teachers addressed reading as part of their disciplinary curriculum, students' reading comprehension would increase.

This reading focus connected with Mr. Howard's desire to help students learn to make sense of their mathematics text. He wanted his students to become more independent learners and not rely solely on him for mathematics information. Therefore, he decided to help his students learn to read their mathematics text as the following dialogue demonstrates. (Refer to Lesson 1-2 first referenced in Chapter 3 and located in the appendix.)

MR. HOWARD: Yesterday, I mentioned that we are going to spend more time this year reading our mathematics book. Today, the focus of the lesson will be totally based on what you read. What is the title of the lesson?

JIMMY: Positive and negative numbers.

MR. HOWARD: What do you all already know about positive and negative numbers?

SAMANTHA: Positives are bigger than zero; negatives are smaller than zero.

JAIME: They're opposites of each other.

MR. HOWARD: So, why it is important to look at the title?

JOAN: It tells you what the lesson is about.

MR. HOWARD: Good. Also, the title helps you to think about what you already know about the topic. You'll be surprised at how much you already know just by looking at the title. We're not going to read the lesson yet. Instead, I want you to scan the pages. Identify the headings that are in this lesson.

[*Mr. Howard gives students about two minutes to skim the lesson.*]

MR. HOWARD: Okay, I want someone to read aloud the major headings. What's one?

CARMEN: Situations with negative numbers.

JAIME: Graphing negative numbers on a number line.

ORTIZ: Comparing positive and negative numbers.

MR. HOWARD: How do you know there aren't any more major headings?

NEAL: There aren't any more labels in red.

MR. HOWARD: Are there any more headings?

JENNIFER: Isn't double inequalities a heading?

MR. HOWARD: What do you all think?

JENNIFER: It is. But it's just like an example of comparing positive and negative numbers.

MR. HOWARD: Okay. Let's look at the first heading: situations with negative numbers. What questions might you want to ask yourself about this section, before you start to read? Let's brainstorm some questions. I'll write them on the board.

ALICE: Where do you see negative numbers?

BEN: Why do I have to use negative numbers?

SAMANTHA: How do you write negative numbers?

MR. HOWARD: Why do you think I asked you to come up with some questions prior to reading the section? [*waits a few minutes, but no one responds*] The questions give you a reason for reading and can help you think about the mathematics you need to learn as you read.

MR. HOWARD: Okay. Ben, read Step 1 under the Activity out loud for us. [*to the class*] Be sure to follow along as Ben reads. [*Ben reads out loud.*] I want someone to explain in their own words what you're supposed to do.

CARLOS: Take all the things in the list and decide which are positive, which are negative, and which are not positive or negative.

MR. HOWARD: Good. Work quietly with the person next to you. How would you classify these sixteen phrases? I'll set the timer for five minutes.

[*Mr. Howard starts a timer that he sets on the table. After five minutes, it starts to beep.*]

MR. HOWARD: Let's see what you found. Were there any phrases that you didn't understand?

ALICE: I didn't know what to do with "7 seconds ago" and "60 seconds from now."

MR. HOWARD: Can anyone help Alice?

CARLOS: I think "ago" means negative 'cause it's in the past.

MR. HOWARD: Well, if Carlos is right about the "seconds ago," what would that mean for time from now?

ALICE: It'd be positive? [*responds with a question in her voice*]

MR. HOWARD: That's right. What are the phrases you thought were negative? [*Students share their thoughts, and then make a list for positives as well.*]
What did the phrase "broke even" mean?

SAMANTHA: Well, if it's even, then it's not positive or negative.

MR. HOWARD: Right. Break even is like being level—you're not above and you're not below. Now, I want you to look at the chart at the bottom of the page. [*gives students some time to read the chart*] What are two correct ways to read this symbol [*points to –5 on the board*]?

CARMEN: Negative five or opposite of five.

MR. HOWARD: Okay. Remember when we looked at the Quiz Yourself on the mathematics textbook survey. What should you do every time you see one of these?

JENNIFER: Try to answer it.

MR. HOWARD: What would your answer be for this first one?

JENNIFER: Negative six and opposite of six.

MR. HOWARD: Good. Now let's go back to the questions we wrote on the board. What would you answer for each of these? [*The class spends a few minutes discussing answers to the questions generated based on the heading.*]

Mr. Howard had similar discussions with his students for each of the other sections of the lesson. He made a conscious decision to work through all three major sections of the lesson with the class to help students think about the types of questions they should ask themselves; he wanted students to have sufficient practice with this process to try it on their own. In particular, he worked through the two examples to make sure that students could translate from words to symbols in Example 1 and from a chart to a graph in Example 2.

After the class finished reading the lesson, he did a quick assessment with them.

MR. HOWARD: Okay. Let's wrap up the lesson to see what we learned. Go back to the beginning of the lesson. Notice that at the top of the lesson there is something labeled *Big Idea*. Read the Big Idea silently to yourself. [*gives students about a minute to do this*] Now that you've read the lesson, you should ask yourself if you understand the Big Idea of the lesson. Can you give situations that would describe negative numbers and other situations that describe positive numbers? If you can't, then you need to read the lesson again or ask someone for help. Also, notice the vocabulary list at the beginning of the lesson. How were these vocabulary words marked in the text?

CARMEN: Bold.

MR. HOWARD: That's right. Terms in bold and terms listed in the vocabulary list are ones that you want to be able to describe in your own words. I'm going to put you in quick groups of three based on where you sit and give each group one word to describe to the class. You have two minutes to come up with a description of the word; then we'll share.

[*Mr. Howard assigns each group one of the words in the vocabulary list. After an opportunity to decide on a description, he has each group share their description.*]

MR. HOWARD: In your notebook, I want you to write one to two sentences to tell what you learned today.

REFLECT

- Refer to the vignette. Identify one practice that Mr. Howard used for each of the three phases of reading: prereading, during reading, and postreading.
- Refer to the lesson from the vignette and the heading "Comparing Positive and Negative Numbers." What are some questions you would encourage students to ask before reading this section?

In the vignette, students read and interpreted all the information needed for the lesson. Prior to reading the Activity, Mr. Howard encouraged students to generate questions to focus their reading (prereading). Then, he checked that students interpreted the information correctly as they read by asking them to respond to the prompts that were provided (during reading). At the end of the lesson, he worked to help students summarize what they had learned by referring to the Big Idea and the Vocabulary List and having students write something about what they had learned (postreading).

In the following sections, we share additional practices that can be used at each stage of the reading process.

Prereading Practices

In the vignette, Mr. Howard used textbook signals (e.g., headings, vocabulary list) to set the stage for learning. In addition to this prereading practice we discuss several other prereading strategies that increase comprehension.

Using Textbook Signals to Generate Questions for Reading

In the vignette, Mr. Howard had students *identify the headings* in the text (i.e., the signals such as the title and the major headings) to gain a sense of the content to be studied. Skimming the title and the headings served as an advance organizer that alerted students to the content to be presented and provided them with a perspective for reading. By having his students identify subheadings, Mr. Howard helped them learn to use the signals that are found in almost all mathematics texts as an aid to comprehension.

Second, Mr. Howard had students *generate questions* to be asked while reading as motivation for their reading. Students did not read passively. Instead, they set a purpose for reading—to find the answers to their questions.

Although Mr. Howard referred back to the vocabulary at the end of the lesson as a summary activity, another prereading strategy is to *identify the vocabulary* in the lesson and have students indicate their knowledge level of the terms, such as *definitely know, have heard but cannot describe in my own words*, or *have no clue*. Then, being able to describe a term in their own words becomes another motivation for reading the lesson.

In the sample lesson, the vocabulary words are listed at the beginning of the lesson to facilitate such a discussion. If their text does not provide such a list, teachers can write the vocabulary terms for a lesson on the board. As we indicated in Chapters 3 and 9, mathematics vocabulary is one of the building blocks of mathematics language; students must become fluent with the vocabulary if they are to become successful mathematics readers and learners.

Using textbook signals to generate questions can be employed daily to help students learn to use their mathematics text effectively. These daily reading practices are similar to daily practices for language development that we described in Chapter 9.

Brainstorming

Brainstorming is an opportunity for students to share what they already know about a topic and access and build important prerequisite knowledge. Particularly at the middle grades level, students have had some exposure to many of the mathematics topics that are studied. For instance, they have worked with whole numbers, fractions, decimals, and their operations; they have studied various geometric figures; they have graphed data in bar graphs and circle graphs; and they have used variables and solved simple equations. Thus, brainstorming activates students' prior knowledge and can also highlight misconceptions or fragile understandings that need to be addressed during the reading or follow-up discussion.

In the vignette, Mr. Howard actually did some brainstorming when he had his students indicate what they already knew about positive and negative numbers. His students indicated they knew how these numbers relate to 0 and they are opposites of each other. Because Mr. Howard was interested in focusing on particular reading strategies in the lesson (i.e., the use of headings to generate questions to motivate reading), he chose not to extend the discussion. He could have continued to have students generate additional thoughts about positives and negatives with questions such as the following:

- Give me two real-world situations where you might use negative numbers.
- Give me two real-world situations where you might use positive numbers.
- Give me a situation where a number is neither positive nor negative.

Such queries would likely have generated a number of scenarios that could then have been compared to the situations in the Activity or in the Examples.

Brainstorming is designed to get many ideas on the table, particularly because some ideas or comments often spark other ideas from peers. As students share at this point, correcting errors or misconceptions is not the goal. However, teachers will want to keep students' misconceptions in mind to ensure that subsequent instruction helps students address their misunderstandings as they make sense of mathematics.

Brainstorming also provides an opportunity for teachers to preview any words or contexts that might be problematic for students. For instance, during one of our recent classroom visits students were working on a problem set in the context of archaeology. The teacher asked students about the meaning of the word *archaeology*. They connected the term to someone learning about the past and digging things up from the ground (like in Egypt). Later, students were solving a problem about the age of a tortoise in the Galapagos Islands and the teacher reminded students that tortoises were like turtles. Although we might not think that attending to words like *tortoise* or *archaeological* are essential to reading mathematics text, unfamiliar contexts can be stumbling blocks that inhibit students from moving forward and making sense of the mathematics. We need to ask students questions about unusual contexts to ensure they have the background necessary to read with success.

In the vignette, Mr. Howard was not sure that students understood the situation related to *breaking even*, so he made a point of discussing this situation with students. He also asked students to identify any situations from the activity that they did not understand, and one of the students raised the issue about *seconds ago*. Although Mr. Howard chose to let questions about these situations arise during the discussion of the reading, he could have raised them during a brainstorming session if he had chosen to use this prereading strategy.

In the lesson related to the vignette, question 15 refers to a golf context and the use of the term *par* (see appendix). Notice that the question describes this term and how it relates to the mathematics that students need to complete. If this is not done as part of the text, it is important that we as teachers describe or discuss words that may be unfamiliar to students.

REFLECT

- Scan the questions from Lesson 1-2 in the appendix referenced in the vignette. Identify any additional words or contexts that you think might be unfamiliar to students.

PreP

PreP, A Prereading Plan, is a strategy designed to stimulate students' interest in a topic, access their background knowledge, and help them refine and extend their knowledge. When students activate their background knowledge, their comprehension generally increases (Langer 1981; Lenski, Wham, and Johns 1999). In addition, *PreP* enables teachers to develop appropriate instruction based on students' prior knowledge.

When used in reading, teachers can model the strategy with one student as other students observe. The teacher identifies the main topic to be read or discussed. Then, with paper and pencil in hand, the teacher talks with the student. "Tell me everything you know about [a topic] and I'll make a list of your ideas." When the student finishes making comments, the teacher reads the list aloud and asks, "Can you think of anything else you know?" Typically, hearing the list repeated causes students to think about other ideas related to the topic. At this point, the teacher and student switch roles. Later in the process, the teacher might ask, "Where did you learn these ideas?" or "How is [Topic A] related to [Topic B]?"

PreP is similar to brainstorming in that students generate ideas about what they already know. However, brainstorming is often accomplished with a large group, whereas *PreP* might be used in pairs or in small groups to generate ideas that can then be shared with a larger group. Also, *PreP* specifically attempts to have students think about where they learned previous facts and how students think concepts relate to one another.

K-W-L (Know, Want to Learn, Learned) Prompts

K-W-L (Ogle 1986, 1989) is a reading comprehension strategy that many teachers use to help students access what they already know about a topic and connect that knowledge to new knowledge. Before reading, students generate a list of what they think they already *know* about a topic (*K*) and what they *want to learn* (*W*). After they read, they indicate what they *learned* (*L*), providing a connection between prereading and postreading learning. In reading circles, *W* often refers to what students *want to know* rather than what they *want to learn* as we have indicated here. Many middle grades students often want to say, "I don't get it" about a topic, rather than reflect on their knowledge to determine what parts of a concept they understand and what parts they don't. As students reflect on their knowledge, they can consider what they "don't get" as the basis for entries in the *W* portion of K-W-L.

Figure 11.1 highlights the first two parts of a K-W-L prompt for the topic of proportions. The K-W-L strategy highlights students' prerequisite knowledge, including any fragile understandings; with this insight, we can plan effective mathematics instruction. When we first introduce K-W-L prompts into instruction, it is important that we have students share their responses to model the types of questions that students should be asking themselves as they read their text.

With both brainstorming and K-W-L prompts, students can be encouraged to organize their initial knowledge into a concept map or other graphic organizer similar to those introduced in Chapter 8. As students read, they can add to their concept map, remove incorrect links, or revise connections.

REFLECT

- What other entries might you expect from middle grades students as part of the K-W-L response in Figure 11.1?

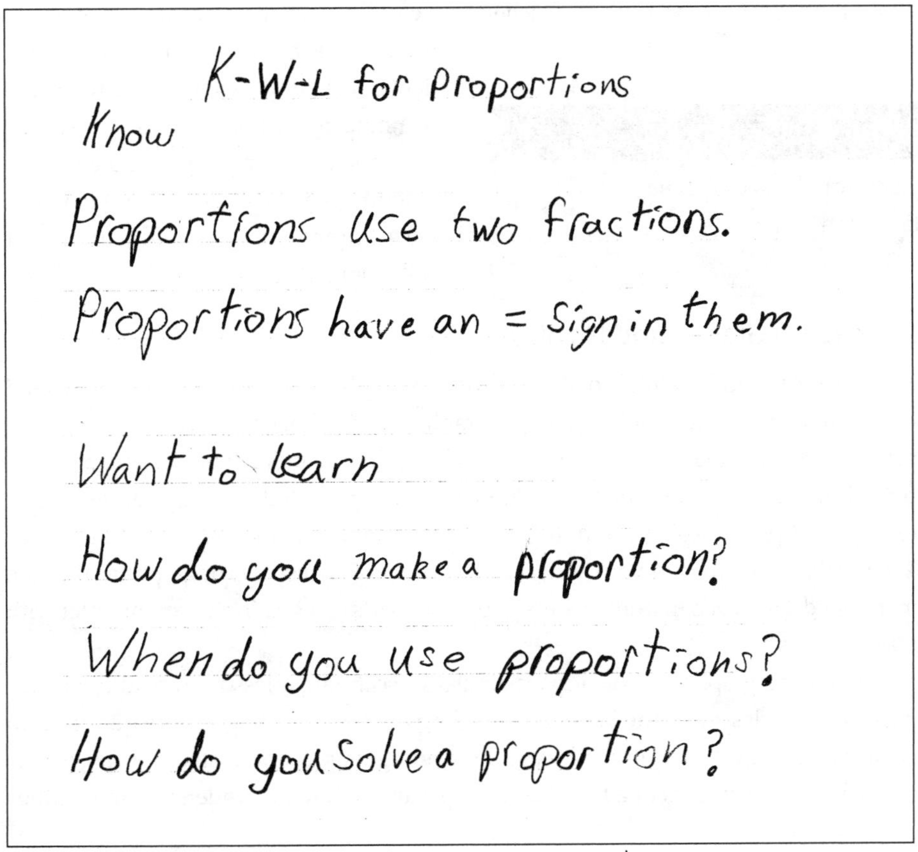

K-W-L for Proportions

Know

Proportions use two fractions.

Proportions have an = sign in them.

Want to learn

How do you make a proportion?

When do you use proportions?

How do you solve a proportion?

FIG. 11.1
A partial K-W-L response for proportions

Anticipation Guides

Anticipation guides (Herber 1978) provide another opportunity for students to connect prereading and postreading knowledge. Teachers create a set of statements related to a particular topic at hand, some of which are true and some of which are not. Prior to reading the text, students review the statements and decide if they think each statement is true or not, according to their current knowledge. After reading, students review the statements to determine if their opinion has changed based on the text and the reading. Anticipation guides can be created for a particular lesson or for a longer unit, such as a chapter. For instance, the following two statements might be used on an anticipation guide before students read about graphs.

- Circle graphs are used when the data exist in categories that don't overlap and that make up the whole.
- A bar graph can be used to show trends over time.

Lesson 1-2 referenced in the vignette is part of a chapter titled "Reading and Writing Numbers." The following three statements might be used on an anticipation guide for this lesson.

- Positive numbers are usually drawn to the left of 0 on a number line.
- $6 < 8 < 12$ is called a double inequality.
- 0 is a positive integer.

Teachers might design anticipation guides with statements based on the most important concepts in the unit, including important vocabulary and symbols. Used at the beginning of a chapter, students' responses alert teachers to what students know well, what misconceptions they might hold, and what they clearly do not know about the content to be studied. Teachers can easily determine whether concepts are understood by a majority of their students; such information can be helpful in planning instruction. Later, prior to a quiz or test, students might revisit their anticipation guides to determine what they have learned and to identify areas that still require study.

> ### REFLECT
> - Identify one other statement from Lesson 1-2 that you would include on an anticipation guide.

Prereading Graphs and Displays

Many readers find it helpful to attempt to read graphs and displays before they read the related text. If they understand the graph from reading it in advance, then their reading of the related text is made simpler. If they do not understand the graph or find something puzzling in it, then they know to read the related text very carefully. Prereading a graph or display is a strategy worth sharing with our students. Too often, they assume they need to read one thing at a time and look at displays or graphs as they are mentioned. However, mature readers often read parts of a text in a different order with many payoffs.

Prereading graphs and displays is similar to scanning a lesson to read the headings. We have described the benefits of reading the headings to generate questions to be answered when reading the lesson. Prereading graphs and displays engages students in visual elements of a text that are typically essential to understanding mathematics; students can generate questions about a graph or display that are to be answered by reading the related text.

During Reading Practices

Prereading strategies activate students' prior knowledge and set a purpose for reading. But we also need to consider practices to help students make meaning as they read. We detail a number of such practices below.

Read Aloud and with a Purpose

The vignette with Mr. Howard illustrated two powerful during reading practices. First, students *read with a purpose*, that is, they read with specific questions in mind that needed to be answered. When students have particular questions to answer, they read with focus as though they are on a scavenger hunt of mathematics.

Second, Mr. Howard had *students read aloud*. Although teachers need to be sensitive to students whose reading level is low and who do not want to read aloud, in visits to many classes we have found that excellent readers (and many who are just average readers) are eager to read to the class and be the center of attention for a few minutes. When teachers have students read aloud, they might be asked to read a specific portion of text, perhaps an introduction through the first example. Teachers should stop intermittently and engage the class in discussing what was read. Students need to translate the text into their own words. Although many students want to repeat the text verbatim, it is when they put the text in their own words that they begin to demonstrate their comprehension. Teachers need to anticipate potential difficulties with concepts and be prepared to ask specific questions when students struggle to put the text into their own words. Verbalizing meanings is part of internalizing mathematics.

One other benefit of having students read aloud, even on short word problems, is that teachers are able to identify words that students struggle to pronounce. We have heard middle grades students struggle to read common words, such as *equivalent, evaluate, indicate, numerically,* or *subtrahend*. Not being able to pronounce a word does not necessarily mean that students do not understand the meaning. But we believe that being fluent in mathematics includes being able to pronounce words appropriately so that students can communicate with others with understanding.

Although mispronouncing words may not signal misconceptions, not being able to verbalize symbolic expressions correctly is a potential source of errors. For instance, we have heard middle grades students read $32 - 8$ as "subtract 32 from 8" even when they did the computation correctly. Another student who hears the verbal expression could be thinking $8 - 32$, which simplifies to -24. So, verbalizing the expression incorrectly potentially leads to misunderstandings as one student obtains an answer of 24 and another wonders why the answer is not -24.

Teacher Think-Alouds

Teacher think-alouds (Daniels and Zemelman 2004; Davey 1983) can be used both before and during reading. Students often need models to know how to engage with technical text such as mathematics. Teachers can model the types of questions they ask themselves, such as those based on the text signals (e.g., headings or bold vocabulary words) to show how to ask good questions. Then, teachers can read aloud particular passages and model how they find the answers to the questions they posed. In the vignette, Mr. Howard worked with his students to pose questions based on the headings they identified in the lesson. Then, he had students share their answers to the questions they had posed (those responses are not included in the vignette). Although Mr. Howard did not do all the work himself aloud, he engaged in the activities that are part of a teacher think-aloud with the entire class, namely having students identify questions and then answer the questions they posed.

In addition to modeling questions, as teachers read a portion of a text, they can stop periodically to identify important points for students to note, vocabulary that students should highlight, and important information in graphic displays. For instance, in reading Example 1 in Lesson 1-2 from the vignette, teachers might want to have students discuss the legend associated with the map. The effort to have students attend to the legend might be beneficial when students address similar graphics in the future. In addition, when reading this lesson, teachers can highlight the caution at the end of the narrative portion of the lesson because the caution addresses a typical error that students make.

Pairs Read

Pairs read (Barton and Heidema 2002) can be used to blend reading with the speaking and listening strategies discussed in Chapter 10. Students read in pairs, taking turns to read a short portion of the text aloud to each other. At the end of each reading segment, the non-reading member summarizes (*reteaches*) what has been read aloud to the other. With this strategy, students must speak mathematics correctly as well as listen to mathematics speech. As they reteach what they heard to the other member, they indicate their comprehension and identify aspects of the concepts that are still unclear.

When teachers introduce this strategy, they might model the strategy aloud with one student, perhaps with the student reading and the teacher providing a summary of what was read. That is, the teacher and student together model the strategy before pairs of students implement it.

QAR (Question-Answer-Relationship)

QAR (Question-Answer-Relationship) (Raphael 1982, 1986) is a strategy to help students enhance their metacognitive skills. Teachers help students learn where to find answers to four different types of questions.

- *Right There* questions are answered verbatim in the text. When students answer these questions, they should provide the page number and paragraph where the answer is found. Right There questions can help students learn to read carefully and for detail. For example in Lesson 1-2 on Positive and Negative Numbers (see the appendix), a Right There question might be, "Is 0 positive or negative?" Notice that on the second page of the lesson, there is a statement, "Zero is an integer but it is neither positive nor negative." So the answer to the question is stated in the narrative.

- *Think and Search* questions require students to make links between related ideas in the text. For example, "Which number is less, –4 or –6?" The answer to this question is not explicitly in the text. However, the text does expect students to place numbers on a number line and to write appropriate inequalities. Thus, students make links between placement of integers on a number line and the order of integers in an inequality to determine which one is less than the other in value.

- *Author and You* questions combine prior knowledge with information in the text so that students must bring personal experiences to bear to answer the question. For example, "Identify one word or phrase not already listed in the activity that suggests a positive number and one that suggests a negative number."

- *On Your Own* questions are relevant to the text but can be answered without reading the text if the student has the appropriate background knowledge. For example, "Mark started a business and at the end of the first month, his accounts show –$2500. What does this mean?"

The use of QAR does require additional effort on the part of the teacher prior to its use in the classroom. Teachers must preview the text and generate a series of questions related to the text content.

R E F L E C T

- Refer again to Lesson 1-2 in the appendix. Write at least one additional question for the lesson for each type of question in QAR.

Sketch the Text

One other strategy students can use while reading is *Sketch the Text* (Daniels and Zemelman 2004; Hoyt 2002; Short, Kauffman, and Kahn 2000; Siegel et al. 1996). This strategy supports conceptual development for many of our students who are visual learners. As students read, they draw pictures to illustrate the concepts and how they are related. In Lesson 1-2 in the appendix, a number line in the second section illustrates those integers that are positive, those that are negative, and zero, which is neither. The number line provides a visual picture of the vocabulary (e.g., positive integers, negative integers) that is introduced in the lesson.

Although students have learned to draw pictures or diagrams when solving word problems, they may not have considered using this strategy in a broader sense. Some diagrams may be in the form of Venn diagrams or concept maps as described in Chapters 8 or 9; others may just be sketches that illustrate relationships. For instance, Figure 11.2 is a visual display of the relationship between gallons, quarts, pints, and cups. Completed pictures or diagrams can be incorporated into word walls or personal glossaries.

Many middle grades students have strong visual literacy skills. As students illustrate a mathematical concept in some type of graphic, they demonstrate their understanding using senses other than hearing or speaking. The adage "A picture is worth a thousand words" is one we should consider if it helps our students make sense of abstract concepts.

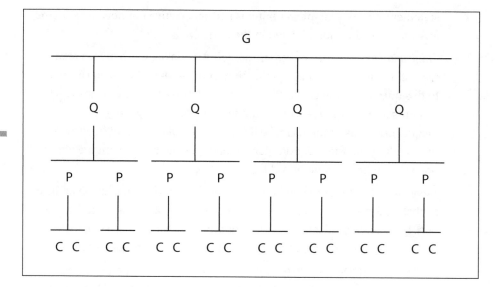

FIG. 11.2
A diagram showing the relationship among gallons, quarts, pints, and cups

Postreading Practices

In the vignette with Mr. Howard, he used at least two postreading strategies. First, he had students *answer the questions* generated during the prereading brainstorming related to the headings. If we encourage students to generate questions mentally, orally, or in writing, then we should expect them to answer them. Otherwise, students are likely to believe that writing or thinking about questions before they read is not important and they will soon disengage from this process.

Second, Mr. Howard had students *summarize what they learned*. At the end of the lesson, he had them write one or two sentences to indicate what they learned. Some teachers call such writing learning logs (Barton and Heidema 2002; Santa and Havens 1991) and expect their students to complete them regularly, either to reflect on what makes sense or what does not. The compiled learning logs are submitted at the end of a unit for a grade.

Some teachers have modified this idea to have students write one or two sentences and use their learning logs as an *exit slip* they present in order to leave class (Daniels and Zemelman 2004). In either format, students have to reflect on their reading and learning in order to respond; teachers obtain insight on any continuing difficulties that can be used to inform instruction.

Many postreading strategies involve writing, and we discuss some beneficial writing strategies in Chapter 12.

Strategies That Engage in All Three Phases of Reading

Some well-known reading strategies are applicable across all three phases of the reading process. Students may have used these strategies in their language arts classes by their formal names and can be encouraged to use them in mathematics as well. The two strategies we highlight incorporate practices we have discussed earlier in this chapter, but they are formalized here in one integrated process.

SQ3R (Survey, Question, Read, Recite, Review)

In *SQ3R* (*Survey, Question, Read, Recite, Review*) (Robinson 1970), students *survey* the lesson to be read by looking at titles and headings. Then, they turn the headings into *questions* to be answered. They *read* the lesson to find answers to the questions. They *recite* what they read without looking at the text or the answers to questions. Finally, they *review* by summarizing the information, perhaps with a graphic organizer (see Chapter 8). Notice that the survey and question parts of SQ3R engage students in the prereading phase. Then using their acquired background knowledge, students read the text. After reading, students recite and review what they have read and learned. Teachers implement the entire SQ3R as they would have the individual parts of the process.

> ### REFLECT
>
> - Refer back to the vignette at the beginning of this chapter. Identify places within the vignette where Mr. Howard and his students engaged in the phases of SQ3R.

DRTA (Directed Reading-Thinking Activity)

DRTA (*Directed Reading-Thinking Activity*) (Gipe 2005; Lenski, Wham, and Johns 1999; Stauffer 1969) is a cyclical strategy that blends practices from three phases of reading. Students take a quick overview by skimming the lesson, looking at the titles or reading the captions for figures and graphs. Students predict what the lesson is about. Then, they read the lesson with a focus to confirm whether or not their predictions are accurate. DRTA helps students think together about the reading process and how they must be actively engaged with the text. In the vignette, Mr. Howard guided his students' actions at each stage of the process. As students gain familiarity and confidence in using the different reading strategies over time, he expects that they will gradually assume responsibility for guiding their own reading and selecting appropriate reading strategies before, during, and after they read.

Reading Word Problems

As teachers, we encourage students to think of word problems as short stories. Therefore, the same strategies that students use when reading stories in language arts or when reading narrative mathematics text as described earlier in this chapter can aid their understanding of word problems in mathematics.

One traditional but problematic strategy for addressing word problems is focusing on key terms. We do *not* encourage the use of this technique because it can result in an incorrect interpretation of the problem. For instance, consider the following problem:

> Janie's cost for dinner is $5 less than Alex's. If Janie's dinner costs $11, how much was Alex's dinner?

Students who look for key words, such as *less than*, are likely to solve the problem as $11 - 6 = 5$; yet, a careful reading of the problem indicates that the solution is $11 + 5 = 16$

because Janie's cost is less than Alex's. We would prefer that students think about the entire meaning of a story in order to approach the problem in a way that makes sense.

For instance, students might use a K-W-L prompt with a word problem to indicate what information they know from the problem, what information they need to know or find out (the question), and what information they learned (the solution to the problem). This approach helps students bring their prior knowledge to bear in the K and W phases and provides a mechanism to help students think about the reasonableness of an answer in the L phase. Consider this brief vignette from a sixth-grade class doing a quick review on computational skills with decimals.

As a review before a quiz, Mr. Jesse had his students do some quick computational problems. After they completed several problems with integers and fractions, Mr. Jesse gave his students the following problem:

> Melissa's cat weighed 22 pounds. It lost 2.3 pounds. How much does it weigh now?

He was astounded that several students gave the answer –1 (because they had computed 22 – 23).

MR. JESSE: I noticed that several of you got negative one for the answer. Let's take another look at the problem. Ben, read the problem out loud for us. [*Ben reads the problem.*] Now what did you know from the problem?

ELIZABETH: The cat weighed twenty-two pounds and lost two point three pounds.

MR. JESSE: And what did you want to find out?

LYNNE: What the cat weighs now.

MR. JESSE: So, if you originally read the amount that the cat lost as twenty-three pounds because you didn't see the decimal point, what should you have thought here?

WALKER: The cat can't lose more pounds than it had to start with.

MR. JESSE: Exactly. So you would have gone back and reread the problem at this point. But if you missed this step, you still had a chance to catch your error when you got an answer. What's wrong with negative one for an answer?

YAN: Cats can't weigh a negative number.

MR. JESSE: Bingo! It's really important to look back at the problem and see if your answer makes sense. You can catch a lot of your own mistakes that way.

The vignette illustrates the need to help students read problems carefully and bring their own knowledge to bear when solving problems. As we illustrated in the vignette in Chapter 5, *Zoom In–Zoom Out* is another strategy that helps students look at word problems for details as well as from a global perspective.

When students work on word problems, we want them to make connections to prior problems and to consider similarities and differences between problem statements and their solutions. *It Reminds*

REFLECT

- Recall a situation when your middle grades students had difficulty with a mathematics problem, not because of the mathematics they needed to complete but because they misread the problem or the numbers. What did you do to help them self-correct?

Me Of (Richards and Gipe 1992) is a strategy to encourage such comparisons. As students peruse a new problem, they might work with a partner to share how the parts of the problem remind them of previously solved problems. They might also share problem-solving approaches that were used with other problems or remember solutions. If students have discussed different approaches to solving similar problems, they can discuss the efficiency of the approaches to determine which one they want to use on the current problem. By helping students make connections among problems, we help them strengthen their problem-solving abilities.

Summary

Over the years, middle grades students have learned many valuable reading strategies. They can apply these same strategies to the reading of mathematics text. Students can use the strategies in Chapter 8 to summarize what they have learned from reading; they can use the strategies in Chapter 9 to focus on making sense of vocabulary; they can use the strategies of Chapter 10 as they discuss reading with each other. If we take the time to model for students how to decipher mathematics text for essential concepts, we will support students to become independent learners.

Expand Your Understanding

1. In each case, consider how the common pairs of words impact meaning in mathematics.
   a. *at least* and *at most*
   b. *each* and *every*
   c. *only* and *exactly*
2. Refer to Example 2 in Lesson 1-2 referenced in the vignette and located in the appendix. What are some features of the example that teachers would likely want to discuss with students?

Connect to Practice

3. Identify a lesson that you expect to teach within the next few weeks.
   a. Develop a plan to engage your students in reading the lesson.
   b. Try the reading lesson with your students and evaluate its success.
4. Review a set of word problems from a lesson or chapter in your middle grades mathematics text. Identify contexts that you think might cause problems for your students.
5. Choose a lesson from your middle grades mathematics text. Create or write three statements, at least one of which is false, that would be appropriate on an anticipation guide for the lesson.

CHAPTER 12

Building Meanings Through Writing

When students challenge me to show what writing has to do with math, I reply, "This is math. You know, it's fine to get the right answer, but what good is that answer if you can't explain it to anyone?"

— Joan Countryman, *Writing to Learn Mathematics*

Writing and talking are ways that learners can make their mathematical thinking visible. Both writing and talking are tools for collaboration, discovery, and reflection.

— Phyllis Whitin and David J. Whitin, *Math Is Language Too*

Writing plays an important role in teachers' mathematics instruction and in students' learning. Students' written products provide teachers with important means to access and assess their mathematical understanding. In writing about mathematics, students solidify their understandings of mathematics concepts as they make decisions about what information to elaborate on or to include or exclude. In addition, they have to consider and use appropriate mathematics vocabulary and symbols to convey the meanings they intend. Overall, "writing promotes metacognition—thinking about mathematical thinking" (Martinez and Martinez 2001). As teachers we engage students in writing in the mathematics classroom to open a window into students' thinking and fluency with language beyond what is obtained when students only express mathematics orally.

When students read or listen, they receive information. When students speak and write, they generate information, but they must focus more closely on what is produced when they write than when they speak. For many of our students, writing mathematics accurately and clearly is the most difficult form of communication. In particular, many students struggle to write in a coherent manner for an intended audience, whether that audience is a teacher or peer. If we want students to become proficient in writing mathematics, we need to provide them with many opportunities to practice and enhance their writing skills. Because writing is a powerful tool to help students make meaning, we believe it should be incorporated into mathematics instruction on a regular basis.

Figure 12.1 lists potential benefits for teachers and students related to writing about mathematics. For many teachers and students, a major benefit of writing is the opportunity for one-on-one communication. Writing provides opportunities for students to communicate with the teacher by asking questions or sharing difficulties in private. Reading students' written work helps us monitor students' mathematical progress. We, in turn, can use this information to modify our instruction in ways that address student concerns, difficulties, and misconceptions.

Potential Benefits to Students	Potential Benefits to Teachers
• Students engage in one-on-one communication with the teacher.	• Teachers engage in one-on-one communication with individual students.
• Students identify their understanding of concepts by explaining them in their own words. They can begin to solidify their emergent understandings.	• Teachers identify students' emerging understandings of concepts.
• Students engage in metacognitive thinking, that is, they think about their own thinking.	• Teachers identify potential misconceptions in students' thinking and can consider ways to modify instruction to address them.
• Students express their learning through an alternative to traditional assessments.	• Teachers gain insights into students' thinking.
• Students activate their prior knowledge of concepts.	• Teachers learn what students already know about concepts to assist in planning instruction.
• Students connect reasons to processes.	• Teachers gain insights on how students reason through mathematical processes.
• Students begin to recognize their feelings or attitudes related to mathematics.	• Teachers learn how students feel about their mathematics learning.
• Students' curiosity is stimulated, motivating their need to develop new understandings.	• Teachers can use writing as a means to arouse interest.
• Students build their fluency with mathematics language.	• Teachers can gauge students' mathematics language fluency.

FIG. 12.1
Potential benefits of writing in mathematics

In this chapter, *writing* includes all forms of written communication in which students make visible their understanding of mathematics or their thoughts and feelings about their learning. Writing in the mathematics classroom includes, but is not limited to:

- describing what is known about a particular concept (e.g., When we studied . . . last year, I remember that . . .);

- showing steps in a solution process (e.g., $2x - 5 = 7$, $2x = 12$, $x = 6$);

- explaining methods used to solve a problem (e.g., To solve this problem, we first had to . . . Then, we decided to . . .);

- justifying their mathematical reasoning (e.g., I know that the answer is . . . because . . . Here is how I reasoned);

- reflecting on mathematics learning experiences or sharing concerns (e.g., In today's lesson, I didn't understand why John said that we should always add when . . .);

- recording information for future study (e.g., taking notes).

R E F L E C T

- How often were you expected to write in mathematics classes? How comfortable are you with writing about mathematics?

- To what extent have you expected your middle grades students to write mathematics, other than to show their steps when solving a problem?

Collectively, the various ways we encourage students to write in mathematics provide additional means to refine, evaluate, and assess mathematics learning.

In the remainder of the chapter, we suggest several strategies teachers might use to engage students in writing about their mathematical understanding.

Mathematics Autobiography

To engage students in writing from the onset of the school year, teachers can ask students to produce a mathematics autobiography (Countryman 1992), a personal account of their mathematics history. This type of writing assignment provides an opportunity for students to reflect on their mathematics learning and share how they have learned mathematics, what difficulties and successes they have faced, what they like or dislike about mathematics, and how they best learn mathematics. As an early writing experience in mathematics, a mathematics autobiography is a nonthreatening writing assignment because students do not need to address content; there are no right or wrong answers. Rather, they provide their thoughts about learning mathematics. Teachers can use the information gleaned from students' writing to plan for instruction.

Students' autobiographical writing is often quite informative. When one of the authors of this text asked middle grades students to write a mathematics autobiography, some students wrote about being good at mathematics until third grade when they had to learn multiplication facts. Others commented about disliking mathematics. Still others commented about being good at mathematics and expecting to excel during the school year. She gained insight into her students' feelings and perceptions about mathematics and their confidence, or insecurities. Therefore, she better understood what actions students found helpful to learn mathematics and what actions made learning difficult. This insight proved helpful as she worked to create a classroom environment in which students felt free to share their thinking about mathematics.

R E F L E C T

- Identify three things that you would include in your own mathematics autobiography.

Writing Opportunities for Concept and Language Development

In the prior sections of this book, we identified various practices that may be used to facilitate students' concept and language development. Many of these practices involve writing and provide an opportunity for students to communicate while building their mathematics language development and fluency. Now we revisit some of these strategies and discuss them in terms of the opportunities they provide for students to write. Writing comes in many forms and styles. Some teachers require students to write in complete sentences; others permit students to write phrases as long as the meaning is clear, and others accept a combination of words and pictures to demonstrate understanding. The methods used to structure writing assignments depend on the instructional goal. Teachers need to guide students as they write so that they understand what type of writing is acceptable under what circumstances.

Personal Glossaries

Because personal glossaries are references that students develop for their own use, the information they write should be mathematically correct. (Also see information about personal glossaries in Chapters 3 and 9.) However, there is room for much flexibility in how students write or rewrite this information. Consider the two entries for polygon in the personal glossaries in Figures 12.2 and 12.3. The entry in Figure 12.2 is a good entry with examples and non-examples and explanations to show why the figures fall into each category. Although the entry in Figure 12.3 is much shorter, it still conveys the essential meaning of the term *polgyon*.

Multiple Representations Chart

The *Multiple Representations (Multi-Rep)* chart (see Chapter 6) requires students to write as they demonstrate their understanding of a concept through a mathematics example, a real-life example, a visual example, and an explanation in words. Depending on the concept, additional representations can be added to the chart, such as a story, rap, or poem about the concept, or an example from a newspaper or magazine.

Analogies

Analogies encourage students to show how terms are related and to demonstrate their understanding of connections between terms. Used in conjunction with Venn diagrams or word origins (see Chapter 9), they are a tool to help students see how related terms are alike and different. In addition to writing the analogy, students can provide an explanation of it; the explanation makes explicit for the student and teacher what connections the student sees.

Polygon

A polygon is made up of straight line segments that don't cross. The start and end come together.

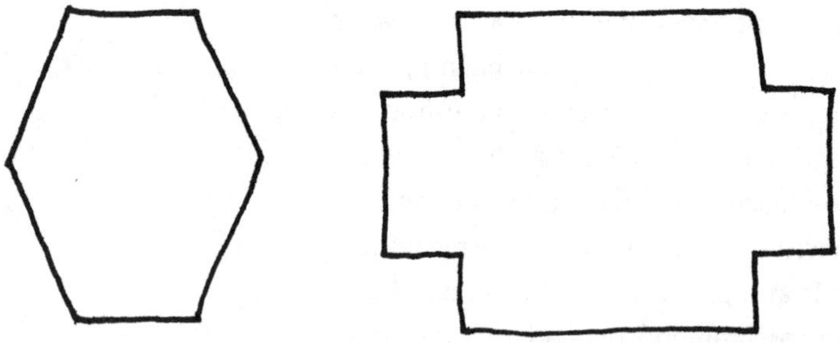

These are polygons because all the sides are segments, they don't cross, and the beginning and end meet.

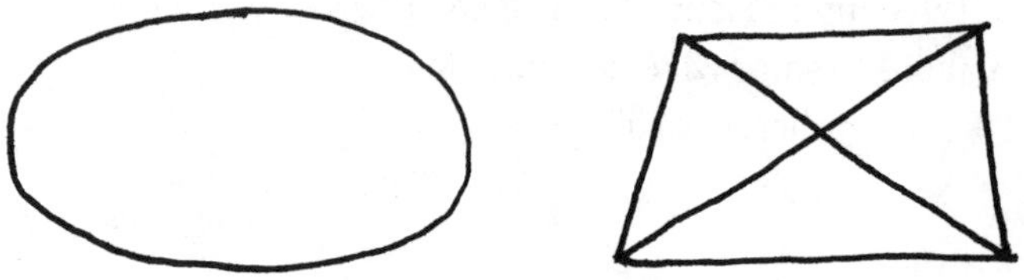

These are not polygons. One figure is not made of line segments. In the other the segments cross but not at the endpoints. That's not allowed.

FIG. 12.2
Personal glossary entry for polygon

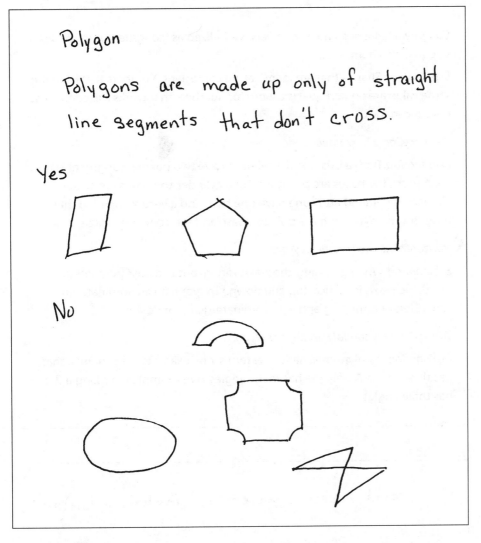

FIG. 12.3
Personal glossary entry for polygon

Figure 12.4 contains four sample analogies with explanations. When students write an analogy and explain it, they need to have more than a surface understanding of the term. They do not just use the vocabulary term; they show how it connects to other terms and concepts. They provide a window into their thinking about the terms that illustrates their understanding.

Consider the analogy in Figure 12.5. Although the response indicates some understanding of connections among the terms *centimeter, meter,* and *kilometer,* we view the explanation as incomplete. It does not provide sufficient information to judge whether the student has made any connections among these measures. This response garners the following questions: Does the student recognize there are 100 centimeters in a meter and 1000 meters in a kilometer? Perhaps a more appropriate analogy would have been the following:

millimeter : meter : : meter : kilometer

In this revised analogy, both relationships are in a ratio of 1000 to 1.

REFLECT

- Write an analogy using the words *sentence, expression, equation,* and *phrase.* Explain your analogy.

FIG. 12.4
Sample analogies

Congruent : shapes :: equal : numbers (verbalized as "congruent is to shapes as equal is to numbers")

Explanation: Shapes that are identical are congruent. Numbers that have the same value are equal. Equal is a word for numbers that works like congruent does for shapes.

Prism : cylinder :: pyramid : cone

Explanation: Both a prism and a cylinder have two parallel congruent bases. For a prism the bases are polygons. For a cylinder, the bases are circles. Similarly, a pyramid and cone have one base and a vertex joined to that base. But the pyramid has a polygon base and the cone has a circle base.

Horizontal : x-axis :: vertical : y-axis

Explanation: When graphing, the *x*-axis is horizontal (across from left to right); the *y*-axis is vertical (up and down.) To graph an *x*-coordinate, go across, left or right; to graph a *y*-coordinate, go up or down.

Trinomial : polynomial :: triangle : polygon

Explanation: A polynomial has many terms; one example is a trinomial that has three terms. A polygon has many angles; one example is a triangle that has three angles.

FIG. 12.5
Sample analogy with incomplete explanation

centimeter : meter :: meter : kilometer

Explanation: Centimeters make up a meter just like meters make up a kilometer. They all measure lengths.

Compare and Contrast

In Chapter 8, we discussed comparing and contrasting as a tool to help students discuss similarities and differences between concepts, particularly through the use of *Venn diagrams* and *These Are/These Are Not* charts. But comparing and contrasting can be used to engage students in more extensive writing. Students can write about related concepts or procedures to draw comparisons and contrasts between them and to address issues that often cause confusion. Writing about what they observe about concepts or procedures encourages students to focus on the nuances that may be inherent to particular aspects of those concepts or procedures. As they look for similarities, they find connections among multiple ideas. As they find differences, they identify distinguishing characteristics of various concepts or symbols. Students can share what they observed and refine their written work based on information gleaned from a class discussion. Figure 12.6

- Compare and contrast the attributes of a rhombus with those of a square.
- Compare and contrast finding $1 - \dfrac{4}{5}$ with $13 - \dfrac{4}{5}$.
- Compare and contrast the graphs of $x < 3$ and $x \leq 3$.
- Compare and contrast solving $-2x + 5 = 11$ with solving $-2x + 5 > 11$.

FIG. 12.6
Sample prompts for comparing and contrasting

contains several prompts that illustrate a range of content for which comparing and contrasting is applicable.

Consider the following vignette from an eighth-grade algebra class that has been studying equations and inequalities. As you read the vignette, think about how writing a few sentences to compare and contrast the solutions and solution processes for the pairs of problems helps students understand the concepts and address common misconceptions.

R E F L E C T

- Choose one of the prompts in Figure 12.6. What comparisons and contrasts might you expect middle grades students to write for the prompt?

Mr. Loman planned to give a quiz to his algebra students on solving linear equations and inequalities. Over the past few days, he noticed that some students were still confused about the differences between *less than* and *less than or equal to,* when to reverse the direction of the inequality, and when the solution was a single value or an interval. He decided to focus the quiz review on helping students make these distinctions.

MR. LOMAN: I notice a number of you are still having problems with some of the differences between solving equations and inequalities and when to use certain operations. So, I thought we would try something today to see if we could solidify those ideas. I'm going to have you work in groups of three. You'll need a piece of newsprint and a marker. I'm going to give each group a pair of problems to solve and graph on a number line. Then I want you to write a few sentences to explain to the rest of the class how your two problems are alike and how they're different. On your newsprint you will need to write both problems, show how you solved them, graph your solution, and then write your explanation. I'm going to give you ten minutes and then we're going to share with the rest of the class. Be sure you write large enough so that someone sitting in the back of the room can see.

[*Mr. Loman gives his eight groups the pairs of problems in Figure 12.7 and sets the timer for ten minutes.*]

MR. LOMAN: I saw some great work and explanations when I was walking around the room. Let's put these up at the front of the room. We'll begin with Group 1. [*The three students go to the front and explain their solution.*]

GROUP 1: On the first equation we subtracted 5 from both sides to start getting the x term by itself. Then we divided by 2. For the second one, we added 5 to both sides

Group 1:	$2x + 5 = 21$	and	$2x - 5 = 21$
Group 2:	$2x + 5 < 21$	and	$2x - 5 > 21$
Group 3:	$3y + 7 < 34$	and	$3y + 7 \leq 34$
Group 4:	$5t + 8 > 43$	and	$-5t + 8 > 43$
Group 5:	$2 - r > 10$	and	$r - 2 > 10$
Group 6:	$8x + 4 = 28$	and	$8x + 4 \geq 28$
Group 7:	$2p + 4 = 12$	and	$2(p + 4) = 12$
Group 8:	$4x - 3 \leq -31$	and	$-4x - 3 \leq -31$

FIG. 12.7

Sample prompts to compare and contrast solving equations and inequalities

and then divided by 2. They're both equations so there's only one answer. Our graphs are dots on the number line. They're different because you have to do the opposite. So to get rid of a plus 5 you subtract, and to get rid of a minus 5 you add. Because the 2 is multiplied by x in both of them, you have to divide to get the x by itself.

MR. LOMAN: Good job. Anybody have any questions for Group 1?

[*Mr. Loman continues with responses from Groups 2 and 3.*]

MR. LOMAN: Group 4, are you ready?

[*The group 4 students stand up and share their response. (See Figure 12.8).*]

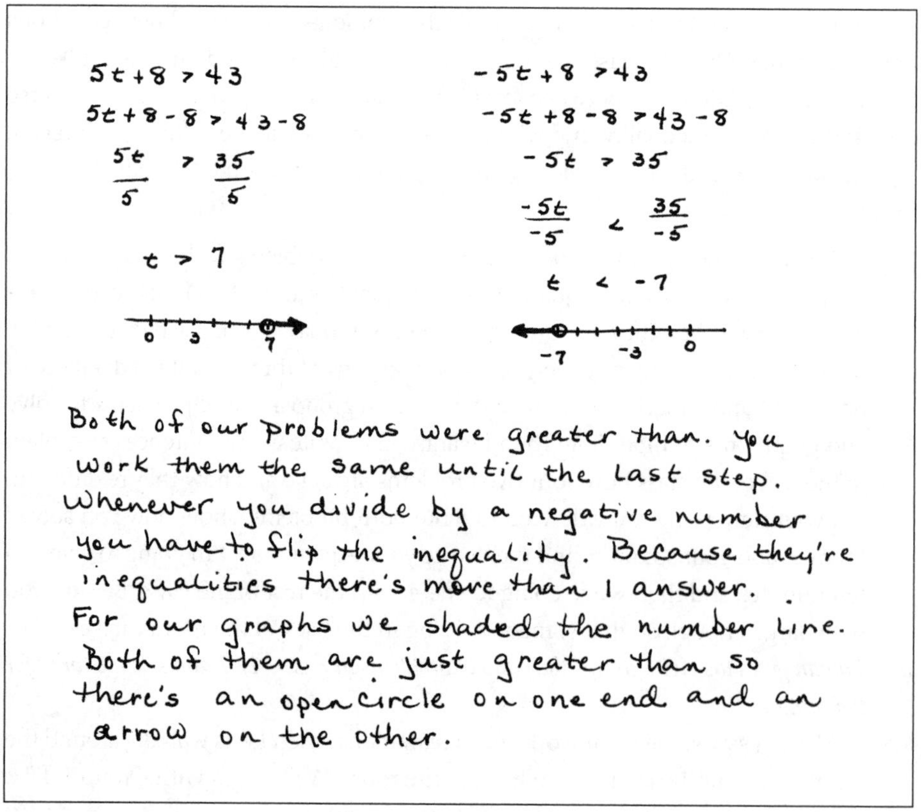

$5t + 8 > 43$
$5t + 8 - 8 > 43 - 8$
$\dfrac{5t}{5} > \dfrac{35}{5}$
$t > 7$

$-5t + 8 > 43$
$-5t + 8 - 8 > 43 - 8$
$-5t > 35$
$\dfrac{-5t}{-5} < \dfrac{35}{-5}$
$t < -7$

Both of our problems were greater than. You work them the same until the last step. Whenever you divide by a negative number you have to flip the inequality. Because they're inequalities there's more than 1 answer. For our graphs we shaded the number line. Both of them are just greater than so there's an open circle on one end and an arrow on the other.

FIG. 12.8

Sample group response to compare and contrast prompts for solving equations and inequalities

MR. LOMAN: I want to stop for a minute and compare the work of Group 3 and Group 4. In Group 3, what was the only difference between the two problems?

GROUP 3 MEMBER: One is less than OR EQUAL TO [*speaks in a slightly louder tone*] and that one has a closed circle on the graph.

MR. LOMAN: Okay. Did you have to switch the inequality sign when you subtracted 7 from both sides? [*Students shake their heads no.*] Why not?

GROUP 3 MEMBER: Because you were subtracting, not multiplying or dividing.

MR. LOMAN: Right. Now look again at the problems that Group 4 had. One of their problems has 5t and the other has –5t. What happened when you went to solve these?

GROUP 4 MEMBER: When we divided by negative five, we had to switch the inequality sign. We were thinking that when we first studied solving inequalities we found that multiplying by a negative one reverses the number line. So we had to reverse the direction of the inequality. We also checked at the end with –10 that was below –7 and it worked.

MR. LOMAN: Right. I'm glad you gave the reason for switching the inequality when you multiplied by a negative number. People often forget that.

[*Mr. Loman then continues to have the rest of the groups present their work.*]

MR. LOMAN: Okay. Now that you've had a chance to look at all the work, I'm going to give each group a few minutes to add anything or correct any errors you found. Then, I want you to put your work on the back wall. We'll want to refer to these when we solve more equations and inequalities tomorrow.

Students can complete writings with comparing and contrasting individually or in small groups as in the vignette. If students work with a partner or in a group, they can produce these writings on newsprint and share their ideas with the class. This approach enables students to analyze different ways that individuals describe similarities and differences in concepts. After sharing with the class, teachers can encourage students, as Mr. Loman did, to revise their entries before they are displayed on the wall or a bulletin board as examples of environmental print as described in Chapter 8 (see page 103).

Writing About Problems or Processes

In addition to writing about language or concepts, at times we want students to provide detailed writing about a problem or a process. Such writing encourages students to indicate their understanding of the problem context and explain their approaches to find a solution.

Symbols-Meanings Writing

Symbols-Meanings Writing offers a chance for students to provide their reasoning about each step they employ when they solve a mathematics problem. Often, when we talk or think about mathematical procedures, we write the symbols, and sometimes, the reasons used for each different step. However, learners often attend to the symbols but not the logic that underlies them. *Symbols-Meanings Writing* enables students to capture explicitly the reasoning and thinking that occurs in proceeding from one step to another.

To complete *Symbols-Meanings Writing*, students fold a piece of paper vertically. In the left column, they write the symbolic notation for the steps they take. In the right column, they write the reasoning and thinking that justified the transitions between steps. That is, the right column includes more than a simple reason; it involves a student talking to himself or herself about why certain actions are taken. Consequently, a student's thinking is made visible for the student to consider again, for peers to compare with their own thinking, or for the teacher to learn what understandings or misconceptions a student may have about a problem. Figure 12.9 illustrates an example of *Symbols-Meanings Writing* for a particular linear equation; this example is a model response in terms of the amount of detail provided.

Problem: A stove costs $428. You make a $50 down payment and monthly payments of $42. How many months will it take to finish paying for the stove?

Symbols	Meanings
The stove costs $428. I paid $50. I will pay $42 per month. Let x = the number of months I pay.	I made sure I understood the story and what the numbers represented. I labeled the variable.
$428 = 50 + 42x$	I know the cost (428) has to be the same as the down payment plus the cost per month times the number of months. 42 dollars/month times some months will equal dollars. There are dollars on both sides of the equation.
$428 = 50 + 42x$ $-50 \quad -50$	I know I paid the down payment. So I can subtract that from both expressions.
$378 = 42x$	I subtracted the $50 from each side of the equation. The equation is still equal.
$\dfrac{378}{42} = \dfrac{42x}{42}$	I will pay $378 at $42 per month. To find the number of months, I divide by 42.
$9 = x$	I will pay for 9 months.
Check: Is $42(9) + 50 = 428$?	I can check by substituting the 9 months.
$9 \times 42 = 378$ $378 + 50 = 428$	The 9 months works.

FIG. 12.9

A sample Symbols-Meanings Writing *for a linear equation*

Given the in-depth nature of this type of writing, we recognize that *Symbols-Meanings Writing* may not be appropriate for daily use. However, we recommend its use to help students recognize and record their metacognitive processes and mathematical reasoning. Students may be asked to complete this type of writing whenever a teacher wants greater knowledge of students' thought processes about a concept or procedure.

Write Your Own Problem

Another writing strategy that was part of the task used in *You Be the Judge* (Chapter 7) is to have students write their own problems, particularly word problems. When students use this practice, they must not only understand the mathematics concepts and important principles but also understand the structure of problems (Countryman 1992; Pugalee 2005, 2007; Rose 1989). Rose notes, "When students write their own problems, they often choose situations from their own experience and thus see how mathematics applies to their own lives, giving them more confidence to read and solve word problems . . . Writing word problems demands clear, specific, and complete instructions, which requires good understanding of the mathematical concept underlying the problem" (19). As students share their problems with their peers, any difficulties in their problems may become apparent. Missing information or unclear contexts or relationships are brought to the fore so that students can revise and modify their work. Such revision is an important part of the writing process.

Notes and Portfolios

Notes about a lesson and portfolios provide opportunities for students to write about an entire lesson, series of lessons, or other instructional segments.

Guided Notes

Guided Notes provide students a structure for organizing notes about a lesson. To assist students, teachers must generate the template that students use to take those notes. These templates can be designed in many forms, with opportunities for students to write sentences, provide examples of concepts, or to work out specific examples. Figure 12.10 is a sample of *Guided Notes* for the lesson on positive and negative numbers that was referenced in Chapters 3 and 11 (see the appendix for the lesson). The use of *Guided Notes* ensures that students have the essential elements of the lesson recorded in a manner that enables them to be used as a learning tool. Although we eventually want students to determine for themselves what aspects of a lesson should be recorded, guided notes can serve as a transition to help adolescents learn how to take notes that are useful for learning.

The *Guided Notes* sheet facilitates use of many of the literacy practices for meaning making that we have discussed in earlier parts of this book. For example, on the note sheet in Figure 12.10, students have several opportunities to provide personal examples of the concepts (items 3 and 10). They are expected to recognize how to verbalize important mathematical symbols (items 7 and 10b). They are expected to read the text examples and then indicate their understanding by solving a similar problem. They are expected to stop at various points in the lesson and answer the questions (Quiz Yourself).

Lesson title: _____

1. Refer to the activity. Put a +, −, or 0 next to each phrase if it would be described with a positive number, a negative number, or zero.

Phrase	Described by +, −, or 0	Situation	Phrase	Described by +, −, or 0	Situation
Profit of $3.21 billion			Loss of $4.6 million		
Sea level			23°F below zero		
Behind 10 points			Broke even		
90°F			Ahead 3 points		
500 feet above sea level			282 feet below sea level		
7 seconds ago			60 seconds from now		
No transaction			Withdrawal of $649.55		
Deposit of $29			Now		

2. The letters below are abbreviations for six situations. Use these abbreviations to label each phrase in the table above with the situation it represents. You may find that a phrase fits multiple situations.

   N business   B bank
   T temperature   F football
   E elevation   I time

3. Make up your own situation that would be described with a negative number.

4. Answer Quiz Yourself 1.

5. a. Describe each set of numbers.
   • Positive integers

FIG. 12.10
Sample Guided Notes *sheet for Lesson 1-2 on positive and negative numbers*

- Negative integers

b. What integer is not on either the positive or negative list?

6. Answer Quiz Yourself 2.

7. Translate each of the following sentences into words.
   $5 > -2$

   $14 < 25$

8. Read Example 1. Suppose another city is 15 feet below sea level.
   a. Write an inequality to compare the elevation of this city to the elevation of New Orleans.

   b. Write an inequality to compare the elevation of this city to the elevation of Amsterdam.

9. Read Example 2. On its first three plays, the middle school football team made these plays: gain of 4 yards, loss of 2 yards, gain of 16 yards. Graph these numbers on the number line below.

10. a. Write an example of a double inequality.

    b. Translate your double inequality into words.

    c. Rewrite your double inequality using the other inequality symbol.

FIG. 12.10
Continued

In addition, the use of *Guided Notes* can save time for students when considerable information needs to be recorded. Although we want students to do the Activity, having them spend time writing out all sixteen situations during class would take the focus away from the mathematics. Hence, in this case, *Guided Notes* facilitate the use of the activity so that the focus is on the underlying mathematics.

Guided Notes should be customized to fit the content of the lesson and the teacher's goals for instruction that day. To guide independent student note taking, teachers can include students in the template development stage by asking them to identify what should be included as part of their notes.

Build Your Test Notes

Successful students are able to think about their own learning. They self-assess to reflect on what they know and what they still need to learn. One writing strategy that hones this metacognitive process is what we call *Build Your Test Notes*. Some authors call this practice *crib sheets* (Mower 2003); students sometimes call them *cheat sheets*. In essence, students generate a set of notes that they are allowed to use on a test or quiz. Although some teachers permit students to use their entire notebook on an assessment, we prefer to modify this practice to require students to think carefully about their understanding of the concepts studied in a unit prior to the assessment and to make judgments about what information to include or exclude from their notes. When students use an entire notebook, we find that they spend too much of their test time flipping through the notebook because they have not taken the time to structure the content to support their own understanding.

To use *Build Your Test Notes*, we generally provide students with a set of specific guidelines. Students write notes to be used on the assessment on a single sheet of paper, or on a 5-by-8-inch index card. We require students to write the notes by hand and in ink. We do not permit them to type the notes on a computer because we want to ensure that each student creates his or her own notes, rather than use a set of notes that another student generated on a computer. We require students to use ink to write so their notes are finalized before the test, not modified during the day as students from different class periods talk about the test. Students also submit their notes with the assessment. When teachers review these notes, they discover students use various approaches and they can identify ways to help students prepare their notes more effectively in the future. As students determine the essential understandings that they need to place on their note sheet, they must ask themselves the following questions:

- What do I know so well that I don't need to put it on the test note page?
- What do I understand, but might need to have a quick reminder about if I get stuck?
- What am I still working on or struggling with that I might need help with during the test?

REFLECT

- Have you ever had a situation where you were permitted to use notes on a formal mathematics assessment? If so, how did the practice contribute to your understanding?

Students' answers to these questions help them decide the concepts and the level of detail they need to include. In addition, answers to these three questions can help students recognize the need for help from a peer or the teacher prior to the assessment. Many students have commented to us that the process of sorting through the concepts and generating the test notes solidified understandings so that they did not need to use their notes during the assessment.

Test Corrections

The goal in our mathematics classes is for students to make sense of mathematics. As teachers, we realize that mathematics concepts build on each other. Shaky understandings of some concepts can make it difficult for students to understand concepts studied later. So, another writing strategy we have found helpful is titled *Test Corrections*. We require the following steps on those problems or questions that students answered incorrectly:

1. Write about what you did incorrectly. What was your misunderstanding?
2. Write about what you should have done and why.
3. Redo the problem.

As students compare and contrast what they did on a problem with what they should have done, they address their understanding of the mathematical concepts. They have an opportunity to make sense of mathematics they did not previously understand correctly so they have the foundations to move forward. Some teachers enable students to improve their exam grades for *Test Corrections* done appropriately.

Portfolios

Student-created *portfolios* give opportunities for students to reflect on their learning by reviewing artifacts they have generated over the course of a marking period or semester. For instance, students might include a problem that initially caused difficulty but that they were finally able to solve, a formal assessment, or other examples of writings that have occurred over the unit. However, portfolios should not just be a collection of work. Students need to write about why they included particular artifacts. How do their choices of artifacts demonstrate growth in understanding, or show how continued struggles on a problem led to success? How do their choices illustrate their thinking over time? When completing a portfolio, students reflect about the mathematics they have learned as they review their work to make portfolio selections and write about their choices.

Journals

Journal writing in mathematics enables students to self-assess as they reflect on and make sense of mathematics. Students must synthesize the concepts or processes they have learned to describe their understandings in a manner that is understandable by others. Journals are records of students' "journey through the course and a way for them to keep track of where they are going, and where they have been, as they struggle with the stuff of mathematics" (Countryman 1992, 27). As we read our students' journal entries, we have access to their thinking, misconceptions, and dispositions about mathematics. As Countryman notes, "Reading math journal entries tells me considerably more about what students grasp and do not understand, like and dislike, care about and reject as they study mathematics than any formal or traditional math assignments. I find myself more aware of what students know, and how they come to construct that knowledge" (28–29).

Prompts may be supplied in a variety of forms, including the beginning of a sentence (a stem) that students must complete, a question or series of related questions, or information that students must explain. To start the journal-writing process, we begin with journal prompts about familiar mathematics (e.g., *What does subtraction mean?*), or about students' feelings toward mathematics or their learning (e.g., *When I solve a new math problem, I . . .* or *I understand . . . but I don't understand . . .*). As students become accustomed to writing, prompts can extend to focus on specific mathematics content or processes. Figure 12.11 contains sample mathematics prompts dealing with affective issues, mathematics content, mathematics processes, mathematics reasoning, or self-monitoring of students' own learning. Writing practices described earlier in this chapter (e.g., comparing and contrasting, *Symbols-Meanings Writing*) can also serve as the basis for a journal-writing opportunity.

R E F L E C T

- How would you respond to the following prompt?

  When I was a student, I did not like . . . in my mathematics classes and don't want to do that with my middle grades students.

Private journal writing between the teacher and the student ensures that teachers better understand students' thinking. The student writes, often in response to a prompt, and the teacher reads and responds to the entry. It is critical that we respond when students write so they recognize we view writing not as a test but as an important part of the learning process.

It Reminds Me Of (Richards and Gipe 1992) is an example of journal writing that specifically helps focus students on making connections to their background knowledge. For instance, the prompt, *This problem reminds me of . . .* , can help students think about previous problems they have solved that are similar to the current problem. We want students to make connections to develop flexibility in thinking. Students can be encouraged to view such writing as an opportunity for personal brainstorming by thinking about what they already know about a problem or a topic and how it relates to other knowledge.

R E F L E C T

- What similarities and differences do you notice between *Symbols-Meanings Writing*, journal writing, and *It Reminds Me Of*?

Creative Writing That Enhances Understanding

Many of our middle grades students are quite creative and become engaged in learning when we give them opportunities to express their creativity. In this section, we suggest several writing activities, such as songs, raps, poems, and graffiti, that enable students to demonstrate their creative side while still demonstrating mathematics understanding. Students who struggle with mathematics in formal settings may shine with more creative writing assignments. Martinez and Martinez (2001) suggest that "creative activities . . . [enable students to] verbalize and contextualize concepts . . . [Such activities assist students as they] liberate mathematical ideas and language from

FIG. 12.11
Sample journal prompts

Affective Prompts

- I like math class when . . .

- I am uncomfortable in math class when . . .

- I am good at math when . . .

- I used what we were learning when . . .

- I understand when . . .

- If I could be a math symbol, I would be . . . because . . .

Mathematics Content

- Describe three objects in the room that are in the shape of a nonrectangular parallelogram.

- Write two different stories that require finding a perimeter.

- Some properties of a square are . . .

- Prisms and pyramids are alike because . . . but they are different because . . .

- Describe everything you know about this graph. Then write two questions you could ask based on the graph.

Mathematics Processes

- How would you explain to a younger student how to add two integers?

- Explain why you cannot divide a number by 0.

- How is multiplying fractions similar and different from dividing fractions?

- How can you use a graphing calculator to solve $3x + 7 = 19$?

- Explain your steps to solve . . .

- Describe two different ways to solve this problem.

Mathematics Reasoning

- Why does adding a positive with a negative number work the way it does?

- Why do we multiply by the reciprocal of the divisor when we divide fractions?

- Describe two different ways to solve this problem. Justify one of your ways.

Self-Monitoring

- To improve my performance in class, I need to . . .

- Before the next test, I need to review . . .

the mathematics class and mathematics exercises and make them part of their real-world, thinking, speaking, and acting" (179).

One benefit of creative writing is that students have opportunities to demonstrate understanding in ways that may be culturally relevant and appealing. Albert (2000) describes an assignment in which students were expected to research and write an essay about a mathematician and the contributions this person made to mathematics. Several of her students wanted to present their report as a rap. The discussions she had with her students revealed that some of her assignments had silenced her students' voices. By permitting her students to use rap to present their research she gave value to their cultural background. She indicates that "culturally relevant teaching can help students feel empowered when constructing and co-constructing mathematical knowledge in learning contexts that matter to them" (87). Creative writing activities are one way to enable students to demonstrate their understanding in ways that are personally meaningful.

We describe several means to engage in creative writing. In each case, students' creativity needs to demonstrate mathematical understanding. However, we are not interested solely in creativity; we are interested in determining students' mathematical understanding by allowing them to make that understanding visible in unusual ways. We believe they are useful writing practices because they help students transmediate, or transfer what they know about mathematics into a different communication form (i.e., sign system). Students need specific guidelines to ensure that understanding is central to the writing (Albert 2000; Mower 2003). All these writing ideas are enjoyable and stimulating ways for students to be creative with mathematical ideas. With guidance, students can benefit from completing these writing assignments as miniprojects or as alternatives to traditional assessments.

Mathematics Bumper Stickers

Mathematics bumper stickers are short statements that convey a message, just like a bumper sticker placed on a car. Here are several sample bumper stickers that we created:

- To divide is to share fairly.
- A trio is prime.
- When I sleep, I have 0 slope.

Mathematics Graffiti

Mathematics graffiti (Dodridge 1987; Schloemer 1993) are visual displays of a word that embed the meaning within the visual display. Again, as students construct these, they can be placed on a bulletin board or wall in the class. Figure 12.12 contains several sample pieces of mathematics graffiti.

R E F L E C T

- Reflect on the sample bumper stickers. What understandings of concepts are demonstrated in each of the bumper stickers?

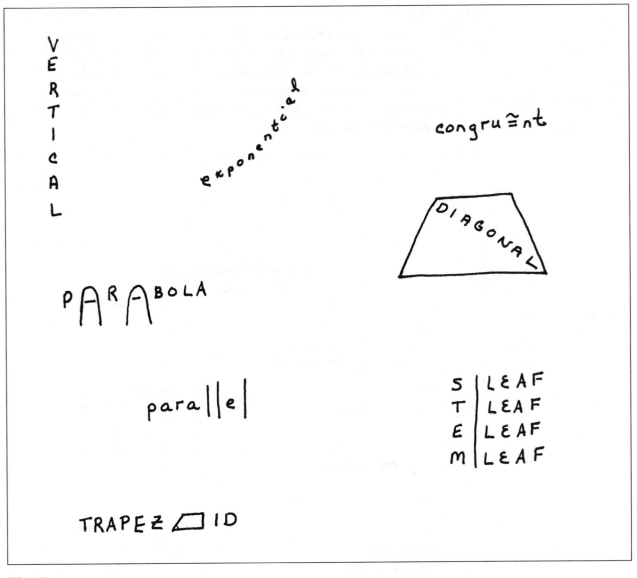

FIG. 12.12
Sample mathematics graffiti

Short Stories, Poems, Songs

Students can also write *short stories, poems, raps,* or *songs* to express mathematics concepts and ideas. We know students who sing songs to themselves during a test to remember important ideas. Figures 12.13, 12.14, and 12.15 contain a story, a rap, and a song, respectively.

FIG. 12.13

Sample mathematics story about the equals sign

In the land of algebra, there lived a creature named EQUALS who could be very jovial when two people visited him if they had the same value. He would pose for pictures with one person on each side. But if the visitors didn't agree in value, he refused to let them in his house. "I won't have my picture taken with you. Go visit Mr. Not Equals or one of his cousins, Mr. Less Than or Ms. Greater Than."

FIG. 12.14

Distributive property rap

Distributive Property Rap
by Rheta N. Rubenstein

Chorus
I know a good math property.
It's the one about distributivity.

Verse
4 times the quantity
2 + 5
equals
4 times 2 plus 4 times 5.

Chorus

Verse
It doesn't matter
What numbers you use.
Follow the pattern
With whatever you choose.

Chorus

Verse
a times the quantity
b plus **c** equals
a times **b** plus **a** times **c**.

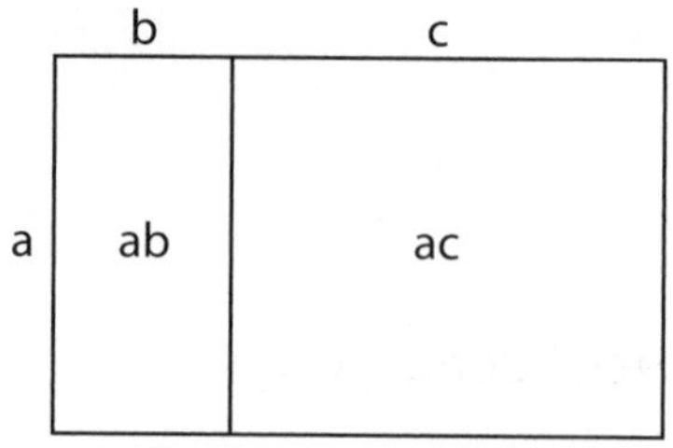

Chorus

$$a(b + c) = ab + ac$$

Verse
Division can be distributed, too.
Find the reciprocal and multiply through.
Like all of (**v** + **u**) over 2
Is half of **v** plus half of **u**.

$$\frac{(v + u)}{2} = \frac{v}{2} + \frac{u}{2}$$

Chorus

Verse
When it comes to negatives I do just fine. $-(x + y) = -x + -y$
Distribute the minus down the line.
So opposite of quantity
$(x + y)$ is
Opposite of **x** plus opposite of **y**.

Chorus

Verse
You may undo distribution, too. $qr + qs = q(r + s)$
Factoring is the thing to do.
Find a factor your terms share.
Put it up front and keep it there.
Take the terms **qr** and **qs**.
What's the same? **q**, I guess.
So the sum **qr** plus **qs**
Is the product now
q times **r** plus **s**.

Chorus

FIG. 12.14
Continued

Summary

Writing provides teachers a window into students' thinking. As students write, they have a conversation with themselves. They reflect on their understanding, clarify what they know, and identify what they still don't know and need to know. They demonstrate the depth of their thinking to themselves and to the readers of their written work. It is not enough for students to read mathematics, listen to mathematics, or even speak mathematics. They also need to transmit their knowledge in written form to be truly mathematically fluent.

Expand Your Understanding

1. Rose (1989) classifies writing as transactional if it is written for an audience, and expressive if it is written primarily for oneself.

   a. Classify the writing practices described in this chapter as transactional or expressive and justify your response.

   b. Which practices do you believe could fit into both categories?

FIG. 12.15
Sample mathematics song

Division by Zero Can't Be Done

(To the tune of "Santa Claus Is Coming to Town")

by Rheta N. Rubenstein

Chorus
You better watch out.
You better not try.
Don't divide by zero,
I'm tellin' you why,
Division by zero can't be done!

Say try to put 0 (oh) into 8.
Ask, "8 is what times oh?"
No matter what you estimate,
There's nothing that will go!

(Chorus)

Denominators must be watched.
Be quick and in the know.
Expressions there can trip you up.
Don't let them be zero.

(Chorus)

Be careful finding slopes of lines.
Zero creeps in here, too.
The ones that go straight up and down—
They have no slope for you.

(Chorus)

A graph may leave you wondering—
Divide by 0 and see.
An asymptote goes up and down
As you near infinity.

(Chorus)

Zero can be a friend or foe.
It factors easily.
But divide by it and down you go—
Avoid it carefully!

(Closing Chorus)

2. What similarities and differences do you notice across all of the writing activities in this chapter?

Connect to Practice

3. Try at least one of the writing practices from this chapter with your middle grades students. How did they react to the assignment? What did you learn about their understanding or ability to communicate in mathematics?

4. Writing prompts may or may not be included in the mathematics text you currently use with your students. Select a unit from your text and identify ways that your text incorporates writing into the unit.

5. Generate a set of guided notes for a lesson and use them with your students. How did students respond to completing these guided notes?

6. Review an upcoming unit in your text.

   a. Identify at least three places in the unit where you believe writing would benefit your students.

   b. Create prompts for the unit that engage students in comparing and contrasting concepts.

   c. Where might you be able to provide an opportunity for students to use *Symbols-Meanings Writing*? What would you be most interested in learning from your students' responses in *Symbols-Meanings Writing*?

7. Write your own short story, poem, rap, or song for a mathematics concept that you will soon be teaching.

Encouraging Meaning Making in Your Classroom

> In classrooms where students are challenged to think and reason about mathematics, communication is an essential feature as students express the results of their thinking orally and in writing.
> —NCTM, *Principles and Standards for School Mathematics*

The chapters in this section have provided an array of teaching practices to support middle grades students' language development in multiple modes of communication (e.g., speaking, reading, writing, listening, kinesthetics) and to help them use language to support concept formation.

If engaging your students as mathematics language learners is new to you, you might wonder how you can get started. We suggest you start slowly. You might begin with one communication activity for a unit or two for a term. Initially, you might engage in activities that can be conducted with the entire class so you can model for students what is expected and help students become comfortable with this new approach. As you become comfortable with focusing on students' language, you might increase the frequency with which you integrate communication activities.

As you progress, we suggest you start with just a few practices and use these same practices repeatedly. This helps you refine your expectations and ascertain what is reasonable for your students. Focusing on just a few practices also helps students learn what constitutes a quality response. If students are constantly exposed to new activities, they never have a chance to hone their responses and learn from early attempts to improve.

In this final set of questions, we encourage you to think about the practices described in this book. Revisit the book as you try ideas. Enjoy the journey with your students in your language-rich classroom.

Connect to Practice

1. Consider the practices introduced in the chapters of this section.

    a. Which practices do you think are simplest to implement for an early-career teacher? Why?

    b. Which practices do you think are most valuable? Why?

    c. Which practices do you expect to implement? Why?

2. Many of the practices in these chapters integrate more than one of the modes of communication. Think about your work with middle grades mathematics students and identify situations in which communication was a concern. These situations might be *incidental* items, such as reading or understanding words, symbols, graphs, or diagrams; verbalizing mathematics correctly; writing words or symbols; misunderstandings in listening or any other communication concern. Other issues might be more *systemic* and represent recurrent challenges in teaching or learning, such as how to motivate students to debate mathematics ideas with one another, how to refrain from telling students too much information, and how to promote engagement and discussion among students.

    a. Identify at least three incidental examples that you have observed in your classroom.

    b. Identify one systemic example that occurred in your classroom.

    c. Report on each example. Describe the context and what happened. What did you do? What were you thinking?

    d. Reflect on each example. What sensitivities or insights did you gain? What are you curious to learn?

    e. What instructional practice would you consider using to address the examples?

3. Take one chapter or unit from your middle grades mathematics text. Design a series of activities to integrate meaning-making practices into this unit.

Sample Middle Grades Mathematics Textbook Lesson

Lesson 1-2

Positive and Negative Numbers

Vocabulary

integers
positive integers
negative integers
positive numbers
negative numbers
inequality symbols
  < (is less than)
  > (is greater than)
double inequality

▶ **BIG IDEA** Situations with two opposite directions lead naturally to uses of negative numbers and zero.

Mental Math

Evaluate.

a. $7 \cdot 5$

b. $7 \cdot 50$

c. $70 \cdot 500$

d. $7,000 \cdot 50$

Situations with Negative Numbers

With the exception of 0, all the numbers mentioned in Lesson 1-1 are positive numbers. Many situations lead to negative numbers and zero as well as positive numbers.

Activity

Step 1   Below are 16 phrases. Which would be described with positive numbers, which with negative numbers, and which with zero? Rearrange the phrases into 3 lists.

profit of $3.21 billion	500 feet above sea level	loss of $4.6 million	282 feet below sea level
sea level	7 seconds ago	23°F below zero	60 seconds from now
behind 10 points	no transaction	broke even	withdrawal of $694.55
90°F	deposit of $29	ahead 3 points	now

Step 2   Here are six situations: business, temperature, elevation, bank, football, and time. Each situation uses 2 or 3 of the 16 phrases. Which phrases go with each situation?

There are three common ways in which the "−" sign for negatives is spoken.

Written	Spoken	Usage
−3	"negative 3"	correct
−3	"the opposite of 3"	correct
−3	"minus 3"	commonly used, but can be confusing since there is no subtraction

🛑 See Quiz Yourself 1 at the right.

▶ **QUIZ YOURSELF 1**

Translate −6 into words in two different correct ways.

Positive and Negative Numbers   **11**

To enter a negative number into a graphing calculator, you can usually use the opposite key, [(-)]. For example, to enter the number –8 into the graphing calculator, key in [(-)] 8. On some calculators, you can use the subtraction symbol [-].

Graphing Negative Numbers on a Number Line

On a horizontal number line, negative numbers are almost always placed at the left. The numbers identified on the number line below are the **integers.** The **positive integers** are the numbers 1, 2, 3, …. The **negative integers** are –1, –2, –3, …. Zero is an integer but it is neither positive nor negative. On the number line below, all numbers to the right of 0 are **positive numbers.** All numbers to the left of 0 are **negative numbers.**

| Negative numbers | Zero | Positive numbers |

–10 –9 –8 –7 –6 –5 –4 –3 –2 –1 0 1 2 3 4 5 6 7 8 9 10

🛑 See Quiz Yourself 2 at the right.

▶ **QUIZ YOURSELF 2**

What is the difference between the whole numbers and the positive integers?

Comparing Positive and Negative Numbers

Numbers are frequently compared. You can compare numbers whether they are positive, negative, or zero. You may recall comparing positive numbers with the **inequality symbols** < and >. The symbol < means **is less than** and the symbol > means **is greater than.** These same symbols are used with negative numbers.

Example 1

Much of the city of New Orleans is situated about 8 feet below sea level. Parts of Amsterdam, the largest city in the Netherlands, are about 18 feet below sea level. Compare these numbers using an inequality symbol.

Solution Both cities are below sea level. The more you descend from sea level, the lower the elevation is. Amsterdam is more feet below sea level than New Orleans; therefore, it is the lower city.

$$-18 < -8$$

You could also write this inequality as –8 > –18.

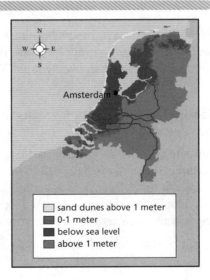

Amsterdam

☐ sand dunes above 1 meter
■ 0-1 meter
■ below sea level
■ above 1 meter

12   Reading and Writing Numbers

Vertical number lines are also used to graph numbers. On vertical number lines, positive numbers are usually placed above 0 and negative numbers are placed below 0.

Example 2

The table below shows the low temperatures on February 28, 2005, for three U.S. cities. Graph these numbers on a vertical number line.

City	Temperature
Boston, MA	24°F
Marquette, MI	−4°F
Duluth, MN	−13°F

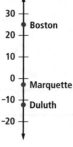

Solution On the vertical number line at the right, the positive numbers are above 0 and the negative numbers are below 0. Notice that on this number line, each tick mark represents a distance of 10 degrees. This is the *scale* of the number line.

You can also graph these numbers on a horizontal number line.

Double Inequalities

Numbers graphed on a number line are also easy to compare, since lesser numbers are usually to the left of or below greater numbers. When the numbers are in order, inequalities can be combined. The three temperatures of Example 2 can be compared using two inequalities.

$$-13 < -4 < 24$$

Because this has two inequality signs, it is called a **double inequality.** It can be read: "negative thirteen is less than negative four, which is less than twenty-four." You could also write:

$$24 > -4 > -13.$$

This is read: "twenty-four is greater than negative 4, which is greater than negative thirteen."

Caution: Do not use > and < in the same double inequality. For example, do not write $24 > -13 < -4$. Although this statement seems correct at first glance, it is not true. In order for it to be true, each individual inequality must be true. Here are the four inequalities in the statement. Whether they are true or false is written below them.

$24 > -13$	$-13 < -4$	$24 > -4$	$24 < -4$
True	True	True	False

Positive and Negative Numbers **13**

Questions

COVERING THE IDEAS

1. Give three examples of negative numbers from the newspaper activity in Lesson 1-1.

2. Write an integer that could be used to represent each situation.
   a. You make a savings-account withdrawal of $40.
   b. You make a savings-account deposit of $60.
   c. You owe $50.
   d. Your team is behind by 5 points.
   e. The game is tied.

3. **Fill in the Blanks**
   a. On a horizontal number line, negative numbers are usually to the ___?___ of the positive numbers.
   b. On a vertical number line, positive numbers are usually ___?___ the negative numbers.

4. What is the scale of a number line?

In 5–7, rewrite the sentence using the symbol < or >.

5. –10 is less than –8.5.

6. –5 is greater than –5.7.

7. An elevation of 38 feet below sea level is lower than an elevation of 25 feet above sea level.

8. Write in words: $79 > 0 > -16$.

9. **Multiple Choice** Which of the following numbers is *not* an integer?

   A 5   B 2.5   C 0   D –3

APPLYING THE MATHEMATICS

10. Give an example of a number that is neither positive nor negative.

11. Suppose time is measured in hours and 0 stands for the time right now.
    a. What number stands for an hour ago?
    b. What number stands for two hours from now?

12. Give an example of a number that is negative but not an integer.

13. Tell whether each number is or is not a positive integer.
    a. $\frac{1}{2}$ b. 0   c. 8   d. $\frac{2}{2}$ e. 1

14   Reading and Writing Numbers

14. Here is a list of some countries in Africa with their lowest points, measured in meters.

Location	Elevation
Chott Melrhir, Algeria	40 m below sea level
Mahoun River, Burkina Faso	200 m above sea level
Gulf of Guinea, Cote d'Ivoire	at sea level
Kulul, Eritrea	75 m below sea level
Shire River, Malawi	37 m above sea level
Sebkha, Morocco	55 m below sea level
Great Usutu River, Swaziland	21 m above sea level

a. Draw a number line with a scale of 20 meters, and place the elevations on it.

b. Write a double inequality relating the lowest points of Burkina Faso, Eritrea, and Morocco.

15. In golf, *par* is the expected number of strokes to play a hole. A golfer's score is often kept by the total number of strokes under or over par, rather than by the total number of strokes. The player with the fewest strokes wins. The vertical number line at the right shows the scores of some players at the end of the fourth round of the 2006 LPGA Championship.

a. Se Ri Pak and Karrie Webb tied for first. Mi Hyun Kim and Ai Miyazato tied for third. Represent their scores above or below par as integers.

b. Here are the scores for other golfers. Copy the vertical number line and place their scores on it.

Golfer	Score
Karen Stupples	9 over par
Marisa Baena	1 over par
Lorena Ochoa	5 under par
Nancy Scranton	par

c. Pak used 280 strokes in four rounds. How many strokes did Stupples use?

16. Manuel wrote the double inequality –15 < 10 > 2. Write a note to Manuel explaining why his inequality is incorrect. Then write a correct double inequality relating the numbers.

REVIEW

17. In 2005, the population of Indonesia was estimated to be about 242 million. Write this number in base 10. **(Lesson 1-1)**

18. The country of Indonesia is an archipelago (ar kuh PEH luh go) of 17,508 islands lying between the Indian Ocean and the Pacific Ocean. Write this number of islands in words. **(Lesson 1-1)**

19. **Multiple Choice** Which of the following is equal to 4^5? **(Previous Course)**

    A $4 + 4 + 4 + 4 + 4$

    B 4×5

    C $4 \times 4 \times 4 \times 4 \times 4$

    D $5 \times 5 \times 5 \times 5$

20. The sum of two whole numbers is 25. **(Previous Course)**

    a. What is the greatest their product can be?

    b. What is the least their product can be?

EXPLORATION

21. Question 14 gives the lowest points in seven countries in Africa. Find the highest points in these countries and graph them on a number line.

22. You are familiar with the Celsius and Fahrenheit temperature scales. There is a third scale called the Kelvin scale. Zero on the Kelvin scale is called "absolute zero." Why is this called absolute zero? What is absolute zero on the Celsius scale? What is it on the Fahrenheit scale?

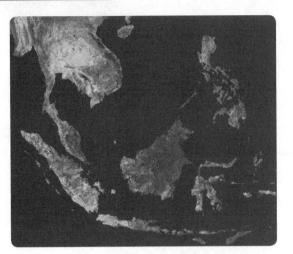

Indonesia includes the chain of islands that curves along the bottom of the photo and all of the islands in the lower right. The large island near the center is shared by Indonesia, Malaysia, and Brunei.

Earth Imaging/Stone Collection/Getty Images

QUIZ YOURSELF ANSWERS

1. negative six, the opposite of six

2. 0 is a whole number but not a positive integer.

References

Albers, Peggy. 2003. "Integrating a Semiotic View of Literacy." In *Integrating Multiple Literacies in K–8 Classrooms: Cases, Commentaries, and Practical Applications*, edited by Janet Richards and Michael C. McKenna, 150–71. Mahwah, NJ: Lawrence Erlbaum.

Albert, Lillie R. 2000. "Lessons Learned from the 'Five Men Crew': Teaching Culturally Relevant Mathematics." In *Changing the Faces of Mathematics: Perspectives on African Americans*, edited by Marilyn E. Strutchens, Martin L. Johnson, and William F. Tate, 81–88. Reston, VA: National Council of Teachers of Mathematics.

Anno, Masaichiro, and Mitsumasa Anno. 1983. *Anno's Mysterious Multiplying Jar*. New York: Philomel Books.

Baldwin, R. Scott, Jeff C. Ford, and John E. Readence. 1981. "Teaching Word Connotations: An Alternative Strategy." *Reading World* 21 (2): 103–108.

Ball, Deborah L. 1997. "From the General to the Particular: Knowing Our Own Students as Learners of Mathematics." *Mathematics Teacher* 90 (9): 732–37.

Baroody, Arthur J., and Bobbye H. Bartels. 2000. "Using Concept Maps to Link Mathematical Ideas." *Mathematics Teaching in the Middle School* 5 (9): 604–609.

Barton, Mary Lee, and Clare Heidema. 2002. *Teaching Reading in Mathematics*. 2nd ed. (*A Supplement to Teaching Reading in the Content Areas Teacher's Manual*, 2nd ed.) Aurora, CO: Mid-continent Research for Education and Learning.

Boud, David. 1989. "The Role of Self-Assessment in Student Grading." *Assessment and Evaluation in Higher Education* 14 (1): 20–30.

Boyle, Joseph R., and Mary Weishaar. 1997. "The Effects of Expert-Generated Versus Student-Generated Cognitive Organizers on the Reading Comprehension of Students with Learning Disabilities." *Learning Disability Research & Practice* 12 (4): 228–35.

Bracket, Josh. 2004. *Content Area Graphic Organizers: Math*. Portland, ME: Walch.

Burns, Marilyn. 1994. *The Greedy Triangle*. New York: Scholastic.

Charles, Randall, Frank Lester, and Phares O'Daffer. 1987. *How to Evaluate Progress in Problem Solving*. Reston, VA: National Council of Teachers of Mathematics.

Christaldi, Kathryn. 1996. *Even Steven and Odd Todd*. New York: Scholastic.

Cobb, Paul, Erma Yackel, and Kay McClain. 2000. *Symbolizing and Communicating in Mathematics Classrooms: Perspectives on Discourse, Tools, and Instructional Design*. Mahwah, NJ: Lawrence Erlbaum.

Coulter, David. 1999. "The Epic and the Novel: Dialogism, and Teacher Research." *Educational Researcher* 28 (3): 4–13.

Countryman, Joan. 1992. *Writing to Learn Mathematics: Strategies That Work, K–12*. Portsmouth, NH: Heinemann.

Crosbie, Michael J. 1993. *Architecture Shapes*. New York: John Wiley.

D'Ambrosio, Beatriz. 2004. "Preparing Teachers to Teach Mathematics Within a Constructivist Framework: The Importance of Listening to Children." In *The Work of Mathematics Teacher Educators: Exchanging Ideas for Effective Practice* (AMTE Monograph 1), edited by Tad Watanabe and Denisse R. Thompson, 135–50. San Diego, CA: Association of Mathematics Teacher Educators.

Daniels, Harvey, and Steven Zemelman. 2004. *Subjects Matter: Every Teacher's Guide to Content-Area Reading*. Portsmouth, NH: Heinemann.

Danielson, Charlotte. 1997. *A Collection of Performance Tasks and Rubrics: Middle School Mathematics*. Larchmont, NY: Eye on Education.

Davey, Beth. 1983. "Think Aloud: Modeling the Cognitive Processes of Reading Comprehension." *Journal of Reading* 27: 44–47.

Davidson, Neil, ed. 1990. *Cooperative Learning in Mathematics: A Handbook for Teachers*. Menlo Park, CA: Addison-Wesley.

Davis, Brent. 1994. "Mathematics Teaching: Moving from Telling to Listening." *Journal of Curriculum and Supervision* 93: 267–83.

———. 1996. *Teaching Mathematics: Towards a Sound Alternative*. New York: Garland.

Dodridge, John. 1987. Session presented at Camborne Teacher's Centre, Cornwall, England.

Drake, Bob M., and Linda B. Amspaugh. 1994. "What Writing Reveals in Mathematics." *Focus on Learning Problems in Mathematics* 16 (3): 43–50.

Elliot, Portia C., and Margaret J. Kenney, eds. 1996. *Communication in Mathematics: K–12 and Beyond*. Reston, VA: National Council of Teachers of Mathematics.

Ellis, Julie. 2004. *What's Your Angle, Pythagoras?* Watertown, MA: Charlesbridge.

Ernest, Paul. 2006. "A Semiotic Perspective of Mathematical Activity: The Case of Number." *Educational Studies in Mathematics* 61: 67–101.

Florida Department of Education. 1994. *Opening the Gate*. Tallahassee: Florida Department of Education.

Fry, Edward. 1977. "Fry's Readability Graph: Clarifications, Validity, and Extension to Level 17." *Journal of Reading* 21 (3): 242–52.

Gardner, Howard. 1983. *Frames of Mind: The Theory of Multiple Intelligences*. New York: Basic Books.

Gavelek, James. 2005. *Toward a Theory of Semiotically Mediated Instruction*. Paper presented at the Annual Meeting of the National Reading Conference, Miami, Florida, December.

Geskus, Elsa L., Jorie Borden, and Jeanie Burnett. 1999. *Using Reading Strategies to Enhance the Teaching of Mathematics* (Monograph No. 27). Ann Arbor, MI: Michigan Council of Teachers of Mathematics.

Gipe, Joan P. 2005. *Multiple Paths to Literacy: Assessment and Differentiated Instruction for Diverse Learners, K–12*. Upper Saddle River, NJ: Pearson Merrill Prentice Hall.

Goldin, Gerald A., and James J. Kaput. 1996. "A Joint Perspective on the Ideas of Representation in Learning and Doing Mathematics." In *Theories of Mathematical Learning*, edited by Leslie P. Steffe and Pearla Nesher, 397–430. Mahwah, NJ: Lawrence Erlbaum.

Griffin, Cynthia C., Linda D. Malone, and Edward J. Kameeni. 1995. "Effects of Graphic Organizer Instruction on Fifth Grade." *Journal of Educational Research* 89 (2): 89–99.

Griss, Susan. 1994. "Creative Movement: A Language for Learning." *Educational Leadership* 51 (5): 78–80.

Guastello, E. Francine, T. Mark Beasley, and Richard C. Sinatra. 2000. "Concept Mapping Effects on Science Content Comprehension of Low-Achieving Inner-City Seventh Graders." *Remedial and Special Education* 21 (6): 356–65.

Hassmen, Peter, and Darwin P. Hunt. 1994. "Human Self-Assessment in Multiple-Choice Testing." *Journal of Educational Measurement* 31: 149–60.

Heimlich, Joan E., and Susan D. Pittelman. 1986. *Semantic Mapping: Classroom Applications*. Newark, DE: International Reading Association.

Herber, Harold. 1978. *Teaching Reading in Content Areas*. 2nd ed. Englewood Cliffs, NJ: Prentice Hall.

Hitt, Fernando. 1998. "The Role of the Semiotic Representations in the Learning of Mathematics." In *Proceedings of the British Society for Research into Learning Mathematics*, edited by L. Bills, 23–28. (Available at bsrlm.org.uk. Accessed December 21, 2005.)

Hoban, Tana. 1974. *circles, triangles, and squares*. New York: Simon & Schuster.

Horton, Phillip B., Andrew A. McConney, Michael Gallo, Amanda L. Woods, Gary J. Senn, and Denis Hamelin. 1993. "An Investigation of the Effectiveness of Concept Mapping as an Instructional Tool." *Science Education* 77: 95–111.

Horton, Steven V., Thomas C. Lovitt, and Donna Bergerud. 1990. "The Effectiveness of Graphic Organizers for Three Classifications of Secondary Students in Content Area Classes." *Journal of Learning Disabilities* 23 (1): 12–22.

Hoyt, Linda. 2002. *Make It Real: Strategies for Success with Informational Texts*. Portsmouth, NH: Heinemann.

Hufferd-Ackles, Kimberly, Karen C. Fuson, and Miriam Gamoran Sherin. 2004. "Describing Levels and Components of a Math-Talk Learning Community." *Journal for Research in Mathematics Education* 35: 81–116.

Huinker, Deann, and Connie Laughlin. 1996. "Talk Your Way into Writing." In *Communication in Mathematics, K–12 and Beyond*, edited by Portia C. Elliot and Margaret J. Kenney, 81–89. Reston, VA: National Council of Teachers of Mathematics.

Hunsader, Patricia D. 2004. "Mathematics Trade Books: Establishing Their Value and Assessing Their Quality." *Reading Teacher* 57 (7): 618–29.

Hyerle, David. 1996. *Visual Tools for Constructing Knowledge*. Alexandria, VA: Association for Supervision and Curriculum Development.

Johnson, Dale D., and P. David Pearson. 1984. *Teaching Reading Vocabulary*. New York: Holt, Rinehart and Winston.

Johnson, David W., and Roger T. Johnson. 1990a. "Social Skills for Successful Group Work." *Educational Leadership* 47 (4): 29–33.

———. 1990b. "Using Cooperative Learning in Math." In *Cooperative Learning in Mathematics: A Handbook for Teachers*, edited by Neil Davidson, 103–25. Menlo Park, CA: Addison-Wesley.

Kagan, Spencer. 1992. *Cooperative Learning*. San Juan Capistrano, CA: Kagan Cooperative Learning.

Kane, Robert B., Mary Ann Byrne, and Mary Ann Hater. 1974. *Helping Children Read Mathematics*. New York: American Book.

Kilpatrick, Jeremy, Jane Swafford, and Bradford Findell, eds. 2001. *Adding It Up: Helping Children Learn Mathematics*. Mathematics Study Learning Committee, National Research Council. Washington, DC: National Academies Press.

Kinchin, Ian M. 2000a. "Concept Mapping in Biology." *Journal of Biological Education* 34 (2): 61–69.

———. 2000b. "Using Concept Maps to Reveal Understanding: A Two-Tier Analysis." *School Science Review* 81 (296): 41–46.

Koivula, Nathalie, Peter Hassmen, and Darwin P. Hunt. 2001. "Performance on the Swedish Scholastic Aptitude Test: Effects of Self-Assessment and Gender." *Sex Roles* 44: 629–33.

Lampert, Magdalene. 2001. *Teaching Problems and the Problems of Teaching*. New Haven: Yale University Press.

Lampert, Magdalene, and Merrie L. Blunk, eds. 1998. *Talking Mathematics in School: Studies of Teaching and Learning.* Cambridge, UK: Cambridge University Press.

Langer, Judith. 1981. "From Theory to Practice: A Prereading Plan." *Journal of Reading* 25: 152–56.

Lappan, Glenda, James T. Fey, William M. Fitzgerald, Susan N. Friel, and Elizabeth Difanis Phillips. 2006. *Connected Mathematics 2.* Boston: Pearson/Prentice Hall.

Lemke, Jay. 2005. *Mathematics in the Middle: Measure, Picture, Gesture, Sign, and Word.* Accessed December, 2005, at http://academic.brooklyn.cuny.edu/education/jlemke/papers/myrdene .htm.

Lenski, Susan, Mary Ann Wham, and Jerry Johns. 1999. *Reading and Learning Strategies for Middle and High School Students.* Dubuque, IA: Kendall/Hunt.

Lipson, Marjorie, and Karen Wixson. 1991. *Assessment and Instruction of Reading Disability: An Interactive Approach.* New York: HarperCollins.

Martinez, Joseph G. R., and Nancy C. Martinez. 2001. *Reading and Writing to Learn Mathematics: A Guide and a Resource Book.* Boston: Allyn and Bacon.

McCallum, Ann. 2006. *Beanstalk: The Measure of a Giant.* Watertown, MA: Charlesbridge.

McMillan, Bruce. 1991. *Eating Fractions.* New York: Scholastic.

McTighe, Jay, and Frank T. Lyman Jr. 1988. "Cueing Thinking in the Classroom: The Promise of Theory-Embedded Tools." *Educational Leadership* 45: 18–24.

Menendez, Ramon, and Tom Musca, screenwriters. 1988. *Stand and Deliver.* Burbank, CA: Warner Bros.

Miller, L. Diane. 1993. "Making the Connection with Language." *Arithmetic Teacher* 40 (6): 311–16.

Monroe, Eula, and Michelle R. Pendergrass. 1997. "Effects of Mathematical Vocabulary Instruction on Fourth Grade Students." *Reading Improvement* 34 (2): 120–32.

Moore, David W., and John E. Readence. 1984. "A Quantitative and Qualitative Review of Graphic Organizer Research." *Journal of Educational Research* 78 (1): 11–17.

Mower, Pat. 2003. *Algebra Out Loud: Learning Mathematics Through Reading and Writing Activities.* San Francisco, CA: Jossey-Bass.

Murray, Miki. 2004. *Teaching Mathematics Vocabulary in Context.* Portsmouth, NH: Heinemann.

National Council of Teachers of Mathematics (NCTM). 1989. *Curriculum and Evaluation Standards for School Mathematics.* Reston, VA: National Council of Teachers of Mathematics.

———. 1991. *Professional Standards for Teaching Mathematics.* Reston, VA: National Council of Teachers of Mathematics.

———. 1995. *Assessment Standards for School Mathematics.* Reston, VA: National Council of Teachers of Mathematics.

———. 2000. *Principles and Standards for School Mathematics.* Reston, VA: National Council of Teachers of Mathematics.

National Research Council. 2000. *Educating Teachers of Science, Mathematics, and Technology.* Washington, DC: National Academy Press.

Neuschwander, Cindy. 1997. *Sir Cumference and the First Round Table: A Math Adventure.* Watertown, MA: Charlesbridge.

———. 2001. *Sir Cumference and the Great Knight of Angleland.* Watertown, MA: Charlesbridge.

———. 2006. *Sir Cumference and the Isle of Immeter.* Watertown, MA: Charlesbridge.

———. n.d. *Sir Cumference and the Dragon of Pi: A Math Adventure.* Watertown, MA: Charlesbridge.

Noonan, James. 1990. "Readability Problems Presented by Mathematics Text." *Early Childhood Development and Care* 54: 57–81.

Novak, Joseph D., and D. Bob Gowin. 1984. *Learning How to Learn*. New York: Cambridge University Press.

Ogle, Donna. 1986. "The K-W-L: A Teaching Model That Develops Active Reading of Expository Text." *The Reading Teacher* 39: 564–70.

———. 1989. "The Know, Want to Know, Learning Strategy." In *Children's Comprehension of Text: Research into Practice*, edited by K. Denise Muth, 205–23. Newark, DE: International Reading Association.

Orton, Anthony. 1987. *Learning Mathematics: Issues, Theory, and Classroom Practice*. London: Casell Education.

Pallotta, Jerry. 2002. *Apple Fractions*. New York: Scholastic.

Peirce, Charles. 1931. *Collected Writings*. Vol. 8. Ed. C. Hartshorse, P. Weiss, and A. Burks. Cambridge, MA: Harvard University Press.

Pimm, David. 1987. *Speaking Mathematically: Communication in Mathematics Classrooms*. New York: Routledge.

———. 1996. "Diverse Communications." In *Communication in Mathematics: K–12 and Beyond*, edited by Portia C. Elliot and Margaret J. Kenny, 11–19. Reston, VA: National Council of Teachers of Mathematics.

Pirie, Susan E. B. 1998. "Crossing the Gulf Between Thought and Symbol: Language as (Slippery) Stepping-Stones." In *Language and Communication in the Mathematics Classroom*, edited by Heinz Steinbring, Maria G. Bartolini Bussi, and Anna Sierpinska, 7–29. Reston, VA: National Council of Teachers of Mathematics.

Pólya, George. 1957. *How to Solve It: A New Aspect of Mathematical Method*. 2nd ed. Princeton, NJ: Princeton University Press.

Probst, Robert E. 1987. "Adolescent Literature and the English Curriculum." *English Journal* 76 (3): 26–30.

Pugalee, David K. 2005. *Writing to Develop Mathematical Understanding*. Norwood, MA: Christopher-Gordon.

———. 2007. *Developing Mathematical and Scientific Literacy: Effective Content Reading Practices*. Norwood, MA: Christopher-Gordon.

Raphael, Taffy. 1982. "Question-Answering Strategies for Children." *The Reading Teacher* 36: 186–90.

———. 1986. "Teaching Question-Answer Relationships, Revisited." *The Reading Teacher* 39: 516–22.

Resnick, Lauren B., and Leopold E. Klopfer. 1989. "Toward the Thinking Curriculum: An Overview." In *Toward the Thinking Curriculum: Current Cognitive Research* (1989 ASCD Yearbook), edited by Lauren B. Resnick and Leopold E. Klopfer, 1–18. Alexandria, VA: Association for Supervision and Curriculum Development.

Richards, Janet C. 2005. "The Reading/Writing Connection." In *Multiple Paths to Literacy: Assessment and Differentiated Instruction for Diverse Learners, K–12*, edited by Joan P. Gipe, 146–75. Upper Saddle River, NJ: Pearson Merrill Prentice Hall.

Richards, Janet C., and Joan P. Gipe. 1992. "Activating Background Knowledge for Beginning and Poor Readers." *The Reading Teacher* 45 (6): 474–76.

Rittenhouse, Peggy S. 1998. "The Teacher's Role in Mathematical Conversation: Stepping In and Stepping Out." In *Talking Mathematics in School: Studies of Teaching and Learning*, edited by Magdalene Lampert and Merrie L. Blunk, 163–89. Cambridge, UK: Cambridge University Press.

Robinson, Francis Pleasant. 1970. *Effective Study*. 4th ed. New York: Harper & Row.

Rose, Barbara. 1989. "Writing and Mathematics: Theory and Practice." In *Writing to Learn Mathematics and Science*, edited by Paul Connolly and Teresa Vilardi, 15–30. New York: Teachers College Press.

Rotman, Brian. 2000. *Mathematics as a Sign*. Stanford, CA: Stanford University Press.

Rubenstein, Rheta N. 1996. "Strategies to Support the Learning of the Language of Mathematics." In *Communication in Mathematics: K–12 and Beyond*, edited by Portia C. Elliot and Margaret J. Kenny, 214–18. Reston, VA: National Council of Teachers of Mathematics.

———. 2000. "Word Origins: Building Communication Connections." *Mathematics Teaching in the Middle School* 5: 493–98.

Rubenstein, Rheta N., Charlene E. Beckmann, and Denisse R. Thompson. 2004. *Teaching and Learning Middle Grades Mathematics*. Emeryville, CA: Key College.

Rubenstein, Rheta N., and Denisse R. Thompson. 2001. "Learning Mathematical Symbolism: Challenges and Instructional Strategies." *Mathematics Teacher* 94 (April): 265–71.

Saenz-Ludlow, Adalira. 2006. "Classroom Interpreting Games with an Illustration." *Educational Studies in Mathematics* 61: 183–218.

Santa, Carol Minnick, and Lynn T. Havens. 1991. "Learning Through Writing." In *Science Learning: Processes and Applications*, edited by Carol Minnick Santa and Donna E. Alvermann, 122–33. Newark, DE: International Reading Association.

Scharer, Patricia L., Gay Su Pinnell, Carol Lyons, and Irene Fountas. 2005. "Becoming an Engaged Reader." *Educational Leadership* 63 (2): 24–29.

Schloemer, Cathy G. 1993. "Bulletin Boards in Mathematics Class." *Mathematics Teacher* 86: 454–55.

Schwartz, David M. 1998. *G Is for Googol: A Math Alphabet Book*. Berkeley, CA: Tricycle Press.

Schwartz, Robert. 1988. "Learning to Learn Vocabulary in Content Area Textbooks." *Journal of Reading* 32: 108–17.

Schwartzman, Steven. 1994. *The Words of Mathematics: An Etymological Dictionary of Mathematical Terms Used in English*. Washington, DC: Mathematical Association of America.

Semali, Ladislaus, and Judith Fueyo. 2005. "Transmediation as a Metaphor for New Literacies in Multimedia Classrooms." *Reading Online* (an Online Publication of the International Reading Association). Accessed December 22, 2005, at http://readingonline.org/newliteracies/semali2.

Sfard, Anna. 2001. "There Is More to Discourse Than Meets the Ears: Looking at Thinking as Communicating to Learn More About Mathematical Learning." *Educational Studies in Mathematics* 46 (1): 13–57.

Shield, Mal, and Kevan Swinson. 1996. "The Link Sheet: A Communication Aid for Clarifying and Developing Mathematical Ideas and Processes." In *Communication in Mathematics, K–12 and Beyond*, edited by Portia C. Elliot and Margaret J. Kenney, 35–39. Reston, VA: National Council of Teachers of Mathematics.

Short, Kathy, Gloria Kauffman, and Leslie Kahn. 2000. "'I just need to draw': Responding to Literature Across Multiple Sign Systems." *The Reading Teacher* 54 (2): 160–71.

Shuard, Hilary, and Andrew Rothery. 1984. *Children Reading Mathematics*. London: John Murray.

Siegel, Marjorie. 1995. "More Than Words: The Generative Power of Transmediation for Learning." *Canadian Journal of Education* 20 (4): 455–74.

Siegel, Marjorie, Raffaella Borasi, Judith M. Fonzi, Lisa Grasso Sanridge, and Constance Smith. 1996. "Using Reading to Construct Mathematical Meaning." In *Communication in Mathematics: K–12 and Beyond*, edited by Portia C. Elliot and Margaret J. Kenny, 66–75. Reston, VA: National Council of Teachers of Mathematics.

Silver, Edward A., and Margaret Smith. 1996. "Building Discourse Communities in Mathematics Classrooms: A Worthwhile but Challenging Journey." In *Communication in Mathematics: K–12 and Beyond*, edited by Portia C. Elliot and Margaret J. Kenny, 20–28. Reston, VA: National Council of Teachers of Mathematics.

Slavin, Robert E. 1983. "When Does Cooperative Learning Increase Student Achievement?" *Psychological Bulletin* 94: 429–45.

Smith, Howard. 1997. "Peirce's Sign and Mathematics Education: An Introduction." *Philosophy of Mathematics Education Journal* 10: 11–14.

———. 2005. *Psychosemiotic*. New York: Peter Lang.

Smith, Margaret Schwan, and Mary Kay Stein. 1998. "Selecting and Creating Mathematical Tasks: From Research to Practice." *Mathematics Teaching in the Middle School* 3: 344–50.

Stauffer, Russell G. 1969. *Directing Reading Maturity as a Cognitive Process*. New York: Harper & Row.

Steinbring, Heinz. 2006. "What Makes a Sign a Mathematical Sign? An Epistemological Perspective on Mathematical Interaction." *Educational Studies in Mathematics* 61: 133–62.

Steinbring, Heinz, Maria G. Bartolini Bussi, and Anna Sierpinska, eds. 1998. *Language and Communication in the Mathematics Classroom*. Reston, VA: National Council of Teachers of Mathematics.

Stevens, Janet. 1999. *Cook-a-Doodle-Doo!* San Diego: Harcourt Brace.

Stigler, James W., and James Hiebert. 1999. *The Teaching Gap: Best Ideas from the World's Teachers for Improving Education in the Classroom*. New York: The Free Press.

Sundby, Scott. 2000. *Cut Down to Size at High Noon: A Math Adventure*. Watertown, MA: Charlesbridge.

Thompson, Denisse R., and Rheta N. Rubenstein. 2000. "Learning Mathematics Vocabulary: Potential Pitfalls and Instructional Strategies." *Mathematics Teacher* 93 (7): 568–74.

Thompson, Denisse R., and Sharon L. Senk. 1993. "Assessing Reasoning and Proof in High School." In *Assessment in the Mathematics Classroom*, edited by Norman L. Webb and Arthur F. Coxford, 167–76. Reston, VA: National Council of Teachers of Mathematics.

Toumasis, Charalampos. 1995. "Concept Worksheet: An Important Tool for Learning." *Mathematics Teacher* 88: 98–100.

Usiskin, Zalman. 1996. "Mathematics as a Language." In *Communication in Mathematics: K–12 and Beyond*, edited by Portia C. Elliot and Margaret J. Kenny, 231–43. Reston, VA: National Council of Teachers of Mathematics.

Van de Walle, John A. 2004. *Elementary and Middle School Mathematics: Teaching Developmentally*. 5th ed. Upper Saddle River, NJ: Allyn & Bacon.

van Kraayenoord, Christina E., and Scott G. Paris. 1997. "Australian Students' Self-Appraisal of Their Work Samples and Academic Progress." *The Elementary School Journal* 97: 523–37.

Whitin, David J. 1995. Exploring Mathematics Through Children's Literature. Talk presented at the Whole Language Umbrella International Conference, Windsor, Ontario, Canada, July.

Whitin, Phyllis, and David J. Whitin. 2000. *Math Is Language Too: Talking and Writing in the Mathematics Classroom*. Urbana, IL: National Council of Teachers of English and Reston, VA: National Council of Teachers of Mathematics.

Wilcox, Sandra K., and Elizabeth M. Jones. 2004. "A Tool for the Teaching Principle: Professional Development *Through* Assessment." In *Perspectives on the Teaching of Mathematics*, edited by Rheta N. Rubenstein and George W. Bright, 239–58. Reston, VA: National Council of Teachers of Mathematics.

Yoshida, Makoto. 2005. "Using Lesson Study to Develop Effective Blackboard Practices." In *Building Our Understanding of Lesson Study*, edited by Patsy Wang Iverson and Makoto Yoshida, 93–100. Philadelphia: Research for Better Schools.

Index

*Note: Capitalized entries identify specific literacy strategies for mathematics

aerobics, mathematics, 104, 106
  examples of, 104
analogies, 118, 153, 155–56. *See
  also* vocabulary strategies;
  writing strategies
  examples of, 156
anticipation guide, 142. *See also*
  reading strategies
assessment, 13, 17, 61, 128, 131,
  150. *See also* writing
  strategies
  Build Your Test Notes,
  164–65
  Give and Take, 130–31, 133
  journals, 6, 57, 62, 165–66,
  167
  Multi-Rep charts, 73–74
  portfolios, 165
  self-assessment, 6, 57, 62, 76,
  164, 165–66
  test corrections, 165
  You Be the Judge, 76–86
autobiography, mathematics,
  152–53. *See also* writing
  strategies

body motion, 103–104, 106. *See
  also* aerobics, mathematics
  examples of, 104
box-and-whisker plot, 34, 104
brainstorming, 139–40, 141. *See
  also* listening strategies;
  reading strategies; speaking
  strategies
Build Your Test Notes, 164–65. *See
  also* writing strategies

bumper stickers, 168. *See also*
  creative writing; writing
  strategies
  examples of, 168

communication, means of, 12
comparing and contrasting,
  96–99, 156–59, 166. *See also*
  writing strategies
  examples of, 156, 157, 158
  These Are/These Are Not,
  98–99, 122, 156–57
  Venn diagram, 97–98, 113–15,
  145
concept development, 41, 89,
  91–92, 153–59
concept maps, 99–101, 104–105,
  141, 145. *See also* graphic
  organizers
  examples of, 100, 101
conceptual understanding,
  91–92. *See also* procedural
  understanding
Co-op, 127–28, 133. *See also*
  cooperative learning
  strategies
cooperative learning activities
  Give and Take, 120–131, 133
  You Be the Judge, 76–86
  Zoom In–Zoom Out, 53–64,
  148
cooperative learning, benefits of,
  87, 92, 110, 124, 128
cooperative learning strategies,
  124–28
  Co-op, 127–28, 133

Jigsaw, 128, 133
  Roundtable, 126–27, 133
  Think-Pair-Share, 46, 49, 125
creative writing, 166, 168–71,
  172. *See also* writing
  strategies
  benefits of, 166, 168
  bumper stickers, 168
  examples of, 168, 169, 170–71,
  172
  graffiti, 166, 168, 169
  poems, 153, 169, 171
  raps, 153, 169, 170–71
  songs, 169, 172
  stories, 153, 169, 170

discourse, 2, 10, 11, 12, 18, 89. *See
  also* math-talk community
discourse community, 10, 18, 30,
  40, 41, 44–52, 89. *See also*
  math-talk community
Distinguished Pairs, 116, 122. *See
  also* reading strategies;
  vocabulary strategies
  examples of, 116
DRTA (Directed Reading-
  Thinking Activity), 147. *See
  also* reading strategies

environmental print, 103, 159. *See
  also* graphic organizers
examples of strategies
  analogies, 156
  bumper stickers, 168
  comparing and contrasting,
  156, 157, 158

examples of strategies (*cont.*)
  concept map, 100, 101
  Distinguished Pairs, 116
  Give and Take, 131
  graffiti, 169
  graphic organizers, 97, 98, 99, 100,
    101, 102, 103
  Guided Note Sheet, 162–63
  invented language, 117
  invented symbols, 118
  journal prompts, 167
  K-W-L, 141
  kinesthetics, 104
  literature connections, 120–21
  Make My Day, 132
  manipulatives for concept
    development, 93, 95
  math aerobics, 104
  middle grades mathematics
    lesson, 178–83
  Multi-Rep chart, 70, 71
  personal dictionary/glossary, 29,
    154, 155
  raps, 170–71
  reading graphs, 33, 34
  Roundtable, 126
  Semantic Feature Analysis Grid,
    102, 103
  Sketch the Text, 146
  songs, 169, 172
  story, 170
  Symbol-Language Glossary, 130
  Symbols-Meanings Writing, 160
  textbook survey, 23
  These Are/These Are Not, 98, 99
  Venn diagram, 97, 114, 115
  word origins, 111, 112
  word wall, 26
exit slip, 146. *See also* reading
    strategies

Give and Take, 130–31, 133. *See also*
    listening strategies; speaking
    strategies
  examples of, 131
graffiti, 166, 168, 169. *See also* creative
    writing; writing strategies
  examples of, 169
graphic organizers, 96–103, 147
  benefits of, 96
  concept maps, 99–101, 104–105,
    141, 145

environmental print, 103, 159
  examples of, 97, 98, 99, 100, 101,
    102, 103
  K-W-L, 140–41, 148
  Multiple Representations chart
    (Multi-Rep), 65–75, 153
  Semantic Feature Analysis Grid,
    99, 101–105
  These Are/These Are Not, 98–99,
    156–57
  Venn diagram, 97–98, 113–15,
    145, 153, 156
graphics, types of, 31–32, 37
graphs, reading of, 31–34, 142–43
  examples of 33, 34
Guided Notes, 161–64. *See also*
    writing strategies
  example of 162–63

invented language, 116–18, 119. *See*
    also vocabulary strategies
  example of, 117
invented symbols, 118
  example of, 118
It Reminds Me Of, 148–49, 166. *See*
    also reading strategies; writing
    strategies

Jigsaw, 128, 133. *See also* cooperative
    learning strategies
journals/journal writing, 6, 57, 62,
    165–66, 167. *See also* writing
    strategies
  examples of prompts, 167

kinesthetics, body motion, 103–104,
    106
  examples of, 104
K-W-L, 140–41, 148. *See also*
    reading strategies; writing
    strategies
  example of, 141

learning logs, 146. *See also* journals;
    writing strategies
listening, 15. *See also* listening
    strategies
listening, modes of, 15–16
listening strategies
  brainstorming, 139–40, 141
  Co-op, 127–28, 133
  Give and Take, 130–31, 133

Make My Day, 132, 133
Pairs Read, 144
PreP, 140
Roundtable, 126–27, 133
Teacher Think-Aloud, 143–44
Think-Pair-Share, 46, 49, 55, 62,
    125
literacy spectrum, 12, 18, 39. *See also*
    listening strategies; reading
    strategies; speaking strategies;
    writing strategies
literature connections, 119–21
  examples of, 120–21

Make My Day, 132, 133. *See also*
    listening strategies
  examples of, 132
manipulatives for concept building,
    92–95, 117. *See also* conceptual
    understanding
  algebra tiles, 94–95
  geoboard, 95
  models, 94–95
  pattern blocks, 92–93
  square tiles, 117
  two-color counters, 94–95
math-talk community, 44, 87–88. *See*
    also discourse
mathematical literacy, 11, 18, 20
mathematics as a language, 2, 5, 10,
    12–13, 25, 26
mathematics language learners, 2,
    11, 13, 18, 20, 26, 38, 40, 121
metacognition, 90, 150, 151, 161,
    164. *See also* assessment, self;
    self-regulation
middle grades mathematics lesson,
    178–83
mnemonic device(s), 9
multiple literacies, 11, 12, 40
Multiple Representations charts
    (Multi-Rep), 65–75, 153. *See*
    also graphic organizers; writing
    strategies
  examples of, 70, 71
  template for, 66
multiple semiotic systems, 40. *See*
    also semiotics

note-taking devices, 103. *See also*
    Guided Notes; writing
    strategies

Pairs Read, 144. *See also* reading strategies

performance task, 76–77, 84

personal dictionaries/glossaries, 29, 36, 110, 114, 153, 154–55. *See also* vocabulary strategies; writing strategies

  examples of, 29, 154, 155

poems, 153, 169, 171. *See also* creative writing; writing strategies

Pólya, 54, 63

portfolios, 165. *See also* writing strategies

PreP, 140. *See also* reading strategies

prereading strategies, 135, 138–43, 151. *See also* reading strategies

prior knowledge, 17, 24, 119, 143, 145, 148

  brainstorming, 139–40

  PreP, 140

problem solving, 54, 63

procedural understanding, 91. *See also* conceptual understanding

QAR (Question-Answer Relationship), 144–45. *See also* reading strategies

raps, 153, 169, 170–71. *See also* creative writing; writing strategies

  example of, 170–71

read-aloud, 143–44. *See also* reading strategies

readability formulas, 34–35

reading, 16–17, 135–49. *See also* reading strategies

  graphs, 31–34, 142–43

  mathematical text, 21

  phases of, 135

  principles of, 24

  tables, 31

reading strategies

  anticipation guide, 142

  brainstorming, 139–40, 141

  Distinguished Pairs, 116–122

  DRTA (Directed Reading-Thinking Activity), 147

  during reading, 135, 138, 143–46, 147

  Guided Notes, 161–64

  It Reminds Me Of, 148–49, 166

K-W-L, 140–41, 148

Pairs Read, 144

postreading, 135, 138, 146, 147

PreP, 140

prereading, 135, 138–43, 144, 147

QAR (Question-Answer Relationship), 144–45

read-aloud, 143–44

read with a purpose, 143

Sketch the Text, 145–46

SQ3R (Survey, Question, Read, Recite, Review), 147

Teacher Think-Aloud, 143–44

textbook signals, 135–39, 144

textbook survey, 23

word problems, 147–49

Zoom In–Zoom Out, 53–64, 148

Roundtable, 126–27, 133. *See also* cooperative learning strategies

  example of, 126

rubrics, 77, 84, 85, 86. *See also* assessment

  example of, 77

self-regulation, 76. *See also* metacognition

Semantic Feature Analysis Grids, 99, 101–105. *See also* graphic organizers; vocabulary strategies; writing strategies

  examples of, 102, 103

semiotics, 1, 4, 6, 8, 9, 1, 15, 38

sentences, mathematics types of, 25

sign systems, 1, 4. *See also* semiotics

  mathematical signs, 7, 38

  multiple sign systems, 18

  sign producer, 12

  sign receiver, 12

  transmediation, 1, 5, 6, 7, 83, 168

Silent Teacher, 129. *See also* speaking strategies

Sketch the Text, 145–46. *See also* reading strategies

  example of, 146

songs, 169, 172. *See also* creative writing; writing strategies

  example of, 170–71, 172

speaking, 16. *See also* speaking strategies

  dialogue, 13, 14

  monologue, 13

speaking strategies

  brainstorming, 139–40, 141

  Co-op, 127–28, 133

  Give and Take, 130–31, 133

  Jigsaw, 128, 133

  Pairs Read, 144

  PreP, 140

  Roundtable, 126–27, 133

  Silent Teacher, 129

  Symbol-Language Glossary, 129–30, 133

  Think-Pair-Share, 46, 49, 55, 62, 125

SQ3R (Survey, Question, Read, Recite, Review), 147. *See also* reading strategies

stories, 153, 169, 170. *See also* creative writing; writing strategies

  example of, 170

strategies. *See* listening strategies; reading strategies; speaking strategies; vocabulary strategies; writing strategies

Symbol-Language Glossary, 129–30, 133. *See also* speaking strategies; symbols

  examples of, 130

symbols

  invented, example of, 118

  issues with, 30–31

  reading of, 24, 30–31, 143–44

  Symbol-Language Glossary, 129–30, 133

  Symbols-Meanings Writing, 159–61, 166, 173

  uses of, 30

  verbalizing of, 30–31, 143–44, 161, 163

  writing of, 159–61

Symbols-Meanings Writing, 159–61, 166, 173. *See also* symbols; writing strategies

  example of, 160

tables, reading of, 31

Teacher Think-Aloud, 143–44. *See also* reading strategies

templates for strategies

  Multi-Rep charts, 66

  rubric, 77

test corrections, 165. *See also* writing strategies

text, types of, 22, 37
textbook signals, 135–39, 144. *See also* reading strategies
textbook survey, 23. *See also* reading strategies
    example of, 23
These Are/These Are Not, 98–99, 122, 156–57. *See also* vocabulary strategies; writing strategies
    examples of, 98, 99
Think-Pair-Share, 46, 49, 55, 62, 125. *See also* cooperative learning strategies
transmediation, 1, 5, 6, 7, 83, 168. *See also* semiotics

Venn diagram, 97–98, 113–15, 145, 153, 156. *See also* graphic organizers; vocabulary strategies
    examples of 97, 114, 115
vignettes
    attaching meaning to words, 108–109
    building a discourse community, 46–48
    building a word wall, 26
    comparing and contrasting, 157–59
    conceptual understanding with manipulatives, 92–93
    cooperative learning, 126, 127–28
    developing meaning for sign systems, 3–4
    dialogue, 14
    invented language, 117–18
    Make My Day, 132
    monologue, 13
    Multi-Rep charts, 66–69

procedural vs. conceptual development, 91
reading comprehension, 148
stages of reading, 135–38
textbook survey, 23–24
You Be the Judge, 78–82
Zoom In–Zoom Out, 54–57
vocabulary. *See also* vocabulary strategies
    challenges of, 25
    sources of difficulty, 28, 107
vocabulary strategies
    analogies, 118
    Distinguished Pairs, 116
    invented language, 116–17
    personal dictionary/glossary, 29, 36, 110, 114, 118
    Semantic Feature Analysis Grid, 99, 101–103
    Symbol-Language Glossary, 129–30, 133
    These Are/These Are Not, 98–99
    word origins, 111–13, 118, 153
    word wall, 26, 110, 113, 114, 116

word origins, 111–13, 118, 153. *See also* vocabulary strategies
    examples of, 111, 112
word problems, reading of, 147–49. *See also* reading strategies
word wall, 26, 110, 113, 114, 116. *See also* vocabulary strategies
    examples of, 26
worthwhile tasks, 41, 49, 88, 89, 92
Write Your Own Problem, 72–73. *See also* writing strategies
writing, 16–17, 76, 150–73. *See also* writing strategies
    benefits of, 65, 151
    purposes of, 152

writing strategies
    analogies, 118, 153, 155–56
    Build Your Test Notes, 164–65
    bumper stickers, 168
    comparing and contrasting, 96–99, 156–59, 166
    concept maps, 99–101
    creative writing, 166, 168–71, 172
    graffiti, 166, 168, 169
    Guided Notes, 161–64
    It Reminds Me Of, 148–49, 166
    journals, 6, 57, 62, 165–66, 167
    K-W-L, 140–41, 148
    learning logs, 146
    mathematics autobiography, 152–53
    Multiple Representations chart (Multi-Rep), 65–75, 153
    personal dictionary/glossary, 29, 36, 110, 153, 154–55
    portfolios, 165
    raps, 153, 169, 170–71
    Semantic Feature Analysis Grids, 99, 101–103
    songs, 169, 172
    Symbols-Meanings Writing, 159–61, 166, 173
    test corrections, 165
    These Are/These Are Not, 98–99
    Venn diagrams, 97–98, 113–15, 145
    Write Your Own Problem, 72–73
    You Be the Judge, 76–86, 161

You Be the Judge, 76–86, 161. *See also* assessment; writing strategies

Zoom In–Zoom Out, 53–64, 148. *See also* reading strategies

About the Authors

Denisse R. Thompson is a professor of mathematics education at the University of South Florida, Tampa. She currently serves as President of the Florida Council of Teachers of Mathematics (2008–2009) and as monograph series editor for the Association of Mathematics Teacher Educators (2005–2008). She previously taught at the middle school, high school, and community college levels, and since 2005 has been Director of Evaluation for the Secondary Component of the University of Chicago School Mathematics Project. She has written extensively on mathematics communication and the use of children's literature to teach mathematics.

Gladis Kersaint is an associate professor at the University of South Florida, Tampa, where she teaches undergraduate, graduate, and doctoral courses in mathematics education. She is an active member of the mathematics education community at the local, state, and national levels. She currently serves as chair of the editorial panel for the NCTM journal, *Teaching Children Mathematics*. She formerly taught secondary mathematics in the Miami-Dade County Public School system. She has written articles that address a broad range of topics in mathematics education.

Janet C. Richards is a professor in the College of Education at the University of South Florida, Tampa, where she teaches courses in literacy theory and methods, writing, and qualitative research. She is Senior Editor of the *Journal of Reading Education*. Richards is a literacy scholar for the International Reading Association and has worked with classroom teachers and higher education faculty in Thailand, Azerbaijan, Estonia, Pakistan, and Romania. She is a former elementary classroom teacher and writes extensively on preservice and inservice teachers' communication skills.

Patricia D. Hunsader is an adjunct professor at the University of South Florida, Sarasota-Manatee, where she teaches courses in mathematics methods for preservice teachers. She has mathematics classroom teaching experience at both the high school and elementary levels, and her research examines how students' literacy skills and self-efficacy influence their problem-solving practices. She received her Ph.D. from the University of South Florida in 2005.

Rheta N. Rubenstein is a professor at the University of Michigan-Dearborn, where she teaches courses in mathematics and methods for undergraduate preservice and graduate inservice teachers. She is active in NCTM, currently serving as general editor for yearbooks on algebra (2008), geometry (2009), and curriculum (2010). She previously taught secondary mathematics in the Detroit Public Schools, education at the University of Windsor, and community college mathematics at Schoolcraft College. She is interested in mathematics communication and curriculum development and has written several textbooks.